T0323757

DOWN WITH COLONIALISM!

This essential new series features classic texts by key figures that took center stage during a period of insurrection. Each book is introduced by a major contemporary radical writer who shows how these incendiary words still have the power to inspire, to provoke and maybe to ignite new revolutions . . .

DOWN WITH COLONIALISM!

◆

HO CHI MINH

INTRODUCTION BY WALDEN BELLO

VERSO

London • New York

Chapters 1-3, 15-19, 21, 23, 25-27, 29, 30, 32-36, 40, 41 and 43-48 first published in
Selected Writings, 1920-1969 by Foreign Languages Publishing House, Hanoi,
copyright © University Press of the Pacific, Honolulu 2001; chapters 4-14, 20, 22, 24,
28, 31, 37, 38, 42 and 49 first published in Ho Chi Minh: Selected Articles and
Speeches, 1920-1967, by International Publishers, New York.
This edition published by Verso 2007
Copyright © Verso 2007
Introduction copyright © Walden Bello 2007

3 5 7 9 10 8 6 4 2

Verso
UK: 6 Meard Street, London W1F 0EG
USA: 388 Atlantic Ave, Brooklyn, NY 11217
www.versobooks.com

Verso is the imprint of New Left Books

ISBN-13: 978-1-84467-177-9

British Library Cataloguing in Publication Data
A catalogue record for this book is available from the British Library

Library of Congress Cataloging-in-Publication Data
A catalog record for this book is available from the Library of Congress

Typeset in Bembo by Hewer Text UK Ltd, Edinburgh
Printed in the USA

CONTENTS

INTRODUCTION

HO CHI MINH: THE COMMUNIST AS NATIONALIST

Walden Bello

Ho Chi Minh was a legend in his time, and like all legends, he manifested a variety of personae to people who worked with him, met him, or studied him. To the Soviet Premier Nikita Khrushchev, Ho was a living 'saint of communism':

> I have met many people in the course of my political career, but none has made such a particular impression on me. Believers often talk of the Apostles. Well, through his way of living and his influence over his peers, Ho Chi Minh was exactly comparable to these 'holy apostles'. An apostle of the Revolution. I will never forget that gleam of purity and sincerity in his eyes. His sincerity was that of an incorruptible communist and his purity that of a man totally devoted to his cause, in his principles and in his actions.[1]

In contrast, for Sophie Quinn-Judge – author of the best study of Ho's activities from 1919 to 1941 – although Ho was motivated 'by sincere patriotism and a deep resentment of French imperialism',

> he was not some sort of communist holy man. He lived with women at various times, made compromises and infiltrated other nationalist parties. He was not always straightforward – in many situations he would have regarded it foolhardy to be honest about his political beliefs. The depth of his attachment to communism is difficult to gauge – the one thing one can say is that he had little interest in

dogma. The path he followed was often chosen from a range of options narrowed by events outside his control.[2]

Ruth Fischer, a contemporary and colleague in the Communist International, offers yet another view, more nuanced than those of Khrushchev and Quinn-Judge:

Amid these seasoned revolutionaries and rigid intellectuals, he struck a delightful note of goodness and simplicity. He seemed to stand for mere common decency – though he was cleverer than he let on – and it was his well earned good name which saved him from being caught up in internal conflicts. Also, he was temperamentally far more inclined strongly toward action than toward doctrinal debates. He was always an empiricist within the movement. But none of this detracted from his colleagues' regard for him, and his prestige was considerable.[3]

THE MAN OF ACTION AS WRITER

The man of action *par excellence*, Ho nevertheless did a lot of writing and thinking. He was, for instance, quite a skilled propagandist. His short piece on lynching, which he subtitled 'A Little Known Aspect of American Civilisation', written in 1924, has lost none of its immediacy and power over eighty years later, and a great part of the reason is his command of irony and sarcasm:

Imagine a furious horde. Fists clenched, eyes bloodshot, mouths foaming, yells, insults, curses. . . . This horde is transported with the wild delight of a crime to be committed without risk. They are armed with sticks, torches, revolvers, ropes, knives, scissors, vitriol, daggers, in a word with all that can be used to kill or wound.

Imagine in this human sea a flotsam of black flesh pushed about, beaten, trampled underfoot, torn, slashed, insulted, tossed hither and thither, bloodstained, dead . . .

In a wave of hatred and bestiality, the lynchers drag the Black to a wood or to a public place. They tie him to a tree, pour kerosene over him, cover him with inflammable material. While waiting for the fire to be kindled, they smash his teeth, one by one. Then they gouge out his eyes. Little tufts of crinkly hair are torn from his head, carrying away with them bits of skin, baring a bloody skull . . .

'Popular justice', as they say over there, has been done. Calmed down, the crowds congratulate the organizers, then stream away slowly and cheerfully, as if after a feast, making appointments with one another for the next time.

While on the ground, stinking of fat and smoke, a black head, mutilated, roasted, deformed, grins horribly and seems to ask the setting sun, 'Is this civilization?'[4]

Though Ho wrote a lot, theoretical innovation was not his forte. This was something he readily admitted. In fact, Ho is rumoured to have said, not without sarcasm, that he did not need to write since Mao Zedong had written all that needed to be written.[5]

So why read Ho? Well, not so much to encounter theoretical originality but to experience how a committed revolutionary with an agile mind sought to translate the concepts and ideas he was coming across as an international activist in Marxist-Leninist circles into the strategy, tactics, and organization that would successfully liberate a colonized country in the first half of the twentieth century, defeating in the process two empires: France and the United States. As we read him, we witness a creative collision of Marxism with colonial realities, resulting in the innovative modification of a paradigm of class and class conflict originating in Europe as it migrated to Asia.

THE YOUNG HO

Ho came to political maturity in the turbulent era unleashed by the First World War. For almost a decade after 1911, the year he left Vietnam, he was mostly at sea as a ship's cook, visiting different parts of the world, including New York and London, before finally settling in Paris for a few years beginning in 1919. An activist for Vietnam's freedom from the very beginning, he first drew attention while lobbying foreign delegations for Vietnam's freedom during the Versailles Conference of 1919. Like many other representatives of colonized nations, he was drawn to the gathering by President Woodrow Wilson's promise of self-determination for subjugated nationalities.

The young Ho or Nguyen Ai Quoc, as he was known then, was not shy about expressing the primacy of the struggle against colonialism as a criterion in determining whom he would work with. At the historic Tours Congress where the French Socialist Party voted to join the triumphant Russian Bolsheviks' Third International, Ho intervened on the floor, saying, 'The Socialist Party must act effectively in favour of the oppressed natives. . . . We shall see in the Socialist Party's joining the Third International the promise that from now on it will attach to the colonial questions the importance they deserve.'

What distinguished Ho from other nationalists and colonial revolutionaries, according to the noted French war correspondent Bernard Fall, was that while he was passionately committed to Vietnamese independence, he understood that Vietnam's status as a colonial country was 'typical of the whole colonial system'.[6] He felt a strong affinity with other peoples caught in the same web of systemic oppression and all his life he held the conviction that liberation had to be not only national but universal. His 'Report on the National and Colonial Questions at the Fifth Congress of the Communist International' [Text 13] was not only a comprehensive description of the system of French colonialism but an angry statement of solidarity with Arabs, Africans, and Pacific peoples that were under French rule.

For Ho, the national question was intimately tied to the class question. Ho's worldview was shaped not only by his youthful experience as the son of an impoverished district chief dismissed from office because of his political beliefs, but also by his class status as a coloured person eking out a living for almost a decade as a messboy on ships plying international routes. There are few work places more international in their work force than ocean-going vessels, and this experience of common hardship with co-workers of all colours could not have failed to be a factor in his embrace of Marxism.

THE ENCOUNTER WITH LENIN

The key link to Ho's socialist future was Lenin. Here it is worth quoting Ho's road-to-Damascus experience that he recounted in an essay entitled 'The Path which Led Me to Leninism' [Text 42]:

What I wanted most to know – and what was not debated in the meetings – was: which International sided with the peoples of the colonial countries?

I raised this question – the most important for me – at a meeting. Some comrades answered: it was the Third, not the Second International. One gave me to read Lenin's 'Theses on the National and Colonial Questions' printed in *L'Humanité.*

In those Theses, there were political terms that were difficult to understand. But by reading them again and again finally I was able to grasp the essential part. What emotion, enthusiasm, enlightenment, and confidence they communicated to me! I wept for joy. Sitting by myself in my room, I would shout as if I were addressing large crowds: 'Dear martyr compatriots! This is what we need, this is our path to liberation!'

Lenin's 'Theses' was probably the most significant document produced by the Third International. It was there that the Russian revolutionary leader made three key points that were to be central in the formulation of the strategies of the Vietnamese and other Asian communist parties later on. First, the 'cornerstone of the Communist International's national and colonial policy must be the uniting of the proletarian and working masses of all nations and countries in a joint revolutionary struggle for the overthrow of the landowners and the bourgeoisie. Only such a union can guarantee the victory over capitalism without which it is impossible to suppress national inequality and oppression.'[7]

Second was the 'necessity of supporting the peasant movement in backward countries against the landowners, against the possession of large estates, against all customs and remnants of feudalism, and of striving to give the peasant movement a revolutionary nature, bringing about a closer union between the West European Communist proletariat and the revolutionary movement of the peasants in the east, the colonies, and in the backward countries in general . . .'[8]

Third, the immediate task with respect to the colonies and oppressed countries was 'to support the bourgeois democratic national movements in the colonies and backward countries' – though this should be 'only on the condition that the elements of the future proletarian parties . . . should be grouped and educated in the knowledge of their special tasks – those of a struggle against the bourgeois democratic movement within their nation.'[9] The socialist revolution would come later.

These theses, which might seem non-controversial today, were of momentous significance when they were first articulated.

The first point addressed head on the neglect of the colonial question which was, in fact, prevalent among European progressives in the inter-war period. During the Fifth Congress of the Comintern in 1925, a frustrated Ho carried Lenin's argument one step further, affirming that, without decisively dealing with the colonial question, socialists could not expect successful revolution in the West.

> You must excuse my frankness, but I cannot help but observe that the speeches by comrades from the mother countries give me the impression that they wish to kill a snake by stepping on its tail. You all know today the poison and life energy of the capitalist snake is concentrated more in the colonies than in the mother countries. . . . Yet in our discussion of the revolution, you neglect to talk about the colonies. . . . Why do you neglect the colonies, while capitalism uses them to support itself, defend itself, and fight you?[10]

The second point, on the revolutionary potential of the peasantry in the colonies, was also something that tended to be slighted. This was not simply because of the socialists' preoccupation with the leading role of the European working class in the world revolution – which was still expected to be ignited in the developed capitalist countries. It was also because of classical Marxism's disdain for the peasantry, as expressed in Marx's comment about the 'idiocy of rural life' and his comparing peasants to a 'sack of potatoes' in terms of their capacity for political organization.

The third proposition was what most attracted Ho. It was also the idea that would elicit the most controversy in the history of the Communist International. This thesis eventually came to be known as the 'two-stage' theory of revolution. It was, from one perspective, simply an effort to formalize the Russian revolutionary experience in 1917 – which began with the February democratic revolution and was followed by the October socialist revolution – to serve as a strategy for progressives in the 'backward societies', with one key modification being that the first stage would not only be a struggle for democratic rights but for national independence.

THEORETICAL AND POLITICAL TENSIONS

Lenin's two-stage formulation became the foundation of Ho's strategy for liberating Vietnam. Looking back at the development of the strategy almost thirty years after the founding of the Indochinese Communist Party, Ho recounted in his 1959 'Report on the Draft Amended Constitution',

> In Vietnam, following World War I, the national bourgeoisie and the petty bourgeoisie were unable to lead the movement for national liberation to success. The Vietnamese working class, in the light of the October Revolution, charted the course of the Vietnamese revolution. In 1930, the Indochinese Communist Party, the political party of the working class, was founded and showed that the Vietnamese revolution should go through two stages: the national democratic revolution and the socialist revolution.

The reality was, however, more complex. The two-stage theory, in fact, bedevilled the Third International and Communists in the East with several tactical controversies. One was how the revolutionary party would relate to its non-Communist allies, especially the 'national bourgeoisie' and pro-independence elements of the landlord class, during the struggle for independence. Another was what would be the main demands of the 'national democratic' stage, especially in regards to the land issue.

It was the Chinese cockpit that provided the grist for the mill for the different sides in the debate on strategy and tactics for the colonial and semi-colonial world. In China, application of the two-stage approach under the direction of the Comintern translated into the Chinese Communist Party's support for the Nationalists or Kuomintang. This was not just a case of forming an alliance with the Kuomintang, but of helping to build the latter organizationally and militarily. The policy ended in a debacle in 1927, when Chiang Kai-Shek turned on the Communists and massacred large numbers of them.

Ho was working for the Comintern in Canton from 1924 to 1927, so he was familiar with the fatal dynamics of the Nationalist-Communist 'United Front'. By the time he was sent by the Comintern to Hong Kong to unify the Vietnamese Communist movement in 1930, the Third International had entered its notorious 'Third Period', where

Communists directed the 'main blow' against the Social Democrats – labelled 'Social Fascists' – in the capitalist countries and abandoned united fronts with bourgeois and petty bourgeois nationalists in favour of 'worker-peasant-soldier' governments in the colonies.

Ho was able to impose a fragile unity among the competing Vietnam-ese communist factions and establish the Indochinese Communist Party. But, contrary to his recollections in 1959, the unification was not on the basis of the two-stage approach but on that of the radical Third Period line. Ho's 'Appeal Made on the Occasion of the Founding of the Indochinese Communist Party' [Text 15], dated February 18, 1930, called on the Vietnamese 'workers, peasants, soldiers, youth, school students' to 'overthrow French imperialism and Vietnamese feudalism and reactionary bourgeoisie', 'to make Indochina completely independent', 'to establish a worker-peasant-soldier government', 'to confiscate the banks and other enterprises belonging to the imperialists and put them under the control of the worker-peasant-soldier government'; and 'to confiscate all the plantations and property belonging to the imperialists and the Vietnamese reactionary bourgeoisie and distribute them to the poor peasants'.

Was this Ho speaking or was it the Comintern? Or had Ho temporarily been won over to the Third Period line? It is difficult to answer this question with the available evidence. What is clear, however, is that Ho opposed the peasant uprisings that the newly unified party instigated in the provinces of Nghe An and Ha Tinh in north-central Vietnam in 1931, and which saw the establishment of village soviets.[11] Ho probably had a premonition that the Third Period line would lead to a disastrous policy in terms of political alliances. And it did. As John McAlister, Jr, notes:

> Perhaps the most fundamental mistake was that the Communist terrorism was almost exclusively directed at lower-echelon Vietnam-ese officials who were exercising authority for the French admin-istration, rather than at the French themselves. . . . The Communists attributed this misstep to the shortcomings of the Theses on the Bourgeois Democratic Revolution in Vietnam, adopted by the Indochinese Communist Party in October 1930. . . . . As one Vietnamese Communist critic has seen it, this program 'committed the error of advocating the overthrow of the national bourgeoisie at the same time as the French colonialists and indigenous feudalists . . .

[for] this bourgeoisie had interests which were in conflict with the imperialists . . . [and] they ought to have been drawn into the ranks of the bourgeois democratic republic and not systematically separated.'[12]

Influenced by Lenin's careful – some would say opportunistic – policies on political alliances, Ho had a strong bias against excluding anyone solely on the basis of class origins and this would not be the last time he would vote against and criticize an exclusionist policy. Asked who were the Communists' allies and who were their enemies, Ho would probably have said, along with Lenin: That depends on conditions, time, and place.

CREATING A BROAD FRONT

The Comintern shifted to 'Popular Front' politics in 1935 following Hitler's coming to power in Germany. With its championing of broad anti-fascist alliances, the new approach appealed more to Ho's instincts about the kind of tactics that would advance the independence struggle. The Third Period line was abandoned in favour of a strategy whose key points were elaborated in the report titled 'The Party's Line in the Period of the Democratic Front (1936–1939)':

1. For the time being the Party should not put forward too exacting demands (national independence, parliament, etc.). To do so is to play into the Japanese fascists' hands.

It should only claim democratic rights, freedom of organization, freedom of assembly, freedom of the press and freedom of speech, general amnesty for all political detainees, and freedom for the Party to engage in legal activity.

2. To reach this goal, the Party must strive to organize a broad Democratic National Front. This Front should embrace not only Indochinese but also progressive French people residing in Indochina, not only the toiling people but also the national bourgeoisie.

3. The Party must assume a tactful, flexible attitude towards the national bourgeoisie, strive to draw them into the Front and keep them there, urge them into action if possible, isolate them politically if necessary. At any rate, we should not leave them outside the Front, lest they fall into the hands of the reaction and strengthen it.

By the time the Second World War broke out, the conditions were in place for the Communists to lead Vietnam's independence struggle. Not only had their tough organizing enabled them to survive fierce French repression in the aftermath of the Nghe An and Ha Tinh soviets. Not only had their only competition, the Vietnam Nationalist Party (VNQDD), been destroyed by the French. But, as in China, they now had an extraordinarily supple tactic – the Democratic National Front – to unite the nation against both the Japanese and the French colonial government that had submitted to Japanese control. Yet even as he invoked the patriotic feelings of all Vietnamese, Ho made it a point in his 'Letter from Abroad' [Text 17], to link the struggle for independence with the class revolution in the country and with the world revolution:

> The hour has struck! Raise aloft the banner of insurrection and lead the people throughout the country to overthrow the Japanese and the French! The sacred call of the Fatherland is resounding in our ears; the ardent blood of our heroic predecessors is seething in our hearts! The fighting spirit of the people is mounting before our eyes! Let us unite and unify our action to overthrow the Japanese and the French.
> The Vietnamese revolution will certainly triumph!
> The world revolution will certainly triumph!

He was not a communist for nothing.

THE LENINIST IN ACTION

Jean Lacouture, one of Ho's biographers, points to the strong influence on Ho of two Leninist ideas: the notion of the 'favourable moment' and the concept of the 'main adversary'.[13] Nowhere was his mastery of these two principles more in evidence than when he declared Vietnam's independence in 1945. The 'favourable moment' is akin to Louis Althusser's concept of an 'overdetermined contradiction', a particular confluence of forces and circumstances that, if taken advantage of, rewards bold political action.[14] Such was Lenin's decision to seize power in October 1917. And such was Ho's decision to launch a general insurrection and declare independence in August and September 1945, taking advantage of a conjuncture where the French had been disarmed by the Japanese, the Japanese themselves had just capitulated to the allies, and the French had as yet no means of reclaiming the colony.[15] It was, like Russia in 1917, a situation virtually inviting the Communists to step in. August and September 1945 saw an insurrectionary takeover, but a relatively bloodless one, with the Communists utilizing to the maximum the legitimacy that they had gained from their leading role in the five-year anti-fascist struggle against the French colonial regime and its Japanese supervisors.

The crafting of the 'Declaration of Independence of the Democratic Republic of Vietnam' [Text 20] showed Ho's command of united front tactics – the main purpose of which was to isolate the 'main adversary' – not only at the national but on the global level. The key problem in 1945 was to prevent the western imperial powers that had vanquished the Japanese from ganging up on the Vietnamese. Ho was very well aware that the US was an imperial power. But he was also conscious that Americans themselves had an anti-colonial tradition, and that this was a fly in the ointment in US post-war policy in Asia – one that made Washington very uncomfortable at being seen as supporting the re-storation of French rule in Indochina, though the Free French government in exile had been a wartime ally of the US.

The good relations established between the Communists and opera-tives of the US Office of Strategic Services (OSS) during the anti-Japanese campaign provided a base for Ho's strategy. His invocation of the first lines of the US Declaration of Independence – 'All men are created equal. They are endowed by their Creator with certain inalien-able Rights; among these are Life, Liberty, and the Pursuit of Happiness' – at the very beginning of Vietnam's declaration of independence was a master stroke designed to deepen the rift between the mightiest global power and a colonial power that had been severely weakened by the war.

The years from 1946 to 1954 saw Ho at his peak as a leader. He negotiated an agreement with the French High Commissioner Jean Sainteny that recognized Vietnam as a 'Free State at the heart of the French Union'. It was a controversial deal, and to gain popular accep-tance, Ho shared the complex rationale of his moves with a hostile audience at the municipal theatre in Hanoi:

We have actually been independent since August 1945 but so far no power has recognized our independence. The agreement with France opens the way to international recognition. It will lead us to an increasingly more solid international position, which is a great political achievement. There will only be fifteen thousand French troops and they will stay for five years. . . . It is a show of political intelligence to negotiate rather than to fight. Why should we sacrifice fifty or one hundred thousand men when we can attain independence through negotiation, maybe within five years? . . . I, Ho Chi Minh, have always led you on the path to freedom. You know that I would rather die than sell out my country. I swear to you that I did not sell you out.[16]

The speech turned the crowd around. It also, incidentally, revealed what Lacouture describes as Ho's penchant for debate as a method for resolving issues: '. . . [O]ne thing about Ho [that] is beyond dispute is his passionate desire to persuade people, his thoroughly democratic urge to win acceptance for measures by argument rather than compulsion.'[17]

Future events would show that Ho's linking the deal with Sainteny was a wise tactic, one which put the French on the defensive, and cast a pall of illegitimacy over their breaking the deal and their subsequent war of reconquest. It was also an audacious military move that gave the Vietnamese, according to Ho in his 'Political Report at the Second National Congress of the Viet Nam Workers' Party' [Text 30], 'nearly one year of temporary peace [that gave] us time to build up our basic forces'.

HO AND PEOPLE'S WAR

War is the pursuit of politics by other means. With no one was this Clausewitzean dictum truer than with Ho, who oscillated masterfully between negotiations and war, always keeping his eye on the ball, which was an independent Vietnam. By December 1946, with the collapse of negotiations with the French, it was back to war.

While General Vo Nguyen Giap is often credited as a military genius owing to the strategic and tactical brilliance with which he conducted the Battle of Dien Bien Phu, Ho's writings also reveal a comprehensive grasp of the principles of people's war. In his 'Appeal Issued after Six Months of Resistance' [Text 23], issued on June 14, 1947, Ho presciently outlined the course of the next seven years:

The enemy wants to win a quick victory. If the war drags on, he will suffer increasing losses and will be defeated.

That is why we use the strategy of a protracted war of resistance in order to develop our forces and gather more experience. We use guerrilla tactics to wear down the enemy forces until a general offensive wipes them out.

The enemy is like fire and we like water. Water will certainly get the better of fire.

Moreover, in the long war of resistance, each citizen is a combatant, each village a fortress. The twenty million Vietnamese are bound to cut to pieces the few scores of thousands of reactionary colonialists.

Dicussions of warfare comprise much of Ho's writings after 1947. In them he continually reiterates the essentials of what he called the 'protracted war of resistance':

– the party must guide military strategy;
– cling to the people because they are the source of strength of the army;
– the aim of guerrilla warfare is 'not to wage large-scale battles but to nibble at the enemy, harass him in such a way that he can neither eat not sleep in peace, to give him no respite, to wear him out physically and mentally, and finally to annihilate him' [Text 33];
– guerrilla war is a necessary phase, but inevitably as the balance of forces shifts towards the people's side, the war passes from the defensive to the phase of active contention to the 'general counteroffensive'. While it is possible to determine the major stages on the basis of the general situation . . . it is not possible to separate one stage completely from the other, like slicing a cake. The length of each stage depends on the situation at home and in the world, and on the changes in the enemy's forces and in ours [Text 30].

The similarity of these prescriptions to Mao's theory of people's war is striking, but it is questionable that Ho, or Giap for that matter, simply lifted them from Mao. The principles appear to have emerged largely from a process of experimentation and learning from mistakes in the monumental process of trial and error that was the Vietnamese Revolution. This is not to say that some cross fertilization between the two roughly simultaneous people's wars did not take place, given Ho and other Vietnamese Communists' close contacts with the Chinese and, in Ho's case, direct participation in the Chinese Revolution at certain points in his revolutionary career.[18]

THE CRUCIBLE OF LAND REFORM

Even as the military struggle went on, the problems encountered in managing the different classes involved in a national independence struggle were not easily resolved, and, in a people's war, resolution of these issues had an impact on the military equation. Here, Ho's writings evince a tension between satisfying the demands of the peasantry that constituted 90 per cent of the population and neutralizing the upper classes, particularly the landed class.

During the Japanese occupation and the first years against the French recolonization, Ho and the party's policy was to postpone land reform and promote rent reduction, along with confiscation of land belonging to the French and pro-French Vietnamese [Text 30].

Rent reduction meant forcing landlords and rich peasants to reduce their rent to 20 per cent from 50 per cent, the operative principle being 'limiting the feudal landlords' exploitation of the peasants while at the same time proceeding with changes in the property system so long as this measure does not impede the United National Anti-Colonialist Front'.[19]

With final victory over the French at hand in 1953, the party decided to finally implement radical land redistribution. Brocheux suggests that it was a challenge from Stalin and the newly triumphant Chinese that prompted Ho to push land reform.[20] This is unlikely given the centrality that he and his comrades had placed on agrarian reform as the 'main content' of the bourgeois democratic stage of the revolution. What is true though is that Ho felt that reform should be carefully planned and implemented owing to the complexity of the rural social structure. Indeed, early in his career as a Communist, he underscored the differences between the European countryside and Asian rural society:

> [The] social conditions of small landlords with ten to one hundred *mau* are complex and unpredictable. With that amount of land, a peasant could end up being exploited, an exploiter, or neutral. . . . [T]he class struggle does not take shape the way it does in the West. The workers lack consciousness, they are resigned and disorganized. . . . In this way, if the peasants have next to nothing, the landlord does not have a great fortune either . . . The one is resigned to his fate, the other moderate in his appetite. So the clash between their interests is softened. That is undeniable.[21]

While he was not directly involved in implementing it, it was Ho that laid out the strategic direction of the land reform program in 1953 [Text 34]:

[T]he key problem remains unsolved: the peasant masses have no land or lack land. This affects the forces of the resistance and the production work of the peasants.

Only by carrying out land reform, giving land to the tillers, liberating the productive forces in the countryside from the yoke of the feudal landlord class can we do away with the poverty and backwardness and strongly mobilize the huge forces of the peasants in order to develop production and push the war of resistance forward to complete victory.

But even as he laid out the strategy of radical land reform, Ho cautioned that the wiping out of feudalism must proceed 'step by step and with discrimination'. Specifically, this meant that 'in the course of land reform, we must apply different kinds of treatment to the landlords according to their individual political attitudes. This means that depending on individual cases we shall order confiscation or requisition with or without compensation, but not wholesale confiscation or wholesale requisition without compensation'.

These cautionary notes were, however, forgotten in the whirlwind that was visited on the countryside, where land reform became, in many places, an organized *jacquerie*. So many abuses were committed and so many people were killed – according to Bui Tin, more than 10,000 people were eliminated, 'most of them Party members or patriots who had supported the Revolution but were reasonably well off'.[22] Ho then personally intervened to 'rectify' the campaign, which involved dismissing Truong Chinh – who was close to the Chinese, who had closely involved themselves in the process – from his post as secretary general. Ho led the process of party self-criticism, but he left it to General Giap, a trusted favourite, to voice his opinions and issue the party's public criticism of itself at the 10th Congress of the Party Central Committee.

(a) While carrying out their anti-feudal task, our cadres have underestimated or, worse still, have denied all anti-imperialist achievements, and have separated the Land Reform and the Revolution. Worst of all, in some areas they have even made the two mutually exclusive. (b) We have failed to realize the necessity of uniting with the middle-level peasants, and we should have concluded some form of alliance with the rich peasants, whom we have treated in the same manner as landlords.

(c) We have attacked the land owning families indiscriminately, according no consideration to those who have served the Revolution and to those families with sons in the army. We showed no indulgence towards landlords who participated in the resistance, treating their children in the same way as we treated the children of other landlords.

(d) We made too many deviations and executed too many honest people. We attacked on too large a front and, seeing enemies everywhere, resorted to terror, which became far too widespread.

(e) Whilst carrying out our Land Reform programme we failed to respect the principles of freedom of faith and worship in many areas.

(f) In regions inhabited by minority tribes we have attacked tribal chiefs too strongly, thus injuring, instead of respecting, local customs and manners.

(g) When reorganizing the Party, we paid too much importance to the notion of social class instead of adhering firmly to the political qualifications alone. Instead of reorganizing education to be the first essential, we resorted exclusively to organizational measures such as disciplinary punishments, expulsion from the Party, executions, dissolution of Party branches and cells. Worse still, torture came to be regarded as a normal practice during Party reorganization.[23]

Though he did not directly guide the land reform and thus could not be held directly accountable for the abuses that were committed, Ho was reproached for not intervening even when he was warned of grave cases of abuse, and for limiting himself to expressing concern.[24] Yet there is no doubt that the Chinese-style land reform contradicted Ho's previous emphasis on uniting rather than dividing, negotiation ahead of battle, education instead of bureaucratic or organizational measures, and rectifying people instead of turning them into pariahs.

Like Mao, Ho had a moralistic streak. But, in his exhortatory essays, Ho adopted a very un-Maoist approach to revolutionary morality, refraining from characterizing people he disagreed with in the party as class enemies or 'capitalist roaders', always urging unity above momentary differences, and always holding up the possibility of redemption, and urging party cadres to assist people who had fallen by the wayside. For instance, in 'To Practise Thrift and Oppose Embezzlement, Waste and Bureaucracy' [Text 32], Ho says:

There are people who are enthusiastic and faithful in struggle; they fear neither dangers, hardships, nor the enemy, thus they have served the revolution well; but as soon as they hold some authority, they grow arrogant and luxurious, indulge in embezzlement, waste, and unconscious bureaucracy, thus becoming guilty in the eyes of the revolution. We must save them, help them recover their revolutionary virtues. Others, while pretending to serve the Fatherland and the people, indulge in embezzlement and waste and harm the Fatherland and the people. We must educate them, and lead them to the revolutionary path.

FROM FOND UNCLE TO STERN FATHER

This did not mean that Ho did not resort to extreme measures. He did when he felt dialogue had become impossible with the Communists' competitors for the loyalties of the Vietnamese. As Lacouture notes,

The fond uncle is quite capable of playing the heavy father when he wishes. In the north, his firm hand was felt by the anti-communist nationalists (VNQDD) . . . and the Catholics between September 1945 and July 1946. And in the South he dealt sternly with the Trotskyites and the Hoa Hao recalcitrants.[25]

The standard story that is brought up to illustrate Ho's tough side is that he caused the arrest of the venerable Vietnamese nationalist Phan Boi Chau in order to rid himself of an attractive rival among Vietnamese political exiles in Canton in 1925. It must be pointed out though that some scholars, like Sophie Quinn-Judge, dispute Ho's role in Phan's apprehension.[26]

With the Trotskyists, he was vituperative in his language and was eager to show his loyalty to Stalin: 'With regard to the Trotskyites there can be no compromise, no concession. We must do everything possible to unmask them as agents of fascism and annihilate them politically'

[Text 16]. That such a strong statement could lead not just to political but to physical elimination by Viet Minh partisans is not surprising. It is reported that the Viet Minh eliminated the Trotskyists by tying several of them together and throwing them into a river to drown. It is also said that in 1946, the Viet Minh 'apprehended Nguyen Ta Thu Than, the most gifted Trotskyite leader and writer, at the train station in Quang Ngai, then took him to a sandy beach and put a bullet through his head'.[27] Ho may not have been personally responsible for these deeds, but he cannot escape accountability for a harsh political line that encouraged such abuses.

FROM NATIONAL DEMOCRACY TO SOCIALISM

During his lifetime, Ho was dogged by the question of whether he was principally a nationalist or a communist. For his rivals in the nationalist movements in Vietnam, as well as for his enemies in Paris and Washington, he was the agent of world revolution, the man of the Communist International *par excellence*. For the Trotskyists, and for some of his rivals in the Indochinese Communist Party, he was either a petty bourgeois nationalist or was guilty of 'nationalist deviation'. Even Stalin is said to have suspected him of unhealthy nationalist tendencies and dared him to enact the radical land reform to smoke him out.[28]

The situation after the defeat of the French in 1954, however, showed Ho to be a faithful Leninist. Faithful, that is, to Lenin's 'Theses on the National and Colonial Question', which contained the theory of a bourgeois democratic revolution followed by a socialist revolution, that had such a big impact on Ho in the early Twenties. With Vietnam divided into the sovereign North and the US-controlled South, Ho adapted the theory to the particular circumstances of the country:

> [T]wo tasks confront the Vietnamese revolution at present: first, the construction of socialism in the North, and second, the completion of the national democratic revolution in the South. These tasks have a common aim: to strengthen peace and pave the way to reunification on the basis of independence and democracy [Text 40].

The demands of socialist revolution and national independence were, in Leninist fashion, creatively reformulated to meet the particular historical conjuncture, but there was no doubt that socialism in an independent nation was the strategic aim. Ho was nearly six years dead by the time the country was rid of the Americans and reunified in March 1975. But, faithful to his Leninist vision, his followers immediately moved to declare the national bourgeois democratic revolution completed in the South, and christen the whole country as the Socialist Republic of Vietnam. For Ho genuine nationalism meant working to bring about socialism to a nation-state that would be part of an international order of independent socialist nation-states.

A MARXIST PRAGMATIST

Ho left no significant theoretical innovations, much less an integrated body of theory. This has, of course, not prevented some in the Vietnamese Communist Party from claiming that Ho left behind 'Ho Chi Minh Thought', which was described as a new development in Marxist-Leninist theory. Not surprisingly, this elicited a certain amount of skepticism since Vietnamese knew that Ho did not leave behind any body of theoretical writing.[29]

Where Ho did excel was in his ability to adapt abstract Leninist ideas to Vietnamese realities, developing a strategy and tactics of national revolution based on these, and creating an organization, the Communist Party, to put this into effect. Perhaps his analytical approach was best articulated in the speech he gave inaugurating the first theoretical course of the Nguyen Ai Quoc School on September 7, 1957:

Reality is problems to be solved and contradictions lying within things. We are revolutionary cadres, our reality is problems to be solved that the revolution puts to us. Real life is immense. It covers the experience drawn from the work and thought of an individual, the Party's policies and line, its historical experiences and issues at home and in the world. In the course of our study these are realities to be kept in touch with.

He continued:

Thanks to its ability in combining Marxism-Leninism with the actual situation of our country, our Party has scored many successes in its work. However, the combination of Marxist-Leninist truth with the practice of the Vietnamese revolution was not complete and brought about many mistakes, namely those committed in the land reform, readjustment of organization, and economic construction. At present, in building socialism, although we have the rich experiences of brother countries, we cannot apply them mechanically because our country has its own peculiarities. Disregard for the peculiarities of one's nation while learning from the experiences of the brother countries is a serious mistake, is dogmatism. But undue emphasis on the role of national peculiarities and negation of the universal value of the great, basic experiences of the brother countries will lead to grave revisionist mistakes.[30]

Ideas do matter in history. And it was Ho's ability to translate revolutionary ideas into a pragmatic but inspiring programme and a tough organization to carry it out successfully, that made him exceptional.

POSTCRIPT

How useful Ho's ideas, especially those that have to do with 'constructing socialism', are today, as Vietnam seeks to break out of underdevelopment and classical socialism has been discredited, is an interesting question. Were Ho alive in the late 1970s, one can certainly see him putting a stop to the expropriation of shops and small factories belonging to the Sino-Vietnamese that triggered the flight of the 'boat people'. One could have imagined him calling a retreat after the programme of accelerated socialist construction created tremendous dislocations in both the countryside and the cities in the late 1970s and early 1980s. Would he have gone so far as to support market reforms, the revival of the private sector, and the courting of foreign investors that have marked Vietnam's political economy in the last two decades? That is an interesting question, the answer to which will probably be debated endlessly.

SUGGESTED FURTHER READING

Collections of Texts and Speeches by Ho Chi Minh

Ho Chi Minh: Selected Articles and Speeches, 1920–1967, International Publishers, 1970.

Selected Writings 1920–1969, University Press of the Pacific, 2001.

Biographies and Studies of Ho Chi Minh

BROCHEUX, Pierre, *Ho Chi Minh: A Biography*, trans. Claire Duiker, Cambridge University Press, 2007.

BUI, Tin, *Following Ho Chi Minh*, Hurst and Co., 1995.

BURCHETT, Wilfred, *Ho Chi Minh, An Appreciation*, W. Burchett Fund and the Guardian, 1972.

DECARO, Peter A., *Rhetoric of Revolt: Ho Chi Minh's Discourse for Revolution*, Praeger Publishers, 2003.

DUIKER, William J., *Ho Chi Minh: A Life*, Hyperion, 2001.

FALL, Bernard (ed.), *Ho Chi Minh on Revolution : Selected Writings, 192066*, Praeger, 1967.

HÉMERY, Daniel, *Ho Chi Minh, l'homme et son héritage*, Duong Moi/La Voie nouvelle, 1990.

HÉMERY, Daniel, *Ho Chi Minh, de l'Indochine au Vietnam*, Découvertes Gallimard, 1990.

LACOUTURE, Jean, *Ho Chi Minh : A Political Biography*, Vintage, 1968.

QUINN-JUDGE, Sophie, *Ho Chi Minh, The Missing Years*, University of California Press, 2003.

WODDIS, Jack (ed.), *Ho Chi Minh : Selected Articles and Speeches, 1920–67*, Lawrence & Wishart, 1969.

GLOSSARY

Note: in Vietnamese, the family name is given first, but persons are referred to by their first name. For example, with Vo Nguyen Giap, the family name is Vo, but he will usually be called Giap.

Annam: central region in Vietnam. Had protectorate status under the French. In Vietnamese: Trung Ky or Trung Bo.

Bao Dai (1913–1997): last emperor of Vietnam, descendant of the Nguyen dynasty. Educated in France, he became King of Annam under the French protectorate, 1926–1945, and then under the Japanese occupation. Abdicated after the August 1945 revolution in favour of the Viet Minh government and briefly became the latter's 'supreme advisor' before leaving the country. Once again appointed head of state in 1948 by the French with the creation of the anti-Viet Minh state. Overthrown in 1955 by his prime minister, he abdicated a second time and ended his life in exile.

Bac Son and Nam Ky uprisings: Communist uprisings in September 1940 on the occasion of the French Second World War defeat. Insurrections took place in Bac Son, Tonkin, then in November in eleven of the twenty provinces of Nam Ky (Vietnamese for Cochinchina). Very severe repression against the Indochinese Communist Party followed.

Carpentier, Georges (1894–1975): French boxer who beat the reigning British champion, Ted Lewis, in 1922. Nicknamed the 'Orchid Man', he was known for his speed, his boxing skills and his hard punch.

Chiang Kai-shek (1887–1975): born in Zhejiang province in China. Took control of the nationalist party the Kuomintang (Guomindang) after the death of Sun Yat-sen in 1925. Broke the alliance with the Chinese Communist Party and militarily crushed the workers' and popular movements, especially in Shanghai and Canton, thus signalling the defeat of the Second Chinese Revolution (1925–27). Became the dictator-president of the Republic of China. Unable to organize an effective resistance against the Japanese invasion (1937–45), he also lost the long civil war against the Communists, who triumphed in the Third Chinese Revolution (1949). Chiang Kai-shek fled to Taiwan where he imposed his regime on the island's population. Despite his defeat, he continued to represent China in international organizations such as the UN until his death.

Cochinchina: southern part of Vietnam. Under French domination, it was a colony, in contrast to Annam and Tonkin, which were protectorates. In Vietnamese : Nam Ky or Nam Bo.

Daladier, Edouard (1884–1970): French politician who, as prime minister, signed the Munich Pact with Nazi Germany in 1938.

Diem [Ngo Dinh] (1901–1933): originally from Quang Binh province in North Vietnam. Catholic. President with dictatorial powers of the Saigon regime from 1955 until his assassination in 1963.

Dien, Raymonde: French pacifist activist engaged in the campaign against the Indochinese war. Particularly active, along with the French Communist Party, in blocking the transport of troops to Vietnam. Arrested in 1950 and imprisoned for a year for offences against state security, she had her French nationality suspended for fifteen years.

Dien Bien Phu: small town to the west of Tonkin, near the frontier with Laos. The French general staff, commanded by General Navarre, decided in 1954 to use this valley as a means of blocking the Viet Minh's mobility. However, the latter, under the command of Vo Nguyen Giap, trapped the elite French forces and, after a month of combat, defeated them. The Vietnamese victory at Dien Bien Phu marked the end of the French occupation of the country.

Geneva Agreements: agreements signed in July 1954 which ended the first Indochinese war. Apart from France and the various Indochinese 'entities', the negotiations were conducted on an international level, with the involvement of the US, the USSR and China. The agreements divided Vietnam into two parts at the level of the 17th parallel, although this was supposed to be temporary and elections to be held in 1956 throughout the country were to have allowed reunification. Knowing that the Communist Party would have won a majority, Washington and the Saigon regime refused to allow the elections to be held.

Ha Huy Tap (1906–1941): from a family based in central Ha Tinh province, studied in the USSR, founding member, in 1930, of the Indochinese Communist Party. Played an active role in the 1930–31 revolutionary movement. Third Party General Secretary from 1936 to 1938. On 28 August 1941, he was executed by the French colonialists at the age of 35.

Hoa Binh Campaign: Hoa Binh was the capital of the Muong tribal minority in Vietnam's highlands. General Jean de Lattre de Tassigny launched the Hoa Binh campaign in November 1951 to try to cut the Viet Minh off from the Mekong Delta. But the campaign ended in February 1952 with the defeat of the French forces, thus marking a turning point in the war.

Hoang Hoa Tham or **De ('Commander') Tham** (d. 1913): leader of a peasant insurrection against the French colonialists in Yen The (Bac Giang, North Vietnam). Started in 1887, this uprising lasted for thirty years. Hoang Hoa Tham was assassinated on 10 February 1913. His name was used for one of the Viet Minh military campaigns in 1951.

Hoang Van Thu (d. 1944): a member of the Tay ethnic group, founding member of the Indochinese CP in 1930. Member of the Central Committee. One of the participants in the Bac Son uprising in 1940. Arrested by the French, tortured and then killed in 1944.

L'Humanité: daily newpaper, founded by Jean Jaurès, first of the French Socialists and then later of the Communist Party.

Khai Dinh (1885–1925): original name Nguyen Bun Dao, emperor of

Vietnam in 1916–25 and an advocate of co-operation with the colonial power, France.

Kolchak and **Wrangel**: Russian leaders of the counterrevolutionary White armies during the Civil War.

Kuomintang (KMT, or Guomindang): the Chinese 'National People's Party' founded in 1912 by Sun Yat-sen and Song Jiaoren. A revolutionary nationalist party particularly strong in the south of the country, it suffered repression (its leaders were exiled in Japan). It re-organized itself with the help of the USSR and allied itself with the Chinese Communists, who joined the party. It played a significant role in 1924–25 at the beginning of the Second Chinese Revolution and the Northern March against the warlords. But, after the death of Sun Yat-sen in March 1925, the key military leader Chiang Kai-shek took control of the party. He used the party as an instrument in the bloody counter-revolution of 1926–27. After the accession of Chiang Kai-shek, the Kuomintang became the party-state of the Republic of China. In 194749, defeated in the civil war against the Red Army, the KMT moved its operations to the island of Taiwan where it imposed a one-party dictatorship.

Le Hong Phong or **Le Huy Doan** (1902–1942): founding member in 1925 of the Than Nien and then, in 1930, the Indochinese CP, of which he became one of the leaders. Studied in Moscow. Husband of Nguyen Thi Minh Khai. In 1935, he led the Vietnamese delegation to the Seventh Congress of the Communist International and became a deputy member of the Executive Committee. Second Party General Secretary from 1935 to 1936. Arrested in 1939 by the French, died at Poulo Condore (Con Dao) prison in 1942 after suffering abuse.

Le Loi (1384/51433): also called Binh Dinh Vuong, or Thuan Thien. Born in Thanh Hoa province. Vietnamese general and emperor who won back independence for Vietnam from China in 1428. Founder of the Le Dynasty. Le Loi is among the most famous figures from the medieval period.

Jean Longuet (1876–1938): leading member of the French Socialist

Party (the SFIO). Son-in-law of Karl Marx. Founded the daily paper *Le Populaire* in 1916.

Luong Ngoc Quyen: member of the nationalist 'Quang Phuc' the Viet Nam Quang Phuc ('Society for the Restoration of Vietnam') created in May 1912 by Phan Boi Chau. One of the leaders of Thai Nguyen garrison uprising, in Tonkin, in August–September 1917.

Marshall Lyautey (Louis Hubert Gonzalve Lyautey) (1854–1934): French officer during the colonial wars, Minister of Defence during the First World War, Marshall of France.

René Maran (1887–1960): poet and novelist from Martinique who lived for a long time in Africa. Was the first black writer to win the Goncourt Prize in 1921 for his novel *Batouala (Batouala: A True Black Novel)*.

Monmousseau, Gaston (1883–1960): before 1914 an anarchist railway worker, Secretary of Railwaymen's Federation in 1920 and General Sectretary of the CGTU in 1922. Joined the French CP in 1925 and became an orthodox Communist.

Nghe An Soviets and Nghe Tinh Soviets: in 1930 and 1931, under the leadership of the Indochinese Communist Party, workers and peasants rose against the French imperialists and the feudal court. This movement took place in Nghe An and Ha Tinh provinces (Central Vietnam), where it overthrew the colonial administration and set up people's power. The colonialists made severe reprisals against the movement.

Ngo Gia Tu (Ngo Si Quyet, Bach) (d. 1935): member of the Thanh Nien, he led a dissident group known as the Indochinese Communist Party just before the creation in 1930, as the product of the fusion of a number of organizations, of the official Indochinese CP. Having also been a founding member of the latter, and due to confusion over names, some have claimed that Ngo Gia Tu was its first General Secretary (who was in fact Tran Phu). Ngo Gia Tu disappeared at sea in 1935, trying to escape by boat from the prison at Poulo Condore.

Nguyen Thi Minh Khai (alias Lan) (d. 1941): originally from Nghe Tinh. From 1930 onwards, worked closely with Ho in relation to the Communist International. Participated in the Seventh Congress of the International in 1935. She married Le Hong Phong in Moscow that same year. As a leader of the CP in Cochinchina, she was arrested in 1940 by the French and executed in April 1941.

Nguyen Van Cu (d. 1941): Fourth General Secretary of the Indochinese CP, March 1938 January 1940. Arrested by the French in 1940 and shot in July 1941.

Nguyen Van To: writer who, in 1941, along with Dao Duy Anh, created in Hanoi a shortlived Confucian journal, *Tri tan ('Knowledge of the New')*.

Le Paria: weekly paper published in Paris by the anti-colonial Union Intercoloniale from 1922 onwards. Ho was a central figure in this organization.

Paris Conference: a consequence of the 1968 Tet Offensive, which convinced Washington of the need to start negotiations, the Paris Conference involved, on the one hand, the Democratic Republic of Vietnam and the National Liberation Front (NLF) and, on the other, the US and the Saigon regime. It resulted in the 1973 accords and the progressive withdrawal of US troops from Vietnam (which Washington tried to compensate for with the policy of 'Vietnamization' of the war and intensive bombing of Cambodia and Laos).

Pathet Lao and Khmer forces: the Pathet Lao ('Land of Laos'), a nationalist movement led by the Communists, was founded in 1950 and presided over by prince Souphanouvong. It collaborated with the Viet Minh and then the NLF in the liberation struggle in Indochina. It gained power in 1975 and maintained its alliance with Vietnam. In contrast, in Cambodia the control over the Communist Party passed to the Pol Pot faction, which was violently anti-Vietnamese. All Khmer Communists suspected of being close to the Vietnamese CP were secretly eliminated. In 1975, the Angkor ('The Organization') turned against Vietnam.

Peng Bai (Peng Pai): educated and cultivated son of rich landowner who, in China, founded the peasant soviets of Hai Lufeng (Guandung) in 1927–28.

Phan Dinh Phung (d. 1895): mandarin and military leader who kept the French at bay until his death in 1895.

Quang Trung (Nguyen Hue) (d. 1792): Vietnamese national hero who led the peasant insurrection of 1771. He reunified the country, hitherto divided into two dynasties, in 1786. Proclaimed emperor in 1788, the following year he inflicted a historic military defeat on the Chinese invasion forces of the Tsing. Also the name given to a Viet Minh military campaign in 1951.

quoc ngu: Vietnamese language written with an adapted Latin alphabet created in the seventeenth century.

Saint, Lucien (1867–1938): Resident General of France in Tunisia between 1921 and 1929. Vigorously opposed the nationalist movement.

Sarraut, Albert-Pierre (1872–1962): French Radical-Socialist statesman most noted for his colonial policy and liberal rule as governor-general of Indochina 1911–14 and 1917–19. Tried to install 'Franco-Annamite collaboration' (under French domination) to forestall radical nationalism.

Sèvres Treaty: peace treaty signed on 10 August 1920 between the allied powers of the First World War and the Ottoman Empire. It marked the dismemberment of the latter.

Siam: name for Thailand until 1939.

Siki (or **Battling Siki**, aka **Louis Mbarick Fall**) (1897–1925): a Senegalese boxer considered one of the more colourful figures in boxing history.

Syngman Rhee (1875–1965): after the Korean War, the first president of South Korea (1948–60). With US support, he installed a dictatorial regime. Was overthrown under the pressure of a democratic student movement in April 1960, only to be replaced by another dictator.

Tassigny, General de Lattre de (1889–1952): commander of the French forces in Indochina until 1951. He died the following year of a sickness.

Tonkin: northern part of Vietnam. Was a protectorate under the French. In Vietnamese: Bac Ky or Bac Bo.

Tours Congress: eighteenth congress of the French Socialist Party (Section française de l'Internationale socialiste, or SFIO) in December 1920. As a consequence of this congress, and the resulting split, the French Communist Party (originally known as the SFIC) was founded.

Tran: name of a dynasty and epoch of Vietnamese history (1225–1400).

Tran Hung Dao (Tran Quoc Tuan) (1228–1300): considered a national hero, he was the military chief who fought the Mongol invasions of the thirteenth century. His name was used for one of the Viet Minh military campaigns in 1951.

Tran Phu (d. 1931): member of the Than Nien, then first General Secretary of the Communist Party in 1930. Arrested by the French, died from the effects of torture in 1931.

Trieu, Lady (Trieu Thi Trinh): female warrior who fought the Chinese occupation in the third century.

Trotskyism (or 'Trotskyites'): name given (in reference to the Russian revolutionary Leon Trotsky) to the anti-Stalinist Left Opposition in the Communist International. In Vietnam, the Trotskyist movement was influential in the 1930s in the SaigonCholon region. During the height of Stalinism, Cochinchina experienced a highly original form of the united front: the Indochinese CP (loyal to the Comintern), the Trotskyists and independent communists joined forces in the legal struggle, publishing an agitational newspaper *La Lutte*, and successfully running for the municipal elections. This united front was broken in 1937 and the Trotskyists gained the majority of the La Lutte group. The best-known of the Trotskyist leaders was Ta Thu Thau, a renowned figure of the Vietnamese communist and nationalist movements. In fact, the Trotskyist movement was divided, with one wing considering the line of La Lutte as opportunist. Ta Thu Thau and several of his comrades were killed by the CP in 1945. Other Trotskyist activists were killed by French occupation forces.

Trung Sisters: two sisters who led the first national uprising against the occupying Chinese in the year 40 AD.

Vaillant-Couturier, Paul (1892–1937): member of the French Socialist Party (SFIO), he participated in the Tours Congress and the foundation of the French CP. A journalist, a deputy and a very popular leader, he was not always in accord with the party leadership.

Viet Bac (Campaign): mountainous zone in North Tonkin. Liberated in 1950, thanks in particular to the victory of the Chinese Revolution.

Viet Minh (or Vietminh): abbreviation for Viet Nam Doc Lap Dong Minh Hoi ('League for the Independence of Vietnam'). National liberation front led by the Communists and founded in 1941. It was under this aegis that the resistance against Japanese occupation (until the August 1945 insurrection) and then against the French (1945–54) was conducted.

Vinh YenPhuc Yen campaign: Vinh Yen is the capital of Phuc Yen province, in the delta of the Red River (Tonkin). The Viet Minh carried out a military campaign there in 1951.

Vo Nguyen Giap (1911): born in the province of Quang Binh. Became politically active in Hanoi as a student and journalist. Imprisoned in 1930, he joined the Indochinese Communist Party in 1931 on his liberation. He met Ho Chi Minh for the first time in 1940. Particularly well known for his role in the battle of Dien Bien Phu (1954), Giap was one of the principal theoreticians, strategists, political leaders and military commanders of Vietnamese Communism. Now retired, he served as a member of the political bureau, commander of the army and minister in numerous governments.

yuan: Chinese currency.

CHRONOLOGY

1931	Ho arrested in Hong Kong
1933	Goes to Moscow
1934	Attends Lenin School
1935	Takes part in Seventh Congress of the Communist International; perhaps goes to Macao for Indochinese Communist Party First Congress
1936	Popular Front Government in France
1937	Japanese invasion of China; Chang Kai-shek makes truce with Chinese Communists
1938	Ho convalesces in Sochi
1939	Goes to Yenan and south-west to Kunming; Second World War begins in Europe
1940	Fall of France; Japanese troops, with French co-operation, occupy Indochina
1941	Ho re-enters Vietnam from China, founds the Vietminh at Bac Bo; Japanese attack Pearl Harbor; US enters war
1942	Re-enters China, is arrested, imprisoned
1944	Released, agreement reached with Chinese Nationalists; Dong Ming Hoi founded

1945

February	Ho sets off for Kunming, meets Lt. Shaw, a rescued US pilot
March	Japanese coup in Indochina against French
April	AGAS-Ho hook-up; he returns to Vietnam as 'agent'
July	Potsdam conference; Indochina to be divided into two zones
August	Second World War ends, Vietminh take over, declare independence; Indochinese Communist Party disbanded
September	Chinese occupy North Vietnam, British take over South

1946

March	French recognize Ho's republic of Vietnam as a free State
May	D'Argenlieu sets up puppet 'Republic of Cochin China'
June	Ho in France to finalize settlement; returns with *modus vivendi*
December	War breaks out between French and Vietminh

1949

| March | France establishes puppet State of Vietnam under Bao Dai |
| October | Communists win struggle in China |

1950

January	Ho's Democratic Republic of Vietnam recognized first by Mao's People's Republic of China, then by Soviet Union
May	The US begins military aid to French in Vietnam

1951

February	Founding of the Lao Dong

1953

March	Death of Stalin leads to Geneva Conference

1954

May	French defeated at Dien Bien Phu
July	Ngo Dinh Diem made Head of State in South Vietnam; Geneva Treaty signed, Vietnam split at the 17th parallel
October	Eisenhower offers aid to Diem

1955

January	First American military supplies arrive in Saigon; Diem rejects proposed elections

1956 French forces leave South, deadline passes for elections; peasant discontent in North Vietnam forcibly put down; Land Reform Campaign fails

1957 Diem's campaign of terror stirs first resistance in the South

1959 Ho decides North must help this resistance movement

1960 Le Duan appointed Party Secretary; National Liberation Front set up in South

1961

November	Kennedy offers increased military aid to Diem
December	US White Paper states United States intentions

1962 International Control Commission censures US and Diem regime for military activity, censures Ho government for aiding NLF

1963

November	Diem assassinated; Kennedy assassinated

1964

January	Coup d'état by General Nguyen Kanh
August	Tonkin Gulf incident; US attacks DRV mainland bases; Buddhist uprising against Kanh regime
September	U Thant makes Ho's negotiation offer to US
November	Johnson re-elected

1965

February	US White Paper prepares for increased military action
April	Johnson's 'Johns Hopkins' speech; DRV's 'Four Points'
May	First US combat troops in action; first pause in US bombing; Nguyen Kao Ky appointed 'Head of State'
November	Massive protests in US to end war
December	Second pause in US bombing

1966

January	Ho appeals to de Gaulle; Sainteny goes to Hanoi; Johnson airs his 'Fourteen Points'; bombing of North resumed
October	Johnson's Manila Conference to promote outside approval

1967

January	Salisbury's *New York Times* reports shock America

1968

February	Tet offensive reveals full weakness of US and South Vietnam; public pressure in US to get out of Vietnam
November	Nixon elected President, promises graduated withdrawal

1969

May	First US troop withdrawal
September	Ho dies

NOTE ON THE TEXT

Chapters 13, 15–19, 21, 23, 25–27, 29, 30, 32–36, 40, 41 and 43–48 are taken from *Selected Writings 1920–1969*, (reprinted by University Press of the Pacific, 2001) and chapters 41–4, 20, 22, 24, 28, 31, 37, 38, 42 and 49 are from *Ho Chi Minh: Selected Articles and Speeches, 1920–1967* (International Publishers, 1970). All notes are taken from the original editions. The Glossary was compiled with the help of Pierre Rousset, author of several studies in French of the Vietnamese Communist movement.

I

SPEECH AT THE TOURS CONGRESS[1]

December 1920

Chairman: Comrade Indochinese Delegate, you have the floor. (*Applause.*)

Indochinese Delegate [Nguyen Ai Quoc, later President Ho Chi Minh]: Today, instead of contributing, together with you, to world revolution as I should wish, I come here with deep sadness and profound grief, as a socialist, to protest against the abhorrent crimes committed in my native land. (*Very good!*)

You all know that French capitalism entered Indochina half a century ago. It conquered our country at bayonet point and in the name of capitalism. Since then we have not only been oppressed and exploited shamelessly, but also tortured and poisoned pitilessly. (I would stress this fact that we have been poisoned, with opium, alcohol, etc.) I cannot, in but a few minutes, reveal all the atrocities perpetrated by the predatory capitalists in Indochina. Prisons outnumber schools and are always overcrowded with detainees. Any native suspected of having socialist ideas is arrested and sometimes put to death without trial. So goes justice in Indochina for in that country there is one law for the Annamese and another for the Europeans or those holding European citizenship. The former do not enjoy the same safeguards as the latter. We have neither freedom of the press, freedom of speech, freedom of assembly, nor freedom of association. We have no right to emigrate or travel abroad as tourists. We live in utter ignorance because we have no right to study. In Indochina the colonialists do all they can to poison us with opium and besot us with alcohol. Thousands of Annamese have been led to a slow death and thousands of others massacred to protect interests that are not theirs.

Comrades, such is the treatment inflicted upon more than twenty million Annamese, that is, more than half the population of France. And yet they are said to be under French protection! (*Applause.*) The Socialist Party must act effectively in favour of the oppressed natives. (*Cheers.*)

Jean Longuet: I have spoken in favour of the natives!

Indochinese Delegate: Right from the beginning of my speech I have imposed the dictatorship of silence . . . (*Laughter.*) The Party must carry out propaganda for socialism in all colonial countries. We shall see in the Socialist Party's joining the Third International the promise that from now on it will attach to the colonial questions the importance they deserve. We are very glad to learn that a Standing Delegation has been appointed for North Africa and we should be very happy if in the near future the Party sends one of its members to Indochina to study on the spot the relevant questions and what should be done about them.

A delegate: With Comrade Enver Pasha?

Indochinese Delegate: Silence, the Parliamentarians! (*Applause.*)

Chairman: Now all delegates must keep silent, including the non-Parliamentarians!

Indochinese Delegate: In the name of the whole of mankind, in the name of all socialists, both those of the left and those of the right, we say to you: Comrades save us! (*Applause.*)

Chairman: Through the applause which greeted him, the Indochinese Delegate can realize that the entire Socialist Party side with him to oppose the crimes of the bourgeoisie.

2

INDOCHINA[1]

1921

It is wrong to say that this country, inhabited by more than 20 million exploited people, is now ripe for revolution; but even wronger to say that it doesn't want a revolution and is satisfied with the regime, as claim our masters. The truth is that the Indochinese people have no means of education and action. They can have neither press, meetings, associations, nor travels. It is a veritable crime for one of them to be found in possession of foreign newspapers or periodicals with somewhat advanced opinions, or a French working-class publication. Alcohol and opium, as well as the subsidized colonial press in the pay of the authorities, complete the government's obscurantist undertaking. The guillotine and prisons do the rest.

Morally and physically poisoned, gagged and penned up, this human herd may be thought to be forever destined to the altar of the capitalist god, to have stopped living and thinking, to be of no use in social transformation. Not at all! *The Indochinese are not dead, they still live, they will live forever.* Systematic poisoning by colonial capitalism has not stamped out their vitality, even less their consciousness. The wind from working-class Russia, revolutionary China or militant India has cured them of intoxication. It is true that they don't get educated by books or speeches, but in another fashion. Suffering, destitution and brutal oppression are their only educators, and while the socialists are remiss about their education, the colonial and native (mandarin) bourgeoisie are paying it affectionate attention. The Indochinese are making tremendous progress and, occasion permitting, will show themselves to be worthy of their masters. Under a mask of passivity, they hide something that is seething, rumbling and will, when the time comes, explode formidably. It is up to the elite to hasten the coming of that moment. The tyranny of capitalism has prepared the ground: the only thing for socialism to do is to sow the seeds of emancipation.

3

THE ANTI-FRENCH
RESISTANCE[1]

1921–26

When the Great War ended, the Vietnamese people like other peoples were deceived by Wilson's 'generous' declarations on the right of peoples to self-determination. A group of Vietnamese, which included myself, sent the following demands to the French Parliament and to all delegations to the Versailles Conference.

CLAIMS OF THE VIETNAMESE PEOPLE

Ever since the victory of the Allies, all the subjected peoples have entertained high hopes about an era of right and justice which should follow the formal and solemn pledges taken before the whole world by the various powers of the Entente in the struggle of civilization against barbarism.

While waiting for the realization of the principle of nationalities through the effective recognition of the sacred right of the peoples to self-determination, the people of the former Empire of Annam, now French Indochina, proposed to the governments of the Entente in general and the French government in particular the following demands:

1. Amnesty for all Vietnamese political detainees;
2. Reform of the Indochinese judicial system by giving the Vietnamese the same judicial safeguards as given to the Europeans and completely and definitively abolishing the special tribunals which are instruments of terror and oppression against the most honest part of the Vietnamese people;

3. Freedom of the press and freedom of opinion;
4. Freedom of association and freedom of assembly;
5. Freedom to emigrate and travel abroad;
6. Freedom of teaching and creation in all provinces of technical and vocational schools for natives;
7. Replacement of the regime of decrees by that of laws;
8. Presence in the French Parliament of a permanent delegation elected by the natives to keep it informed of their aspirations!

(. . .)

To these demands we added a tribute to the peoples and to feelings of humanity.

However, after a time of waiting and study, we realized that the 'Wilson doctrine' was but a big fraud. The liberation of the proletariat is the necessary condition for national liberation. Both these liberations can only come from communism and world revolution.

4

SOME CONSIDERATIONS ON THE COLONIAL QUESTION[1]

25 May 1922

Since the French Party has accepted Moscow's 'twenty-one conditions' and joined the Third International, among the problems which it has set itself is a particularly ticklish one – colonial policy. Unlike the First and Second Internationals, it cannot be satisfied with purely sentimental expressions of position leading to nothing at all, but must have a well-defined working programme, an effective and practical policy.

On this point, more than on others, the Party faces many difficulties, the greatest of which are the following:

I. THE GREAT SIZE OF THE COLONIES

Not counting the new 'trusteeships' acquired after the war, France possesses:

In Asia 450,000 square kilometres, in Africa 3,541,000 square kilometres, in America 108,000 square kilometres and in Oceania 21,600 square kilometres, or a total area of 4,120,000 square kilometres (eight times its own territory), with a population of 48,000,000 souls. These people speak over twenty different languages. This diversity of tongues does not make propaganda easy, for, except in a few old colonies, a French propagandist can make himself understood only through an interpreter. However, translations are of limited value, and in these countries of administrative despotism, it is rather difficult to find an interpreter to translate revolutionary speeches.

There are other drawbacks: though the natives of all the colonies are equally oppressed and exploited, their intellectual, economic and political development differs greatly from one region to another. Between Annam and the Congo, Martinique and New Caledonia, there is absolutely nothing in common, except poverty.

2. THE INDIFFERENCE OF THE PROLETARIAT OF THE MOTHER COUNTRY TOWARDS THE COLONIES

In his theses on the colonial question, Lenin clearly stated that 'the workers of colonizing countries are bound to give the most active assistance to the liberation movements in subject countries'. To this end, the workers of the mother country must know what a colony really is, they must be acquainted with what is going on there, and with the suffering – a thousand times more acute than theirs – endured by their brothers, the proletarians in the colonies. In a word, they must take an interest in this question.

Unfortunately, there are many militants who still think that a colony is nothing but a country with plenty of sand underfoot and of sun overhead; a few green coconut palms and coloured folk, that is all. And they take not the slightest interest in the matter.

3. THE IGNORANCE OF THE NATIVES

In colonized countries – in old Indochina as well as in new Dahomey – the class struggle, and proletarian strength, are unknown factors for the simple reason that there are neither big commercial and industrial enterprises, nor workers' organizations. In the eyes of the natives, Bolshevism – a word which is the more vivid and expressive because frequently used by the bourgeoisie – means either the destruction of everything or emancipation from the foreign yoke. The first sense given to the word drives the ignorant and timorous masses away from us; the second leads them to nationalism. Both senses are equally dangerous. Only a tiny section of the intelligentsia knows what is meant by communism. But these gentry, belonging to the native bourgeoisie and supporting the bourgeois colonialists, have no interest in the communist doctrine being understood and propagated. On the contrary, like the dog in the fable, they prefer to bear the mark of the collar and to have their piece of bone. Generally speaking, the masses are thoroughly rebellious, but completely ignorant. They want to free themselves, but do not know how to go about doing so.

4. PREJUDICES

The mutual ignorance of the two proletariats gives rise to prejudices. The French workers look upon the native as an inferior and negligible human being, incapable of understanding and still less of taking action. The natives regard all the French as wicked exploiters. Imperialism and capitalism do not fail to take advantage of this mutual suspicion and this artificial racial hierarchy to frustrate propaganda and divide forces which ought to unite.

5. FIERCENESS OF REPRESSION

If the French colonialists are unskilful in developing colonial resources, they are masters in the art of savage repression and the manufacture of loyalty made to measure. The Gandhis and the de Valeras would have long since entered heaven had they been born in one of the French colonies. Surrounded by all the refinements of courts martial and special courts, a native militant cannot educate his oppressed and ignorant brothers without the risk of falling into the clutches of his civilizers.

Faced with these difficulties, what must the Party do?

Intensify propaganda to overcome them.

5

ANNAMESE WOMEN AND FRENCH DOMINATION[1]

1 August 1922

Colonization is in itself an act of violence of the stronger against the weaker. This violence becomes still more odious when it is exercised upon women and children.

It is bitterly ironic to find that civilization – symbolized in its various forms, viz. liberty, justice, etc., by the gentle image of woman, and run by a category of men well known to be champions of gallantry – inflicts on its living emblem the most ignoble treatment and afflicts her shamefully in her manners, her modesty and even her life.

Colonial sadism is unbelievably widespread and cruel, but we shall confine ourselves here to recalling a few instances seen and described by witnesses unsuspected of partiality. These facts will allow our Western sisters to realize both the nature of the 'civilizing mission' of capitalism, and the sufferings of their sisters in the colonies.

'On the arrival of the soldiers,' relates a colonial, 'the population fled; there only remained two old men and two women: one maiden, and a mother suckling her baby and holding an eight-year-old girl by the hand. The soldiers asked for money, spirits and opium.

'As they could not make themselves understood, they became furious and knocked down one of the old men with their rifle butts. Later, two of them, already drunk when they arrived, amused themselves for many hours by roasting the other old man at a wood fire. Meanwhile, the others raped the two women and the eight-year-old girl. Then, weary, they murdered the girl. The mother was then able to escape with her infant and, from a hundred yards off, hidden in a bush, she saw her companion tortured. She did not know why the murder was perpetrated, but she saw the young girl lying on her back, bound and gagged, and one of the men, many times, slowly thrust his bayonet into her stomach and, very slowly, draw it out again. Then he cut off the dead girl's finger to take a ring, and her head to steal a necklace.

'The three corpses lay on the flat ground of a former salt marsh: the eight-year-old girl naked, the young woman disembowelled, her stiffened left forearm raising a clenched fist to the indifferent sky, and the old man, horrible, naked like the others, disfigured by the roasting with his fat which had run, melted and congealed with the skin of his belly, which was bloated, grilled and golden, like the skin of a roast pig.'

6

AN OPEN LETTER TO M. ALBERT SARRAUT, MINISTER OF COLONIES[1]

1 August 1922

Your Excellency,

We know very well that your affection for the natives of the colonies in general, and the Annamese in particular is great.

Under your proconsulate the Annamese people have known true prosperity and real happiness, the happiness of seeing their country dotted all over with an increasing number of spirit and opium shops which, together with firing squads, prisons, 'democracy' and all the improved apparatus of modern civilization, are combining to make the Annamese the most advanced of the Asians and the happiest of mortals.

These acts of benevolence save us the trouble of recalling all the others, such as enforced recruitment and loans, bloody repressions, the dethronement and exile of kings, profanation of sacred places, etc.

As a Chinese poem says, 'The wind of kindness follows the movement of your fan, and the rain of virtue precedes the tracks of your carriage.' As you are now the supreme head of all the colonies, your special care for the Indochinese has but increased with your elevation. You have created in Paris itself a service having the special task – with special regard to Indochina, according to a colonial publication – of keeping watch on the natives, especially the Annamese, living in France.

But 'keeping watch' alone seemed to Your Excellency's fatherly solicitude insufficient, and you wanted to do better. That is why, for some time now, you have granted each Annamese – dear Annamese, as Your Excellency says – private *aides-de-camp*. Though still novices in the art of Sherlock Holmes, these good people are very devoted and particularly sympathetic. We have only praise to bestow on them and compliments to pay to their boss, Your Excellency.

We are sincerely moved by the honour that Your Excellency has the extreme kindness to grant us and we would have accepted it with all gratitude if it did not seem a little superfluous, and if it did not excite envy and jealousy.

At a time when Parliament is trying to save money and cut down administrative personnel; when there is a large budget deficit; when agriculture and industry lack labour; when attempts are being made to levy taxes on workers' wages; and at a time when repopulation demands the use of all productive energies: it would seem to us anti-patriotic at such a time to accept personal favours which necessarily cause loss of the powers of the citizens condemned – as *aides-de-camp* – to idleness and the spending of money that the proletariat has sweated hard for.

In consequence, while remaining obliged to you, we respectfully decline this distinction flattering to us but too expensive to the country.

If Your Excellency insists on knowing what we do every day, nothing is easier: we shall publish every morning a bulletin of our movements, and Your Excellency will have but the trouble of reading.

Besides, our timetable is quite simple and almost unchanging.

Morning: from 8 to 12 at the workshop.
Afternoon: in newspaper offices (leftist of course) or at the library.
Evening: at home or attending educational talks.
Sundays and holidays: visiting museums or other places of interest.

There you are!

Hoping that this convenient and rational method will give satisfaction to Your Excellency, we beg to remain . . .

7

MURDEROUS CIVILIZATION![1]

I August 1922

We have of late pointed out from this platform a series of assassinations perpetrated by our 'civilizers' which remain unpunished. Alas! The gloomy black list lengthens every day.

Quite recently, a fifty-year-old Annamese employed for 35 years in the Railways Department of Cochin-China was murdered by a white official. Here are the facts.

Le Van Tai had in his charge four other Annamese employed in preventing trains from crossing a bridge while it was opened to let navigation pass. The order was to close the bridge to navigation ten minutes before the trains were due to cross the bridge.

On 2 April, at 4.30 p.m., one of these Annamese came to close the bridge and lower the signal. Just then a government launch appeared with a naval dockyard official on board returning from a hunt. The launch whistled. The native employee went to the middle of the bridge and waved a red flag as a sign to the boat that a train was going to pass and that navigation was accordingly suspended. Here is what happened. The launch came alongside a pillar of the bridge. The official jumped out and made furiously for the Annamese employee. Prudently, the latter fled in the direction of Tai's house. The Frenchman pursued him, throwing stones at him.

When he heard the noise, Tai came out to meet the representative of civilization who addressed him thus, 'You stupid brute, why don't you raise the bridge?' In reply, Tai, who could not speak French, pointed to the red signal. This simple gesture exasperated M. Long's collaborator who, without more ado, fell upon Tai and, after giving him a thorough drubbing, pushed him into a brazier nearby.

Horribly burnt, the Anamese crossing-keeper was carried to hospital where he died after six days of atrocious suffering. The French official was not charged.

In Marseille, the official prosperity of Indochina is on display; in Annam, people are dying of starvation. Here loyalism is praised, there assassination is perpetrated! What do you say to this, oh thousands of times over Majesty Khai Dinh and Excellentissimo Sarraut?

PS   While the life of an Annamese is not worth a cent, for a scratch on the arm M. Inspector General Reinhardt receives 120,000 francs compensation. Equality! Beloved equality!

8

THE MARTYRDOM OF
AMDOUNI AND BEN-BELKHIR[1]

1 November 1922

In the war fought to uphold the rule of law, to safeguard justice, civilization, etc. . . . 100,000 Tunisian infantrymen were mobilized, 60 per cent of whom did not come back. At that time, Tunisians were covered with flowers and showered with affection. Franco-Tunisian brotherhood was chanted with much love and tenderness, 'a brotherhood sealed for ever in blood and glory'. A censorship was even established to prevent publication in the press of any matter likely to offend native opinion.

Today, this fraternity has changed its form. It is no longer expressed by caresses and flowers. It is expressed more eloquently by revolver shots or riding whips. The following facts are proof of this.

Seeing three natives grazing their sheep in his olive groves, a French settler sent his wife for his rifle and cartridges. When they were brought to him, our civilizer laid in wait behind a bush, and, bang! bang! bang! three shots went off and the three natives fell gravely wounded.

Another French settler had working for him two natives, Amdouni and Ben-Belkhir. It seemed that these had taken a few bunches of grapes. The settler sent for them and beat them mercilessly with a bull's pizzle until they fainted. When they recovered their senses, our protector had their arms bound behind their backs and had them strung up by their hands. Though the two unfortunates lost consciousness, the odious punishment lasted for four hours and ended only when a neighbour protested.

Taken to hospital, the unfortunates each had to have one hand amputated, and it is not known whether the other hand can be saved.

There it is, fra-ter-ni-ty!

The honourable M. Lucien Saint is too busy expelling communists and journalists to think of the lives of his native protégés.

9

ABOUT SIKI[1]

1 December 1922

Ever since colonialism has existed, the whites have been paid to bash in the faces of the blacks. For once, a black has been paid to do the same thing to a white. Being an opponent of all acts of violence, we disapprove of either procedure.

With a punch – if not scientifically aimed, at least amazingly well placed – Siki definitely removed Carpentier from his pedestal to climb on to it himself.

The boxing championship has changed hands, but national sporting glory has not suffered, because Siki, a child of Senegal, is in consequence a son of France, and hence a Frenchman.

In spite of this, it so happens that every time Carpentier wins, it is naturally due to his skill and science. But every time he is beaten, it is always because of the brute strength of a Dempsey, or the dirty legwork of a Siki. This is the reason why at the Buffalo match they wished to say – they had even made the statement – that Siki, though having won the match, lost it 'just the same'. But the public, the good public, did not wish to see it in that light. And popular justice was triumphant: Siki was proclaimed champion of the world and of France.

After being knocked out by a black, Carpentier calmly went to visit Russia, the land of the reds. We congratulate Siki on his victory. We also congratulate Carpentier on his open-mindedness.

Fortune smiles only upon the rich, says the SDN (read *sagesse des nations* and not Société des Nations (League of Nations)). René Maran and Siki have caused much black ink to flow. Siki, furthermore, caused red blood to flow. People are behaving as if both our African brothers need as much ink again. Following Maran's ironical pen, Siki's gloves have stirred everything, including even the political sphere. And M.

Luquet, Councillor of the Seine Department, immediately tabled a motion attempting to ban boxing matches. M. Luquet must allow us to tell him respectfully that what he did was an anti-patriotic act. Here is our explanation: from the point of view of international policy, a featherweight champion makes as much propaganda for our moral influence abroad as an immortal, a glorious man, a songwriter or ten army corps (see the newspapers). From the national viewpoint, boxers are indispensable as an example of and stimulation to the physical excellence of the young generation. From the colonial viewpoint, a Carpentier–Siki match is worth more than one hundred gubernatorial speeches to prove to our subjects and protégés that we want to apply to the letter the principle of equality between races. Will this threefold advantage be sacrificed to a vague humanitarianism? No! Isn't that so, M. Sarraut?

We learn from the newspapers that Siki has just been suspended for nine months from all boxing rings in France. Reason: for having railed at M. Cuny.

What happened? Before, Siki was glorified because he made Carpentier's nose swell; today, he has not touched a hair of M. Cuny's head and yet he is disgraced. We are surely not going to be made to believe that M. Cuny's face is any more fragile or any more peculiar than Carpentier's and that . . . but no. That is no way to understand it at all. We are rather inclined to think this way: Siki, a black, will never be forgiven for having defeated Carpentier, a white, and if Carpentier bears no grudge, the chauvinism of others does. And this charge is only a pretext . . . motivated by . . .

We learn from the same newspapers that the British Home Ministry has banned the expected match between Joe Beckett and Siki in London. This does not surprise us. As His British Excellency could digest neither Kemal [Atatürk]'s croissant nor Gandhi's chocolate, he wants to have Battling Siki swallow his purge even though the latter is a Frenchman. Understand?

10

MENAGERIE[1]

1 February 1923

We have racked our yellow brains in vain, yet we cannot succeed in discovering the reason which led the men and women of France to found the remarkable institution called the Society for the Prevention of Cruelty to Animals. First, the reason escapes us because we see that there are still so many unfortunate human beings who appeal without result for a little care. Then, because all these animals do not deserve so much benevolence and are not as unhappy as all that. Except for the black lion who is useful to people accustomed to wrapping their feet in animal pelts, most of these creatures are wicked, very wicked indeed.

Does not the bulldog – with his ugly teeth – come to tear away the entire structure of the Paris Conference? Which obliges the Flemish monkey and the Gallic cock to confront the German eagle in the Ruhr alone. Did not the Tiger [Clemenceau], while he was still chained, devour several ministries of the Republic? Were not millions and billions uselessly expended through the agency of our glorious friends Kolchak and Wrangel to buy the skin of the Muscovite bear who, today more than ever, has no mind to let people have it all their own way? (Ah! What an animal!)

Which of our friends in France has not cause to complain of the vultures' misdeeds? Are not crows disastrously destructive in the moral field? And what do the *'chats fourrés'* [judges] do if not profit by dissensions and discords in society? Is there not one animal which impudently permits that all disrespectful sons-in-law call their mothers-in-law by its name? Are there not expensive lovebirds which darken the conjugal bliss of many a family? And are not cat burglars the age-old enemies of those who move from home?

Without taking account of the fact that the stronger wolf is always right and that black sheep are a plague to honest society, we . . . but let us speak a little, before concluding, of colonial beasts.

Just at the moment when M. Guinal is ready to present to the Academy of Sciences, through the medium of M. Mangin, a note relating to the utilization of shark skin, M. Albert Sarraut goes to the Isle of Dogs to deliver some of his ministerial speeches to the frozen cod of Saint-Pierre et Miquelon, and M. Citroen, for his part, launches his civilizing 'caterpillar' across the Sahara. Both these missions – official and semi-official – will very probably obtain the happy result that people have a right to expect from them, to whit, to know how to make a mouse bring forth a mountain and consolidate the position of the colonial sharks.

It is generally believed that our protectors always carry out an ostrich policy. What a mistake, my friends! Here is proof to the contrary: on the mere invitation of the sardine at the 'old port' [Marseille], the colonial government has not hesitated a moment to cause to be spent by:

Indochina	3,190,846
French West Africa	5,150,000
French Equatorial Africa	348,750
The Cameroons	390,000
Madagascar	1,837,600
Martinque	108,300
Guadeloupe	55,000
Guiana	62,500
New Caledonia	75,000
New Hebrides	60,000
Oceania	65,000
French settlements in India	135,000
Somaliland	97,000
Reunion	85,000
Saint-Pierre-et-Miquelon	14,000 francs

to bring a few camels, cows and crocodiles from the colonies to Marseille. No effort, it must be admitted, was spared by our civilizers to deck out a handful of native sparrows – very obedient and very docile ones – in peacock feathers to turn them into parrots or watchdogs. And if the African and Asian peoples are aware of this 'peace' and this 'prosperity', who then are the busy beavers but those untiring 'disseminators of democracy'?

In short, the lot of all these animals is relatively easy. If the members of the lofty SPCA had time to spare, they would perhaps do more useful work in taking care of the monkeys martyrized by Doctor Voronoff and the poor native sheep which are forever being shorn.

II

THE COUNTER-REVOLUTIONARY ARMY[1]

7 September 1923

We are aware that colonial rivalry was one of the main causes of the 1914–18 imperialist war.

What all Frenchmen should realize is that colonial expeditions are largely responsible for aggravating the depopulation from which their country is now suffering. If one looks at the statistics of military losses in killed and wounded sustained in the colonies, one is frightened by the gap they have caused in an ever-decreasing population such as that of France. From January to June 1923, in Morocco alone, 840 soldiers were killed or wounded for the greater glory of Marshal Lyautey!

What the French working class must realize is that colonialism relies on the colonies to defeat all attempts at emancipation on the part of the working class. No longer having absolute confidence in the white soldiers, who are more or less contaminated by the idea of classes, French militarism uses African and Asian natives in their stead. Out of 159 regiments in the French army, 10 are composed of colonial whites, i.e., semi-natives, 30 of Africans, and 39 of natives from other colonies. One half of the French army is thus recruited in the colonies.

Now, an Annamese soldier is in service for four years and an Algerian for three years. Thus, according to the reckoning of French militarism, two native soldiers are worth almost five French.

Moreover, being ignorant of the language and politics of the country, thinking that all whites belong to the race of his exploiters, and finally spurred on by his white superiors, the native soldier will march forward submissively and blindly, where the French soldier, more conscious, might refuse to go. Therein lies the danger.

One wonders for what reason 31 of the native regiments will be stationed on French territory? For what purpose are they intended? Are the French going to be civilized by these natives? The intention of French capitalism is thus clear. It is up to the French workers to act. They should fraternize with the native soldiers. They should make them understand that the workers of the mother country and the soldiers from the colonies are equally oppressed and exploited by the same masters, that they are all brothers of the same class, and that when the hour of struggle strikes, they will have, one and the other, to struggle against their common masters, and not between brothers.

12

THE WORKERS' MOVEMENT IN TURKEY[1]

1 January 1924

With a courage and spirit of sacrifice worthy of admiration, the Turkish people have torn up the odious Sèvres Treaty and recovered their independence. They have defeated the plotting of imperialism and overthrown the throne of the Sultans. They have turned their exhausted, torn and trampled nation into a united and strong republic. They have had their revolution. But like all bourgeois revolutions, the Turkish revolution is profitable only to one class: the moneyed class.

The Turkish proletariat, which greatly contributed to the struggle for national independence, is now obliged to embark on another struggle: the class struggle.

In this struggle, the Turkish working class is facing many obstacles. In Turkey, there are no trade unions such as those existing in the West. There are only corporations or friendly societies grouping workers of the same trade living in the same town. Workers of different trades living in the same town or workers of the same trade living in different towns have no connection between them. This prevents any effective common action.

Notwithstanding this state of affairs, the year that has just ended was disturbed many times by a ferment of the workers. Several strikes were launched in Constantinople, at the Golden Horn, at Aidine, etc. Printers, railwaymen, coastal vessel workers and workmen in petroleum storehouses and breweries waged struggles. Ten thousand workers participated in the movement. Following these experiences, the Turkish workers have realized that organization and discipline are necessary in order to triumph.

THE CONSTANTINOPLE CONGRESS FOUNDS THE *BIRLIK*

Recently, a Workers' Congress was convened in Constantinople. Two hundred and fifty delegates were present. They represented 19,000 Constantinople workers, 15,000 Zongouldak coal miners and 10,000 workers from the lead mines at Balyakaraidin.

It was decided to unite the 34 existing *demek* [associations] into a *birlik*, or federation. This bold decision frightened the government, which refused to recognize the *birlik*. It is to be noted that the government's attitude towards workers has changed a great deal since the end of the war. The government was always in favour of the workers when it was a question of driving out foreigners, but when it is a matter of organizing workers, it shows itself to be as reactionary as all other capitalist governments. Its opposition therefore surprises nobody. Besides, everybody knows that, since the Lausanne event, Turkish capitalism is flirting with foreign capital, which, after having caused the deaths of thousands of poor Greeks and Turks without succeeding in colonizing Turkey, is now penetrating peacefully into the Land of the Crescent. The refusal of the government to recognize the *birlik* is tantamount to a gracious smile directed to the foreign capital in the country, three-fifths of which is French.

But the Turkish proletariat has made its first step. It will go on.

13

REPORT ON THE NATIONAL AND COLONIAL QUESTIONS AT THE FIFTH CONGRESS OF THE COMMUNIST INTERNATIONAL[1]

1924

Comrades, I only wish to supplement Comrade Manuilsky's criticism of our policy on the colonial question. But before entering upon that subject, I deem it necessary to supply some figures which will help us to see its importance even more clearly.

Countries	METROPOLITAN COUNTRIES		COLONIES	
	Area (sq.km)	Population	Area (sq.km)	Population
Great Britain	151,000	45,500,000	34,910,000	403,600,000
France	536,000	39,000,000	10,250,000	55,600,000
United States	9,420,000	100,000,000	1,850,000	12,000,000
Spain	504,500	20,700,000	371,600	853,000
Italy	286,600	38,500,000	1,460,000	1,623,000
Japan	418,000	57,070,000	288,000	21,249,000
Belgium	29,500	7,642,000	2,400,000	8,500,000
Portugal	92,000	5,545,000	2,062,000	8,738,000
Holland	83,000	6,700,000	2,046,000	48,030,000

Thus, nine countries with an aggregate population of 320,657,000 and a total area of 11,407,600 square kilometres are exploiting colonies with a total population of 560,193,000 and covering areas adding up to 55,637,000 square kilometres. The total area of the colonies is five times that of the metropolitan countries, whose total population amounts to less than three-fifths that of the colonies.

These figures are even more striking if the biggest imperialist countries are taken separately. The British colonies taken as a whole are eight and a half times more populous and about 252 times bigger than Great Britain. France occupies an area 19 times bigger than her own. The population of the French colonies exceeds that of France by 16,600,000.

Thus, it is not an exaggeration to say that so long as the French and British communist parties do not apply a really active policy with regard to the colonies, and do not come into contact with the colonial peoples, their vast programmes will remain ineffective, and this because they go counter to Leninism. Let me explain what I mean. In his speech on Lenin and the national question Comrade Stalin said that the reformists and the leaders of the Second International dared not put the white and the coloured people on the same footing, that Lenin had rejected that inequality and smashed the obstacle separating the civilized slaves of imperialism from the uncivilized ones.

According to Lenin, the victory of the revolution in Western Europe depends on its close contact with the national liberation movement against imperialism in the colonies and dependent countries; the national question, as Lenin taught us, forms a part of the general problem of proletarian revolution and proletarian dictatorship.

Later, Comrade Stalin condemned the counter-revolutionary viewpoint which held that the European proletariat could achieve success without a direct alliance with the liberation movement in the colonies.

However, if we base our theoretical examination on facts, we are entitled to say that our major proletarian parties, except the Russian Party, still hold to the above-mentioned viewpoint because they are doing nothing in this matter.

What have the bourgeoisie in the colonialist countries done in order to keep the colonial masses under their oppressive rule? Everything. Besides using all the means given them by their state administrative machine, they have carried out an intense propaganda. They have crammed the heads of the people of the metropolitan countries with colonialist ideas through speeches, films, newspapers, exhibitions – to mention only the more important means – while dangling before their eyes pictures of the easy, honourable and rich life which is said to await them in the colonies.

As for our communist parties in Great Britain, Holland, Belgium and other countries whose bourgeoisie have invaded the colonies, what have they done? What have they done since the day they assimilated Lenin's theses in order to educate the proletariat of their countries in the spirit of genuine proletarian internationalism and close contact with the toiling masses in the colonies? What our parties have done in this domain amounts to almost nothing. As for me, born in a French colony and a member of the French Communist Party, I am sorry to say that our party has done very little for the colonies.

It is the task of the communist press to acquaint our militants with colonial questions, to awaken the toiling masses in the colonies and win them over to the cause of communism, but what have we done in this respect? Nothing at all.

If we compare the space devoted to colonial questions by such bourgeois newspapers as *Le Temps*, *Le Figaro*, *L'Oeuvre* or by those of other tendencies such as *Le Populaire* or *La Liberté* with that reserved for the same questions in *L'Humanité*, the central organ of our party, we must say that this comparison is not to our advantage.

The Ministry of Colonies has worked out a plan for transforming many African regions into large private plantations, and turning the people of these regions into veritable slaves attached to the new owners' lands; and yet our newspapers have remained wholly silent. In the French West African colonies, unprecedented measures have been carried out to force people into the army and yet our newspapers have not reacted. The colonialist authorities in Indochina have acted like slave traders, and sold Tonkinese people to plantation owners on the Pacific islands; they have extended the duration of the natives' military service from two to four years; ceded the greater part of the colony's land to the sharks of financial capitalism; and raised by a further 30 per cent taxes that already exceeded the natives' ability to pay. And this while the natives were being driven to bankruptcy and dying of hunger in the wake of floods. And yet our newspapers have kept silent. No wonder the natives are following such liberal democratic organizations as the Ligue des droits de l'homme and other similar organizations which take care of them or pretend to take care of them.

If we go a bit further, we shall see incredible things, which suggest that our party disregards all that concerns the colonies. For instance: *L'Humanité* did not publish the appeal made by the Peasants' International to the peoples of the colonies, sent to it by the Communist International for publication.

Prior to the Lyons conference[2] it published all the theses except that on the colonial question. *L'Humanité* carried many articles on the successes achieved by the Senegalese boxer Siki, but did not raise its voice when the dockers at Dakar port, Siki's fellow workers, were arrested in the middle of their work, hauled onto lorries, taken to jail then to the barracks to be forcibly put into uniforms and turned into 'guardians of civilization'. The central organ of our party daily informed its readers of the feats of the pilot Oisy, who flew from Paris to Indochina. But when the colonial administration pillaged the people of 'noble Annam', robbed them of their lands in favour of French speculators, and sent out bombers to bring to reason the pitilessly despoiled natives, it did not find it necessary to inform its readers of these facts.

Comrades, the French bourgeoisie, through its press, is perfectly aware that the national and colonial questions cannot be separated from each other. But in my opinion, our party has not thoroughly understood this. The lesson of the Ruhr, where colonial troops had been sent out to 'quiet' the starving German workers and had encircled the suspected French regiments; the example of the Army of the Orient in which colonial forces were issued machine guns to 'raise the morale' of French troops worn out by the hard and protracted war; the events which occurred in 1917 at places in France where Russian troops were stationed;[3] the lesson of the strike of agricultural workers in the Pyrenees in which colonial troops were forced to play the shameful part of blacklegs; and finally the presence of 207,000 colonial troops in France itself – all these facts have not made our party think and realize the necessity of laying down a clear and firm policy on colonial questions. The Party has missed many good opportunities for propaganda. The new leading organs of the Party have acknowledged its passivity in this matter. This is a good sign, because once the leaders of the Party have realized and recognized this weak point in the Party's policy, there is hope that the Party will do its utmost to rectify its errors. I firmly believe that this congress will be a turning point and will induce the Party to correct its past shortcomings. Although Comrade Manuilsky was quite right in his remarks on the elections in Algeria, I must say, to be more objective, that our party has indeed missed a good opportunity here but has retrieved its error by nominating colonial candidates in the elections for the Seine department. This is not much but it will do for a beginning. I am very happy to see that our party is again inspired by the best intentions and enthusiasm – something new for us – and that it needs only to translate all this into practical deeds to arrive at a correct policy on the colonial question.

What practical deeds? It is not enough, as has been done so far, to work out long theses and pass high-sounding resolutions which are, after the congress, sent to museums. What we need are concrete measures. I propose the following ones:

1. To publish regular articles on colonial questions in *L'Humanité* (at least two columns each week);
2. To increase propaganda and recruit Party members among the natives of the colonial countries where the Communist International has set up branches;
3. To send comrades from the colonial countries to study at the Eastern Toilers' University in Moscow;
4. To come to an agreement with the Confédération générale des travailleurs unitaire (United General Confederation of Labour)[4] on the organization of toilers from colonial countries working in France;
5. To make it a duty for Party members to pay greater attention to colonial questions.

In my opinion, these proposals are logical ones, and if the Communist International and the delegates of our party approve them, our delegation to the next congress will be able to say that the united front of the French people and the colonial peoples has become a reality.

Comrades, as disciples of Lenin, we must concentrate all our forces and energies on the colonial question as well as on all other questions in order to implement his precious teachings.

Comrade Douglas (an English delegate): . . .

Comrade Smeran: . . .

Comrade Nguyen Ai Quoc: The French colonies occupy an area of 10,241,510 square kilometres with 55,571,000 inhabitants and are scattered over all four continents. In spite of the differences in race, climate, custom, tradition and economic and social development, there are two common points which can lead to their unity in struggle:

1. The economic situation: in all the French colonies, industry and commerce are little developed and the majority of the population are engaged in agriculture. Ninety-five per cent of the people are peasants.
2. In all the colonies, the native peoples are unremittingly exploited by French imperialist capital.

I have not enough time to make a thorough analysis of the situation of the peasants in each colony. Therefore, I shall use only a few typical examples to give an idea of the peasants' life in the colonies.

I shall begin with my own country, Indochina, which naturally I know best.

During the French conquest, military operations drove the peasants away from their villages. When they returned they found their lands occupied by colonists who had followed in the wake of the occupying troops and who had shared among themselves the land that the native peasants had cultivated for generations. Thus, our peasants were turned into serfs forced to cultivate their own lands for foreign masters.

Many of those unfortunate people who could not endure the harsh conditions imposed by the occupiers left their lands and wandered about the country. They were called 'pirates' and hunted down by the French.

The lands robbed in this way were allotted to planters, who had only to say a word in order to get concessions of sometimes more than 20,000–25,000 hectares.

These planters not only occupied lands without any payment but also obtained all that was necessary to exploit them, including manpower. The administration sent prisoners to work for them without pay, or ordered the villages to supply them with manpower.

Besides this wolfish administration, one should mention the Church. The Catholic Mission alone occupied one quarter of the areas *under cultivation* in Cochin China. To lay hands on those lands it used unimaginable methods: bribery, fraud and coercion. Here are a few examples. Availing itself of crop failures it gave the peasants loans, with their ricefields as security. The interest rates being too high, the peasants were unable to pay off their debts and their mortgaged fields went to the

Mission. Using all kinds of underhand methods, the Church succeeded in laying hands on secret documents that could harm the authorities, and used these to blackmail them into granting it all it wanted. It entered into partnership with big financiers for the exploitation of the plantations granted free to them and the lands stolen from the peasants. Its henchmen held high positions in the colonial government. It fleeced its flock no less ruthlessly than the planters did. Another of its tricks was to get poor people to reclaim waste land with promises that it would be allotted to them. But as soon as the crops were about to be harvested, the Mission claimed ownership of the land and drove out those who had toiled to make it productive. Robbed by their 'protectors' (religious or lay), our peasants were not even left in peace to work on their remaining tiny plots of land. The land registry service falsified the results of the cadastral survey so as to make the peasants pay more taxes. These were made heavier every year. Recently, after handing over thousands of hectares of land belonging to Annamese highlanders to speculators, the authorities sent bombers to fly over these regions so that the victims dared not even think of rebelling.

If the despoiled peasants, ruined and driven away, were again able to reclaim virgin land, the administration would seize it once it was put under cultivation and would oblige them to buy it back at prices fixed by the authorities. Those unable to pay would be driven out pitilessly.

Last year, the country was devastated by floods; yet taxes on ricefields increased 30 per cent.

In addition to those iniquitous taxes that have ruined them, our peasants still have to bear numerous burdens: corvées, poll tax, salt tax, forced buying of government bonds, forced contribution to fund-raising campaigns, etc.

French capitalists in Algeria, Tunisia and Morocco have carried out the same policy of robbery and exploitation. All the good irrigated land was occupied by the colonists. The natives were driven away to areas at the foot of mountains or to arid spots. Financial companies, profiteers and high functionaries divided the land of these colonies among themselves.

In 1914, through direct and indirect operations, the banks in Algeria and Tunisia reaped profits amounting to 12,258,000 francs from a capital of 25 million francs.

The Bank of Morocco, with a capital of 15,400,000 francs, made 1,753,000 francs' profit in 1921.

The Franco-Algerian Company has occupied 324,000 hectares of the best land in the colony.

The Algerian Company has occupied 100,000 hectares.

A private company has been granted 50,000 hectares of forest, while the Capzer Phosphate and Railway Company has occupied 50,000 hectares of land with rich deposits, and in addition has secured priority rights over 20,000 hectares of land in the neighbourhood.

A former French deputy has occupied 1,125 hectares of land with rich mineral deposits, valued at 10 million francs and producing a yearly income of 4 million francs. The natives, the real owners of these mines, receive annually only one centime (one hundredth of a franc) per hectare.

French colonial policy has replaced collective ownership by private ownership. It has also abolished small holdings to the advantage of big plantations. It has robbed the colonial peasantry of more than 5 million hectares of their best land.

In 15 years, the peasants of Kabylia were dispossessed of 192,090 hectares.

From 1913 onwards, each year Moroccan peasants have been ousted from 12,500 hectares of land under cultivation. Since France won the war 'fought for the sake of justice', that figure has risen to 14,540 hectares.

At present, in Morocco 1,070 French people occupy 500,000 hectares of land.

Like their Annamese brothers, the peasants in Africa lead an unbearably hard life, subjected to continuous corvées and heavy taxation. Their misery and sufferings are beyond description. Reduced to eating wild vegetables and tainted cereals they fall a prey to typhoid fever and tuberculosis. Even in good harvest years, peasants are seen rummaging in rubbish heaps and disputing scraps of food with dogs. In lean years fields and roads are strewn with corpses.

Peasants' life in West Africa and French Equatorial Africa is still more horrible. These colonies are in the hands of about 40 companies. They control everything: land, natural resources and even the natives' lives; the latter lack even the right to work for themselves. They are compelled to work for the companies, all the time, and only for the companies. To force them to work for nothing, incredible means of coercion are used by the companies. All lands and fields are confiscated. Only those who agree to do the farming required by the companies are allowed to have some tiny plots of land. People are affected with all kinds of diseases through malnutrition, and the death rate, especially among the children, is very high.

Another method is to hold old people, women and children hostage. They are penned up in crowded huts, ill-treated, beaten up, starved and sometimes even murdered. In some localities the number of hostages equals that of the workers, in order to discourage the latter from running away. The natives are not allowed to till their own land before finishing work on the plantations. Hence the frequent famines and epidemics in the colonies.

The few tribes who have fled to the forest to escape the planters' exploitation live like animals, feeding on roots and leaves, and die from malaria and the unwholesome climate. Meanwhile the white masters are devastating their fields and villages. Here is an excerpt from an officer's diary which gives a clear, concise and gruesome description of the way the colonial peasants are repressed:

Raid on Kolowan village.
Raid on the Fan tribe at Cuno. Villages and orchards destroyed.
Raid on the Bekamis. Village burnt down; 3,000 banana trees cut down.
Raid on Kua village. Village destroyed. Plantations razed.
Raid on Alcun. All houses burnt down, all farms destroyed.
Raid on Esamfami village. Village destroyed. All hamlets along the Bom river burnt down.

The same system of pillage, extermination and destruction prevails in the African regions under Italian, Spanish, British and Portuguese rule.

In the Belgian Congo, the population fell from 25 million in 1891 to 8.5 million by 1911. The Herero and Camard tribes in the former German colonies in Africa were completely exterminated: 80,000 were killed under German rule and 15,000 during 'pacification' in 1914. The population of the French Congo was 20,000 in 1894. It was only 9,700 in 1911. In one region there were 10,000 inhabitants in 1910. Eight years later there remained only 1,080. In another region with 40,000 black inhabitants, 20,000 people were killed within two years, and in the following six months 6,000 more were killed or disabled.

Densely populated and prosperous regions along rivers were turned into deserts within a mere fifteen years. Ravaged oases and villages were strewn with bleached bones.

The plight of the survivors was atrocious. The peasants were robbed of their tiny plots of land, the artisans lost their crafts, and the herdsmen their cattle. The Matabeles were cattle-breeders: before the arrival of the British, they had 200,000 head of cattle. Two years later only 40,900 were left. The Hereros had 90,000 head of cattle. Within twelve years the German colonists had robbed them of half that number. Similar cases are numerous in all the black countries which have come into contact with the whites' civilization.

In conclusion, let me quote these words of the African writer René Maran, author of *Batuala*:

> Equatorial Africa was a densely populated area, rich in rubber and dotted with orchards and farms full of poultry and goats. Within seven years everything was destroyed. Villages were in ruin, gardens and farms laid waste, poultry and goats killed. The people were exhausted by continuous hard work for which they got no pay. They had neither strength nor time left to till their own fields. Disease and famine caused the death rate to increase. And yet they are the descendants of strong and healthy tribes full of combativeness and stamina. Here civilization has disappeared.

To complete this tragic picture, let me add that French capitalism has never hesitated to drive whole regions to misery and famine if this proves of advantage to it. In many colonial countries, e.g., the Reunion Islands, Algeria, Madagascar, etc., cereals have been replaced by other crops required by French industry. These crops bring more profits to the planters. Hence a rising cost of living and chronic famine.

In all the French colonies popular anger has followed in the wake of misery and famine. The native peasants are ripe for insurrection. In many colonies, they have indeed risen up but their rebellions have all been drowned in blood. The reason for their present passivity is the lack of organization and leaders. The Communist International must help them to reorganize, supply them with leading cadres and show them the road to revolution and liberation.

14

LENIN AND THE
COLONIAL PEOPLES[1]

27 January 1924

'Lenin is dead!' This news struck the people like a bolt from the blue. It spread to every corner of the fertile plains of Africa and the green fields of Asia. It is true that the black or yellow people do not yet know clearly who Lenin is or where Russia is. The imperialists have deliberately kept them in ignorance. Ignorance is one of the chief mainstays of capitalism. But all of them, from the Vietnamese peasants to the hunters in the Dahomey forests, have secretly learned that in a faraway corner of the earth there is a nation that has succeeded in overthrowing its exploiters and is managing its own country with no need for masters and Governors General. They have also heard that that country is Russia, that there are courageous people there, and that the most courageous of them all was Lenin. This alone was enough to fill them with deep admiration and warm feelings for that country and its leader.

But this was not all. They also learned that that great leader, after having liberated his own people, wanted to liberate other peoples too. He called upon the white peoples to help the yellow and black peoples to free themselves from the foreign aggressors' yoke, from all foreign aggressors, Governors General Residents, etc. And to reach that goal, he mapped out a definite programme.

At first they did not believe that anywhere on earth could there exist such a man and such a programme. But later they heard, although vaguely, of the communist parties, of the organization called the Communist International which is fighting for the exploited peoples, for all the exploited peoples including themselves. And they learned that Lenin was the leader of that organization.

And this alone was enough to make these peoples – though their cultural standard is low, they are grateful folk and of goodwill – wholeheartedly respect Lenin. They look upon Lenin as their liberator. 'Lenin is dead, so what will happen to us? Will there be other courageous and generous people like Lenin who will now spare their time and efforts in concerning themselves with our liberation?' This is what the oppressed colonial peoples are wondering.

As for us, we are deeply moved by this irretrievable loss and share the common mourning of all the peoples with our brothers and sisters. But we believe that the Communist International and its branches, which include branches in colonial countries, will succeed in implementing the lessons and teachings the leader has left behind for us. To do what he advised us, is that not the best way to show our love for him?

In his lifetime he was our father, teacher, comrade and adviser. Nowadays, he is the bright star showing us the way to the socialist revolution.

Eternal Lenin will live forever in our work.

15

APPEAL MADE ON THE OCCASION OF THE FOUNDING OF THE INDOCHINESE COMMUNIST PARTY

18 February 1930

Workers, peasants, soldiers, youth and school students! Oppressed and exploited fellow countrymen! Sisters and brothers! Comrades!

Imperialist contradictions were the cause of the 1914–18 World War. After this horrible slaughter, the world was divided into two camps: one is the revolutionary camp which includes the oppressed colonial peoples and the exploited working class throughout the world. Its vanguard is the Soviet Union. The other is the counter-revolutionary camp of international capitalism and imperialism, whose general staff is the League of Nations.

That war resulted in untold loss of life and property for the peoples. French imperialism was the hardest hit. Therefore, in order to restore the forces of capitalism in France, the French imperialists have resorted to every perfidious scheme to intensify capitalist exploitation in Indochina. They have built new factories to exploit the workers by paying them starvation wages. They have plundered the peasants' land to establish plantations and drive them to destitution. They have levied new heavy taxes. They have forced our people to buy government bonds. In short, they have driven our people to utter misery. They have increased their military forces, firstly to strangle the Vietnamese revolution; secondly to prepare for a new imperialist war in the Pacific aimed at conquering new colonies; thirdly to suppress the Chinese revolution; and fourthly to attack the Soviet Union because she helps the oppressed nations and the exploited working class to wage revolution. World War Two will break out. When it does the French imperialists will certainly drive our people to an even more horrible slaughter. If we let them prepare for this war, oppose the Chinese revolution and attack the Soviet Union, if we allow them to stifle the Vietnamese revolution, this is tantamount to letting them wipe our race off the surface of the earth and drown our nation in the Pacific.

However, the French imperialists' barbarous oppression and ruthless exploitation have awakened our compatriots, who have all realized that revolution is the only road to survival and that without it they will die a slow death. This is why the revolutionary movement has grown stronger with each passing day: the workers refuse to work, the peasants demand land, the students go on strike, the traders stop doing business. Everywhere the masses have risen to oppose the French imperialists.

The revolution has made the French imperialists tremble with fear. On the one hand, they use the feudalists and comprador bourgeoisie to oppress and exploit our people. On the other, they terrorize, arrest, jail, deport and kill a great number of Vietnamese revolutionaries. If the French imperialists think that they can suppress the Vietnamese revolution by means of terror, they are grossly mistaken. For one thing, the Vietnamese revolution is not isolated but enjoys the assistance of the world proletariat in general and that of the French working class in particular. Secondly, it is precisely at the very time when the French imperialists are frenziedly carrying out terrorist acts that the Vietnamese communists, formerly working separately, have united into a single party, the Indochinese Communist Party, to lead the revolutionary struggle of our entire people.

Workers, peasants, soldiers, youth, school students!
Oppressed and exploited fellow-countrymen!

The Indochinese Communist Party has been founded. It is the party of the working class. It will help the proletariat lead the revolution waged for the sake of all oppressed and exploited people. From now on we must join the Party, help it and follow it in order to implement the following slogans:

1. To overthrow French imperialism and Vietnamese feudalism and reactionary bourgeoisie;
2. To make Indochina completely independent;
3. To establish a worker–peasant–soldier government;
4. To confiscate the banks and other enterprises belonging to the imperialists and put them under the control of the worker–peasant–soldier government;
5. To confiscate all the plantations and property belonging to the imperialists and the Vietnamese reactionary bourgeoisie and distribute them to the poor peasants;
6. To implement the eight-hour working day;
7. To abolish the forced buying of government bonds, the poll tax and all unjust taxes hitting the poor;
8. To bring democratic freedoms to the masses;
9. To dispense education to all the people;
10. To realize equality between man and woman.

16

THE PARTY'S LINE IN THE PERIOD OF THE DEMOCRATIC FRONT[1]

1939

1. For the time being the Party should not put forward too exacting demands (national independence, parliament, etc.). To do so is to play into the Japanese fascists' hands.

It should only claim democratic rights, freedom of organization, freedom of assembly, freedom of the press and freedom of speech, general amnesty for all political detainees, and freedom for the Party to engage in legal activity.

2. To reach this goal, the Party must strive to organize a broad Democratic National Front.

This Front should embrace not only Indochinese but also progressive French people residing in Indochina, not only the toiling people but also the national bourgeoisie.

3. The Party must assume a tactful, flexible attitude towards the national bourgeoisie, strive to draw them into the Front and keep them there, urge them into action if possible, isolate them politically if necessary. At any rate, we must not leave them outside the Front, lest they should fall into the hands of the reaction and strengthen it.

4. With regard to the Trotskyites there can be no compromise, no concession. We must do everything possible to unmask them as agents of fascism and annihilate them politically.

5. To increase and consolidate its forces, to widen its influence and work effectively, the Indochinese Democratic Front must maintain close

contact with the French Popular Front which also struggles for freedom and democracy and can give us great help.

6. The Party cannot demand that the Front recognize its leadership. It must instead show itself to be the Front's most loyal, active and sincere element. It is only through daily struggle and work, when the masses of the people have acknowledged the correct policies and leading capacity of the Party, that it can win the leading position.

7. In order to carry out this task the Party must uncompromisingly fight sectarianism and organize the systematic study of Marxism-Leninism in order to raise the cultural and political level of the Party members. It must help the non-Party cadres raise their standard. It must maintain close contact with the French Communist Party.

8. The Central Executive Committee must supervise the Party press to avoid technical and political mistakes (e.g. in publishing comrade R.'s biography, the *Labour* revealed where he had been and how he had come back, etc. It also published without comment his letter saying that Trotskyism is a product of personal vanity, etc.).

17

LETTER FROM ABROAD

6 June 1941

Venerable elders! Patriotic personalities! Intellectuals, peasants, workers, traders and soldiers! Dear fellow countrymen!

Since France was defeated by Germany, its power has completely collapsed. Nevertheless, with regard to our people, the French rulers have become even more ruthless in carrying out their policy of exploitation, repression and massacre. They bleed us white and carry out a barbarous policy of all-out terrorism and massacre. In the foreign field, bowing their heads and bending their knees, they resign themselves to ceding part of our land to Siam and shamelessly surrendering our country to Japan. As a result our people are writhing under a double yoke of oppression. They serve not only as beasts of burden to the French bandits but also as slaves to the Japanese robbers. Alas! What sin have our people committed to be doomed to such a wretched fate? Plunged into such tragic suffering are we to await death with folded arms?

No! Certainly not! The twenty-odd million descendants of the Lac and the Hong are resolved not to let themselves be kept in servitude. For nearly eighty years under the French pirates' iron heels we have unceasingly and selflessly struggled for national independence and freedom. The heroism of our predecessors, such as Phan Dinh Phung, Hoang Hoa Tham and Luong Ngoc Quyen and the glorious feats of the insurgents of Thai Nguyen, Yen Bai, Nghe An and Ha Tinh provinces will live for ever in our memory. The recent uprisings in the South and at Do Luong and Bac Son testify to the determination of our compatriots to follow the glorious example of their ancestors and to annihilate the enemy. If we were not successful, it was not because the French bandits were strong, but only because the situation was not yet ripe and our people throughout the country were not yet of one mind.

Now, the opportunity has come for our liberation. France itself is unable to help the French colonialists rule over our country. As for the Japanese, on the one hand bogged down in China, on the other hampered by the British and American forces, they certainly cannot use all their strength against us. If our entire people are solidly united we can certainly get the better of the best-trained armies of the French and the Japanese.

Fellow countrymen! Rise up! Let us emulate the dauntless spirit of the Chinese people! Rise up without delay! Let us organize the Association for National Salvation to fight the French and the Japanese!

Dear fellow countrymen! A few hundred years ago, in the reign of the Tran, when our country faced the great danger of invasion by Yuan armies the elders ardently called on their sons and daughters throughout the country to stand up as one man to kill the enemy. Finally they saved their people and their glorious memory will live for ever. Let our elders and patriotic personalities follow the illustrious example set by our forefathers.

Notables, soldiers, workers, peasants, traders, civil servants, youth and women who warmly love your country! At present national liberation stands above everything. Let us unite and overthrow the Japanese, the French and their lackeys in order to save our people from their present dire straits.

Dear fellow countrymen!

National salvation is the common cause of our entire people. Every Vietnamese must take part in it. He who has money will contribute his money, he who has strength will contribute his strength, he who has talent will contribute his talent. For my part I pledge to follow in your steps and devote all my modest abilities to the service of the country and am ready for the supreme sacrifice.

Revolutionary fighters!

The hour has struck! Raise aloft the banner of insurrection and lead the people throughout the country to overthrow the Japanese and the French! The sacred call of the fatherland is resounding in our ears; the ardent blood of our heroic predecessors is seething in our hearts! The fighting spirit of the people is mounting before our eyes! Let us unite and unify our action to overthrow the Japanese and the French.

The Vietnamese revolution will certainly triumph!

The world revolution will certainly triumph!

18

INSTRUCTIONS FOR THE SETTING UP OF THE ARMED PROPAGANDA BRIGADE FOR THE LIBERATION OF VIET NAM[1]

December 1944

1. The name of the Armed Propaganda Brigade for the Liberation of Viet Nam shows that greater importance is attached to its political than to its military action. It is a propaganda unit. In the military field, the main principle for successful action is concentration of forces. Therefore in accordance with the new instructions of our organization, the most resolute and energetic cadres and men will be picked from the ranks of the guerrilla units in the provinces of Bac Can, Lang Son and Cao Bang, and an important part of the available weapons concentrated in order to establish our main-force brigade.

Ours being a national resistance by the whole people we must mobilize and arm the whole people. While concentrating our forces to set up the brigade, we must maintain the local armed forces which must co-ordinate their operations and assist each other in all respects. For its part, the main-force brigade has the duty to guide the cadres of the local armed units, assist them in training, and supply them with weapons if possible, thus helping these units to develop unceasingly.

2. With regard to the local armed units, we must gather their cadres for training, send trained cadres to various localities, exchange experience, maintain liaison and co-ordinate military operations.

3. Concerning tactics, we must apply guerrilla warfare; maintain secrecy, quickness of action and initiative (now in the east now in

the west, arriving unexpectedly and departing without leaving any traces).

The Armed Propaganda Brigade for the Liberation of Viet Nam is the first-born unit. It is hoped that other units will soon come into being.

Its initial size is modest but it faces brilliant prospects. It is the embryo of the Liberation Army and can expand from north to south, throughout Viet Nam.

19

APPEAL FOR GENERAL INSURRECTION

August 1945

Dear fellow countrymen!

Four years ago, I called on you to unite, for unity is strength and only strength will enable us to win back *independence and freedom.*

At present, the Japanese army has collapsed. The National Salvation Movement has spread to the whole country. The League for the Independence of Viet Nam (Viet Minh) has millions of members from all social strata: intellectuals, peasants, workers, businessmen, soldiers, and from all nationalities in the country: Viet, Tho, Nung, Muong, Man, and others. In its ranks our compatriots march side by side regardless of age, sex, religion and fortune.

Recently, the Viet Minh convened the Viet Nam People's National Congress[1] and appointed the *National Liberation Committee* to lead the entire people in the resolute struggle for national independence.

This is a great advance in the history of the struggle waged for nearly a century by our people for their liberation.

This is a source of powerful encouragement for our compatriots and great joy for myself.

However, we cannot content ourselves with that. Our struggle will be a long and hard one. The Japanese defeat does not mean that we shall be liberated overnight. We still have to make further efforts and carry on the struggle. Only unity and struggle will bring us independence.

The Viet Minh is at present the basis for the unity and struggle of our people. Join the Viet Minh, support it, make it even greater and stronger!

At present, the National Liberation Committee is the equivalent of a provisional government. Let us rally around it and see to it that its policies and orders are carried out throughout the country!

This way, independence is certain to come to our people soon.

Dear fellow countrymen!

The decisive hour has struck for the destiny of our people. Let all of us stand up and rely on our own strength to free ourselves.

Many oppressed peoples the world over are vying with each other in wresting back independence. We should not lag behind.

Forward! Forward! Under the banner of the Viet Minh, let us valiantly march forward!

20

DECLARATION OF INDEPENDENCE OF THE DEMOCRATIC REPUBLIC OF VIET NAM[1]

2 September 1945

'All men are created equal. They are endowed by their Creator with certain unalienable Rights; among these are Life, Liberty and the pursuit of Happiness.'

This immortal statement appeared in the Declaration of Independence of the United States of America in 1776. In a broader sense, it means: All the peoples on the earth are equal from birth, all the peoples have a right to live and to be happy and free.

The Declaration of the Rights of Man and the Citizen, made at the time of the French Revolution, in 1791, also states: 'All men are born free and with equal rights, and must always remain free and have equal rights.'

Those are undeniable truths.

Nevertheless, for more than eighty years, the French imperialists, abusing the standard of Liberty, Equality and Fraternity, have violated our fatherland and oppressed our fellow citizens. They have acted contrary to the ideals of humanity and justice.

Politically, they have deprived our people of every democratic liberty.

They have enforced inhuman laws; they have set up three different political regimes in the North, the Centre and the South of Viet Nam in order to wreck our country's oneness and prevent our people from being united.

They have built more prisons than schools. They have mercilessly massacred our patriots. They have drowned our uprisings in seas of blood.

They have fettered public opinion and practised obscurantism.

They have weakened our race with opium and alcohol.

In the field of economics, they have sucked us dry, driven our people to destitution and devastated our land.

They have robbed us of our ricefields, our mines, our forests and our natural resources. They have monopolized the issue of banknotes and the import and export trade.

They have invented numerous unjustifiable taxes and reduced our people, especially our peasantry, to extreme poverty.

They have made it impossible for our national bourgeoisie to prosper; they have mercilessly exploited our workers.

In the autumn of 1940, when the Japanese fascists invaded Indochina to establish new bases against the Allies, the French colonialists went down on their bended knees and opened the doors of our country to welcome the Japanese in.

Thus, from that date, our people were subjected to the double yoke of the French and the Japanese. Their sufferings and miseries increased. The result was that towards the end of last year and the beginning of this year, from Quang Tri province to the North, more than two million of our fellow-citizens died from starvation.

On the 9th of March this year, the French troops were disarmed by the Japanese. The French colonialists either fled or surrendered, showing that not only were they incapable of 'protecting' us, but that, in a period of five years, they had twice sold our country to the Japanese.

Before the 9th of March, how often the Viet Minh had urged the French to ally themselves with it against the Japanese! But instead of agreeing to this proposal, the French colonialists only intensified their terrorist activities against the Viet Minh. After their defeat and before fleeing, they massacred the political prisoners detained at Yen Bai and Cao Bang.

In spite of all this, our fellow citizens have always manifested a lenient and humane attitude towards the French. After the Japanese putsch of 9 March 1945, the Viet Minh helped many Frenchmen to cross the frontier, rescued others from Japanese jails and protected French lives and property. In fact, since the autumn of 1940, our country had ceased to be a French colony and had become a Japanese possession.

When the Japanese surrendered to the Allies, our entire people rose to gain power and founded the Democratic Republic of Viet Nam.

The truth is that we have wrested our independence from the Japanese, not from the French.

The French have fled, the Japanese have capitulated, Emperor Bao Dai has abdicated. Our people have broken the chains which have fettered them for nearly a century and have won independence for Viet Nam. At the same time they have overthrown the centuries-old monarchic regime and established a democratic republican regime.

We, the Provisional government of the new Viet Nam, representing the entire Vietnamese people, hereby declare that from now on we break off all relations of a colonial character with France; cancel all treaties signed by France on Viet Nam, and abolish all privileges held by France in our country.

The entire Vietnamese people are of one mind in their determination to oppose all wicked schemes by the French colonialists.

We are convinced that the Allies, which at the Teheran and San Francisco conferences [in November–December 1943 and April–June 1945 respectively] upheld the principle of equality among the nations, cannot fail to recognize the right of the Vietnamese people to independence.

A people who have courageously opposed French enslavement for more than eighty years, a people who have resolutely sided with the Allies against the fascists during these last years, such a people must be free, such a people must be independent.

For these reasons, we, the Provisional government of the Democratic Republic of Viet Nam, solemnly make this declaration to the world:

Viet Nam has the right to enjoy freedom and independence and in fact has become a free and independent country. The entire Vietnamese people are determined to mobilize all their physical and mental strength, to sacrifice their lives and property in order to safeguard their freedom and independence.

21

TO THE PEOPLE'S COMMITTEES IN THE WHOLE COUNTRY (NORTH, SOUTH, CENTRE) AND AT ALL LEVELS (PROVINCE, DISTRICT AND VILLAGE)

October 1945

Dear friends,

Our country was oppressed by the French for more than eighty years and by the Japanese for nearly five years. The misery we suffered was beyond description. Even now it is a heartbreaking thing to remember it. Our people's unity and the government's wise guidance have allowed us to break the bonds of slavery and win back our independence and freedom.

Without the people, we shall have no strength; without the government, no guidance. Therefore, the government and the people must form a monolithic whole. We have now founded the Democratic Republic of Viet Nam. But without happiness and freedom for the people, independence would be meaningless.

Our government has promised that it will strive to bring every citizen his share of happiness. Building our country and putting things in order will have to be done gradually and cannot be completed within a month or a year. But we must make a correct start. We must bear in mind that all government organs, from the central to the village level, are the people's servants, that is to say they must work in the public interest, not oppress the people as government organs did under the French and Japanese rule.

What is of benefit to the people we must strive to do.

What is harmful to them we must strive to avoid.

We must love the people: they will love and respect us.

I know that many of you have correctly carried out the government's policies and won the people's hearts. But others among you have committed very serious mistakes, the main ones being:

1. *Violation of legality* – Traitors whose guilt is clearly established must of course be punished, and no one can complain. But sometimes arrests are made and property confiscated out of personal enmity, causing discontent among the population.

2. *Abuse of power* – Abusing their positions as members of such and such committees, some people are doing as they please in defiance of public opinion, having no regard for the people and forgetting that they have been elected by the people to serve them, not to browbeat them.

3. *Corruption* – Good food, fine clothing, wasteful expenditure, frivolous amusement – where does the money for all this come from?

    Some may go so far as to divert public property to their own use, casting aside integrity and honesty. Mister Commissar rides in official cars, then his wife does, then even his children. Who is going to pay for these expenses?

4. *Favouritism* – Some build their own group of followers, appoint their friends and relatives to positions for which they have no ability, shove aside people who are competent and honest but are not to their liking. They forget that this is a matter of public concern, not a private affair.

5. *Sowing of discord* – Some oppose one section of the people to another instead of urging mutual concession and concord. In some places, fields lie fallow and the peasants are complaining. Some cadres forget that at present they must work for the unity of the whole people, irrespective of age and fortune, in order to safeguard our independence and fight the common enemy.

6. *Arrogance* – As officials, some consider themselves to be sacrosanct, and look down upon the people. Their every gesture shows them to be 'mandarin revolutionaries'. They fail to realize that their

arrogance will lose them the people's confidence, and harm the government's prestige.

Mistakes are not to be feared, but they must be corrected when discovered. He who has not fallen into the above-mentioned errors should try to avoid them and make further progress. He who has committed such errors must endeavour to correct them. If he fails to do so, the government will not condone his mistakes.

It is for the sake of the people's happiness and the national interest that I have made these comments. We must engrave upon our minds the words 'justice' and 'integrity'.

I hope you will make progress.

22

APPEAL TO COMPATRIOTS TO CARRY OUT DESTRUCTION, TO WAGE RESISTANCE WAR[1]

6 February 1947

Compatriots who love our country,

Why must we wage the resistance war?

– Because if we do not wage the resistance war, the French will occupy our country once more. They will enslave our people once more. They will force our people to be their coolies and soldiers, and to pay them every kind of taxes. They will suppress all our democratic freedoms. They will plunder all our land and property. They will terrorize and massacre our brothers, sisters and relatives. They will burn down or destroy our houses, pagodas and temples. You will realize this by seeing what they have done in Hanoi and Haiphong.

– Because we do not want to be buffaloes and horses to the French, because we must protect our country, we must fight the French colonialists.

To fight we must carry out destruction. If we do not do so, the French will. If our houses are solid enough to be used as bases, they will mobilize tanks and vessels to attack us, and they will burn or plunder all our property. This is why we must carry out destruction before the French can make use of our property. Suppose we want to keep sluices, roads and houses for our own use, we can't, because the French will occupy all or destroy all.

Now we must carry out destruction to stop them, to prevent them from advancing, and from using our roads and houses.

For the sake of the fatherland we must make sacrifices and endure hardships for a certain time. When the Resistance comes out victorious, we will pool our forces for construction and repair work and this will not be difficult at all.

On the battlefront the fighters are sacrificing their lives for the fatherland without regret; why do we regret a section of road, a sluice or a house which the French can use to attack our fatherland?

You all love your country, no doubt you will have no heart to regret so.

Therefore, I earnestly call on you to exert all your efforts to carry out destruction work. We must destroy roads widely and deeply so that the French cannot use them. A pick stroke into the roads has the value of a bullet shot by our soldiers at the enemy.

I solemnly promise to you that after victory, I will endeavour to repair everything with you. We will build more beautiful roads, bridges and sluices and better houses worthy of a free and independent nation.

Long live our victorious resistance war!

Long live independent Viet Nam!

23

APPEAL ISSUED AFTER SIX MONTHS OF RESISTANCE

19 June 1947

Fellow citizens,

Fighters in the army, militia and self-defence corps,

The reactionary French colonialists have mobilized scores of thousands of men in their ground, naval and air forces and spent scores of millions of piastres daily for their military expenses. By using overwhelming forces in lightning attacks they hoped to occupy our country within a few months. They also hired a clique of stooges with the aim of undermining our resistance and dividing our people. But their schemes, both military and political, have utterly failed. Today the war of resistance has been going on in Nam Bo for two years, and in the whole country for six months. Our forces are growing ever stronger, our successes ever more obvious. Why?

(a) *Because we are fighting a just war*

We only defend our own country. We only fight for the unity and independence of our fatherland.

As for the French reactionary colonialists, they seek to occupy our country, enslave our people. Therefore, we are in the right: justice will prevail.

(b) *Because our compatriots are closely united*

Our entire people share a common resolve: never to fall back into slavery; a common will: never to lose their country; a common aim: to win back unity and independence for the fatherland.

Our oneness of mind stands like a bronze wall defending our fatherland. However cruel and perfidious the enemy, running into this wall he is sure to fail.

(c) *Because our fighters are courageous*

We have but inferior weapons and little experience, but our fighters' determination and spirit of sacrifice have defeated the enemy's brutal force and they have scored glorious, resounding feats of arms.

(d) *Because our strategy is correct*

The enemy wants to win a quick victory. If the war drags on, he will suffer increasing losses and will be defeated.

That is why we use the strategy of a protracted war of resistance in order to develop our forces and gather more experience. We use guerrilla tactics to wear down the enemy forces until a general offensive wipes them out.

The enemy is like fire and we like water. Water will certainly get the better of fire.

Moreover, in the long war of resistance, each citizen is a combatant, each village, a fortress. The twenty million Vietnamese are bound to cut to pieces the few scores of thousands of reactionary colonialists.

(e) *Because we have many friends*

The reactionary colonialists' aggressive war is unjust and hated by all. Our resistance for national salvation is a just cause and is therefore receiving support from many people. The majority of the French people want to live in peace and friendship with us.

The peoples of the colonies sympathize with us.

The Asian peoples support us. World opinion is favourable to us.

On the moral plane, the enemy has already failed completely and we have won total victory.

Fellow citizens!

Combatants!

Our long war of resistance will have to go through many more difficult periods.

We must endure sacrifices and hardships and make great efforts. But we are ready to face sacrifices and sufferings and to exert ourselves for five, ten years in order to break the chains which have held us in slavery over the past eighty years, and regain unity and independence forever. On behalf of the government,

I order all combatants to fight even more vigorously and emulate one another in attacking the enemy;

I call on all our people to strive to increase production, build up food reserves in secure areas, watch over the dykes, and assist the troops;

I urge all political, administrative and technical personnel to redouble their efforts to overcome difficulties, correct shortcomings and become model cadres.

We are of one heart and of one mind. We are bound to win.

Forward!

Smash the French reactionary colonialists!

The Vietnamese and French peoples are friends!

The long war of resistance will certainly end in victory!

Long live independent and reunified Viet Nam!

24

TWELVE RECOMMENDATIONS[1]

5 April 1948

The nation has its root in the people.

In the resistance war and national reconstruction, the main force lies in the people. Therefore, all the people in the army, administration and mass organizations who are in contact or live with the people, must remember and carry out the following twelve recommendations.

Six forbiddances:

1. Not to do what is likely to damage the land and crops or spoil the houses and belongings of the people.
2. Not to insist on buying or borrowing what the people are not willing to sell or lend.
3. Not to bring living hens into mountainous people's houses.
4. Never break our word.
5. Not to give offence to people's faith and customs (such as to lie down before the altar, to raise feet over the hearth, to play music in the house, etc.).
6. Not to do or speak what is likely to make people believe that we hold them in contempt.

Six permissables:

1. To help the people in their daily work (harvesting, fetching firewood, carrying water, sewing, etc.).
2. Whenever possible to buy commodities for those who live far from markets (knife, salt, needle, thread, pen, paper, etc.).
3. In spare time, to tell amusing simple and short stories useful to the Resistance, but not betraying secrets.

4. To teach the population the national script and elementary hygiene.

5. To study the customs of each region so as to be acquainted with them in order to create an atmosphere of sympathy first, then gradually to explain to the people to abate their superstitions.

6. To show to the people that you are correct, diligent and disciplined.

STIMULATING POEM

The above-mentioned twelve recommendations
Are feasible to all
He who loves his country,
Will never forget them.
When the people have a habit,
All are like one man,
With good army men and good people,
Everything will be crowned with success.
Only when the root is firm, can the tree live long
And victory is built with the people as foundation.

25

TO THE NATIONAL
CONGRESS OF MILITIAMEN

April 1948

On this occasion, I affectionately wish you good health, and ask you to convey my greetings to all our militiamen and guerrillas. Here are a few suggestions about your work.

Generally speaking, militiamen and guerrillas have rendered good services to the resistance. In many places, they have fought the enemy either in close co-ordination with the National Defence Army or on their own; they have displayed great energy and reaped good successes in combating spies and bandits, annihilating puppet administrative organs, destroying the enemy's communication lines, learning the national script, and increasing production.

Such villages as Dinh Bang and many others have earned a reputation of heroism because of their guerrilla activities. Many fighters have distinguished themselves: Pham Van Trac, Le Binh, Nguyen Van Y, Do Van Thin, Dang Van Gieng, Pham Van Man . . ., and others. We must also congratulate those guerrilla units made up of old folk and women who have bravely attacked the enemy.

These are *good points* which we should further develop.

But our militiamen and guerrillas have also shortcomings which must be corrected at once. In many places the meaning of guerrilla warfare has not been clearly and thoroughly grasped, hence an erroneous tendency to wage big battles, and attack strong fortified positions. Besides, the watchword of self-supply and self-sufficiency has not been put into practical effect, and the intensification of production not properly emphasized. There is still lack of close co-ordination with the National Defence Army and lack of initiative in attacking the enemy. Concerning organization and training, too much attention is paid to matters of form, too little to practical deeds. These shortcomings must be resolutely and rapidly corrected. We must:

1. Effectively organize and train militiamen and guerrillas in *each village; take the village militiamen and guerrillas as basis*, while consolidating the guerrilla units released from production duty;
2. Drive home to each fighter where our strength lies, and inspire him with faith in this strength and in our rudimentary weapons;
3. Combine guerrilla action very closely with operations by the National Defence Army;
4. Make each fighter fully conscious of his glorious duty;
5. Give them a clear grasp of guerrilla tactics: to keep the initiative, to seek out and attack the enemy, to harass him and engage in sabotage work; and to keep gaining small successes which will add up to a big victory;
6. Realize self-supply and self-sufficiency by effectively increasing production;
7. Bring about these things through emulation. Let village vie with village, district with district, province with province, zone with zone.

I promise that the government will reward the most outstanding fighters and units in this *emulation* drive.

With the clear and *practical* plan to be worked out by the Congress, with the enthusiasm of all militiamen and guerrillas, with the help of our compatriots, I am sure that our militiamen and guerrillas will fulfil their glorious task: to kill many enemy troops, to capture many guns, to achieve many feats of arms in order to speed up the victory of the long war of resistance, and the realization of national reunification and independence.

Cordial greetings. We shall win!

26

TO THE 6TH CONGRESS OF PARTY CADRES

18 January 1949

Present at this congress are delegates of the North, Centre and South and high-ranking Party cadres in the administration, army, economy and finance, Party apparatus, mass organizations, control organs, etc. This is very good.

The problems raised for discussion have been many but all have been directed to one goal: the victory of the Resistance, the building of a new democracy in preparation for an advance to socialism.

The course having been charted, let us follow it. We shall certainly reach our destination.

These are our tasks for this year:

1. To boost our military effort; to put the war of resistance, the armed struggle above everything else. All activities must aim at winning victory for the Resistance.
2. To put in order the administrative machinery at all levels, from village upwards. If rearrangement is made from the base up, and vice versa, we shall naturally achieve success.
3. To produce much and to spend little. No unnecessary expenditure. Such is the content of all our economic and financial policies.
4. To reorganize the mass organizations. Our successes are due to the people. Yet at present many mass organizations are still very weak.
5. To perform the above tasks, we must first of all perfect our party's organization. We must set forth the chief tasks and concentrate on them.

We can liken the Party to a power generator, and the above tasks to electric lights. The more powerful the generator, the brighter the lights.

Here are some urgent tasks for our party:

(a) We lack too many cadres. We must gradually train a sufficient number of them. To this end, the Party must help its members study and learn through their own efforts. For their part, the cadres must study hard.

Many of our comrades have good practical experience, but only an elementary education. The intellectual comrades have read a great deal but have only little practical experience, and are not used to the Party's working methods.

So, it is necessary to raise the theoretical level of veteran cadres while teaching the intellectual cadres to do mass work.

(b) There are two shortcomings in the present style of work in the Party:

    – veteran cadres work the 'handicraft' way;

    – new cadres work the scientific way but they go too far and fail to adapt themselves to the conditions of the war of resistance.

We should correct our working methods, make them ever more rational and suit them to the present circumstances, and avoid formalism and mechanicalness.

(c) Before the masses, we won't win their love and esteem by merely inscribing the word 'communist' on our foreheads.

The people only love and respect those with good conduct and morality. Those who want to guide the masses must set good examples for them. Many comrades have done so, but others have degenerated. Our party must help them cleanse themselves.

When you call on people to practise thrift, you yourself must do it. Our comrades must acquire the four revolutionary virtues: industry, thrift, integrity and uprightness.

To make the revolution, one must first and foremost remould oneself.

(d) Although we may come from different nationalities and classes, we follow the same doctrine, pursue the same goal, are bound together for life and death, and share weal and woe. That is why we must sincerely unite. To reach our destination, to organize ourselves is not enough: we must besides be sincere in our minds.

There are two ways to achieve ideological unity and inner cohesion: *criticism and self-criticism.*

Everyone, from the top down, must use them to achieve ever closer unity and greater progress.

(e) To keep discipline:

Though comprising a large number of people, our party goes to combat united as one man. This is due to discipline. Ours is an iron discipline – that is, a severe and conscious one.

We must strive to maintain this iron discipline of our party.

This conference is being held at a time when the world revolutionary movement is progressing rapidly. This is especially evident in the victory of the Chinese people and Party.

Our party is the Indochinese Communist Party but we must also contribute to the liberation of Southeast Asia. It ranks next to the Chinese Communist Party in strength and was the first to come to power in Southeast Asia. This is said not for the sake of vanity but so that we should strive to fulfil our responsibility.

The world's people today number about 2,000 million; the communist parties have a total membership of over 20 million; so there is one communist for every hundred persons or so. In Indochina, according to current figures, this ratio is one to a hundred and twelve. This is a heartening fact. If everybody fully discharges his duties, our war of resistance will certainly gain quick victory and national construction swift success.

Long live the Indochinese Communist Party!

Long live the victory of world revolution!

27

TO PEASANT CADRES

November 1949

Ours is an agricultural country.

More than nine-tenths of our people are peasants.

More than nine-tenths of our peasants are middle, poor and landless peasants.

The National Defence Army, the regional forces, the militia and guerrilla units are mostly made up of peasants.

The production work to feed the army, the workers and the functionaries is carried out by the peasants.

The work of doing sabotage to check the enemy, repairing roads, ensuring communications and transport, is mostly done by the peasants.

In a word, the peasants constitute an immense force of the nation and a most loyal ally of the working class.

For the war of resistance and national construction to be successful, for genuine independence and reunification to be achieved, reliance should be placed on the peasant forces.

Our peasants make up a tremendous force, inspired by ardent patriotism, determination to struggle and readiness for sacrifices.

Political work among the peasants consists in:

- Tightly organizing them.
- Closely uniting them.
- Fully awakening their political consciousness.
- Leading them to struggle vigorously for their own interest and that of the fatherland.

To carry out *political agitation* among the peasants means to stir them up; that is, to make them clearly understand the interests of the nation and those of their class, to get them to join the National Salvation Peasants' Association in great numbers in order to struggle for their own objectives and actively participate in the war of resistance and in national construction.

To achieve this end, peasant cadres must avoid subjectiveness, formalism and red tape.

Provincial cadres must go to districts and villages.

District cadres must go to villages and hamlets.

Cadres must go to the base to see and hear for themselves, talk to people, ponder over things and act accordingly.

They must conduct practical investigations, give assistance, exercise control, draw lessons and exchange experiences, with a view to helping the peasants and learning from them.

In the organs of power and in the leading bodies of the Peasants' Association, poor peasants and landless peasants must have an effective share.

If our cadres (peasant cadres and administrative cadres) strictly adhere to these principles, and this they should do at all costs, we shall surely reap fine results in all these fields:

- Emulation in production to stave off famine;
- Emulation in learning *quoc ngu* to liquidate illiteracy;
- Emulation in assisting the army, and fostering the militia and guerrilla forces to annihilate the foreign aggressors.

28

INSTRUCTIONS GIVEN AT THE CONFERENCE REVIEWING THE SECOND LE HONG PHONG MILITARY CAMPAIGN[1]

Fall 1950

About this review conference, I have some opinions:

At this conference, there are officers who directly took part in the campaign and are back here to review both their achievements and shortcomings. There are also cadres and officers from the various interzones, army units and public services who did not take part in the campaign but who are here to learn experiences. To make criticism and self-criticism, to review our work, to popularize and draw experiences are very good things which should be developed into a style of work in the army, administration and mass organizations. In this review, I want to draw your attention to some points.

I. HEIGHTEN DISCIPLINE

Discipline must be observed at all levels. Critical reviews must be made at all levels, from lower levels upward and from higher levels downward. We must help all the men and officers of the army to understand thoroughly the necessity for this work. Only then can we achieve success.

2. STRICTLY CARRY OUT ORDERS FROM HIGHER LEVELS

Orders from higher levels must be unconditionally and strictly carried out. There is a Chinese proverb saying that 'military orders are as firm as mountains', that is, whenever an order from a higher level is issued, it must be carried out at any cost. Don't misunderstand democracy. When no decision is yet taken, we are free to discuss. But when a decision is taken, we should not discuss any longer. Any discussion then could be only discussion on the ways and means to carry out the decision quickly and not to propose that it should not be carried out. We must prohibit any such act of unruly freedom.

3. LOVE THE SOLDIERS

The officers must love the men under their command. As regards sick armymen or invalids, the officers must look after them and inquire into their health. The commanders and political commissars must be the brothers, sisters and friends of the soldiers. So long as they are not so, they have not yet fulfilled their tasks. Only when officers are close to soldiers like the limbs of the same body, can the soldiers love the officers like their kith and kin. Only so can the instructions, orders and plans from higher ranks be actively and strictly implemented by the armymen. We must congratulate and reward all armymen who have achieved meritorious services, promote all progressive officers and men, especially those who have a long service in the army.

4. RESPECT THE PEOPLE

We must respect the people. There are many ways of showing respect to the people. It is not sufficient to greet people in a polite manner. We must not waste the manpower and property of the people. When mobilizing the people, we must see to it that their contributions do not exceed the requirements in order to avoid waste. We must avoid anything which is prejudicial to the people's life. To know how to assist the people is also to respect them. Help them to harvest crops, and organize literacy classes for local militia and armymen.

5. TAKE GOOD CARE OF PUBLIC PROPERTY AND WAR BOOTY

Public property is the fruit of the collective labour of the people. The army must preserve and take good care of it and must not waste it. Put an end to such acts as selling the rice contributed by the people, damaging tools and wasting ammunition. War booty is also public property. It belongs to the nation, not to the enemy. Munitions, medicine, equipment and food are the sweat and blood of our people. Our soldiers had to shed blood to recover them. We must prize and take good care of them, and not waste them or make them our personal property. When looking after them, we must arrange them neatly and protect them carefully against rain and sun.

6. WE MUST SINCERELY MAKE CRITICISM AND SELF-CRITICISM

In your reports to the conference, you must pay attention to this point. When making criticism and self-criticism, we must sincerely expose our shortcomings. If we make mistakes but don't want to expose them, that is like a patient who refuses to tell his disease to the doctor. When we do a lot of work it is difficult for us to avoid making mistakes. So we use the method of criticism and self-criticism to help one another in correcting our errors, and to be determined to correct them in order to make progress together. Besides exposing our shortcomings we must also report our achievements in order to develop them. In order to achieve good results in criticism and self-criticism, cadres at all levels, especially high-ranking cadres, must *be exemplary before anyone else.*

Many experiences, good and bad alike, may be drawn from this campaign. We must review them, popularize them and learn from them. They may be summed up in the following main points:

1. The leadership of the Central Committee is clearsighted. The leading committees at all levels have also adopted correct lines of leadership. The various organs of the army, mass organizations and administration have united, closely co-ordinated their actions, and adopted a unified plan of work.

2. Our soldiers are very zealous and heroic. This has been amply proved by the examples of the man who had his broken arm chopped off

to facilitate his movement in the assault, of another man who rushed into an enemy stronghold with a charge of dynamite in his hands, or of many others who did not eat anything for three or four days but continued to fight with all their ardour and heroism, and other examples.

3. Our people are very good. Never before have such big contingents of women of the Kinh, Man, Tho, Nung and other nationalities volunteered to carry supplies to the front as in the recent campaign. Hardship, privation and danger could not lessen their ardour, cheerfulness and heroism. That is really admirable. This is thanks partly to Comrade Tran Dang Ninh and other cadres of the Viet Bac Interzone who have correctly implemented the policies of the Party and the government and partly to the ardent patriotism and self-sacrificing spirit of our compatriots.

4. The enemy was subjective and underestimated his adversary. He did not think that we were so powerful or could make such rapid progress. That is why he did not take appropriate measures of defence, and exposed his weaknesses.

These are major experiences which must be pointed out in the reviewing report.

OTHER NOTABLE POINTS

I. CONCERNING PROPAGANDA WORK

In practice, the enemy has been making much more propaganda for us than we have ourselves. We have not concentrated all means and mobilized all our abilities for propaganda. That is why our information is still very slow and does not reach broad masses. The campaign closed on 15 October, yet until 30 October, the people and cadres in many localities did not yet know anything or only knew very little of it. Or if they had heard about it, they did not know how to popularize the news. Our propaganda among the prisoners of war and enemy troops as well as abroad is still very weak. We did not know how to make excerpts from enemy newspapers which expressed anger at the colonialist military commanders, politicians and administrative authorities who only cared for having a good time and disputed about personal interests while their soldiers died on the battlefields 'without a wreath being laid or a tear being shed for them'. We have failed to base ourselves on this material to write leaflets for agitation among the enemy's ranks, give explanations to the prisoners of war and make propaganda among the population in enemy-held areas.

2. LET US NOT INDULGE IN SUBJECTIVISM AND UNDERESTIMATE THE ENEMY

Do not indulge in naïve subjectivism and think that from now on victory will always be ours and there will be no more difficulties or failure. This victory is only a preliminary success. We still have to make great efforts and win many more victories like this or even greater ones before we can switch over to a general counteroffensive. From now to the day of complete victory, we shall meet with many difficulties and perhaps shall go through many failures. In a war, to win a victory or suffer a defeat are common things. The essential is that we must win final victory. We must help all officers and men and the people to bear that firmly in mind so that they will not be self-complacent when winning and disappointed when losing, but instead will always make utmost efforts to overcome difficulties and hardships and advance towards final victory.

Do not underestimate the enemy. The enemy is pulling himself in, not to lie still, but actually to leap forward again. He is striving to win time and prepare to hit back. In the meantime, they will seek to bomb and strafe the areas under our control with the aim of intimidating us, as was the case in Ha Giang, Tuyen Quang and Bac Giang recently.

3. WE MUST WIN TIME

We too must win time in order to make preparations. That is a condition for defeating the opponent. In military affairs, time is of prime importance. Time ranges first among the three factors for victory, before the terrain conditions and the people's support. Only by winning time can we secure the factors for defeating the enemy. It is precisely to win time that this conference should be a short one. The reports must be concise and raise the main and necessary problems. Don't be wordy. This would only waste time and bring no result at all.

4. LASTLY, WE MUST KEEP ABSOLUTE SECRECY

Secrecy is a very important thing. Everybody must keep secrecy. We must seek every means to keep secret all activities and in all circumstances: in an inn, in our talks and in our work, we must observe secrecy. It is not sufficient for the army and public offices alone to keep secrecy. We must teach the people to keep secrecy if we want to keep our work in complete secrecy. If we succeed in keeping secrecy, that is already one step towards our success.

From all the questions I raise above, this conference should try to solve some. After the conference, if you decide to solve the remaining ones, we will surely succeed in our future battles.

The Party, government and people call upon all officers and men to carry out these recommendations.

29

ON THE FIFTH ANNIVERSARY OF THE AUGUST REVOLUTION AND NATIONAL DAY

2 September 1950

Fellow countrymen at home and abroad,
Members of the National Defence Army, regional forces, militia and guerrilla units,
Cadres of the administration and mass organizations,
Young people and children!

Today we celebrate the fifth anniversary of the August Revolution and National Independence Day. Our Resistance has also lasted five years.

Let us briefly review the situation in the course of these five years so as to define our forthcoming tasks.

Prior to the August Revolution we were confronted with *two direct enemies*, Japanese imperialism and French colonialism, and an indirect enemy, the reactionary Chinese Kuomintang. That means that our enemies had immense forces.

Prior to the August Revolution, power was not in our hands and we had no regular army; the national front was still small and worked underground. That means that our forces were most deficient.

However, thanks to our skill in turning to account the international situation and in *uniting and mobilizing our people*, we were able to turn our weakness into strength, defeat the three enemies, bring the revolution to victory and gain national independence.

No sooner had our country regained her independence than the French colonialists attacked us.

Relying on their powerful army, well officered and armed with modern weapons, they intended to wage a *lightning war* and win a *quick victory*.

With only freshly organized troops and rudimentary weapons, we decided to *carry out a long war of resistance*.

Facts have proved that *our strategy has got the better of the enemy's*.

Since the outbreak of hostilities in Viet Nam, the French government has been overthrown over a dozen times; French commanders-in-chief have been replaced five or six times; French troops have been worn down; France's finances have dwindled with every passing day. The French people's anti-war movement has spread ever more extensively. Our people have grown ever more united and resolute.

Now the French colonialists have openly admitted that *they are exhausted and cannot prolong the war unless they are helped by the USA*.

While begging for US help, they are afraid lest the Americans oust them from Indochina, as the Japanese did a few years ago.

Ever since the war started, the *Americans have done their best to help the French*. But at present they go one step further by *directly interfering in Viet Nam*.

So, apart from our principal enemy, the French colonialists, we have now *another foe, the American interventionists*.

As far as we are concerned, the war of resistance waged these last few years *has won Viet Nam the greatest success in her history:* the two largest countries in the world, the Soviet Union and People's China, and the new democracies, have recognized the Democratic Republic of Viet Nam as an equal member in the great family of democratic countries of the world. This means that we have definitely joined the democratic camp and the eight hundred million people fighting against imperialism.

Surely these political successes will pave the way for *future military victories*.

The USSR and the new democratic countries are growing ever more powerful.

China has defeated the US interventionists and the reactionary Kuomintang clique, and is embarking on the path of new democracy.

The Korean people have risen against the US interventionists and all their satellites. They make up a huge allied force supporting our Resistance for national salvation and especially our struggle against the US interventionists.

The US reactionaries have failed in face of the unity in struggle of the Chinese people. They will fail in face of the unity in struggle of the peoples of Viet Nam, Korea and the world.

Facts over the past years have demonstrated that *our long war of resistance will certainly end in victory.*

This is beyond all question.

But *victory and long resistance must go hand in hand:*

'He who wishes to gather fine fruit should plant good trees'; this saying expresses eternal truth.

Therefore, our urgent tasks are:

- to strengthen our *unity* even further;
- to *unite all our people in a patriotic emulation movement for general mobilization* in order promptly to switch over to the general counteroffensive; first and foremost to encourage the supply of manpower and food;
- to urge the National Defence Army, regional forces, militia and guerrilla units to emulate one another in *wiping out enemy forces and performing brilliant exploits*;
- to urge the workers and peasants to *vie with one another in production*;
- to urge the youth to *rival one another in all fields*: enlistment in the army, production, transport, study, etc;
- to encourage all administrative and mass organization cadres to put into practice the motto: *industry, thrift, integrity, uprightness*;
- to urge our compatriots living in enemy-controlled areas to get ready to fight the enemy and support our troops.

Dear fellow countrymen!

Dear soldiers!

The *August Revolution* brought us unity and independence. At that time, apart from our spirit of solidarity, we possessed only small forces; but we carried the day.

Now we are waging a long war of resistance to defend our unity and independence; we have powerful forces and enjoy favourable national and international conditions: we are bound to win.

However, we must be aware of the following:

- The enemy will grow even more reckless and ferocious, they will probably extend their attacks even more before being wiped out.

– We shall meet with even greater difficulties and hardships before winning final victory.

Therefore we must be vigilant and resolute; we shall neither be discouraged by temporary setbacks, nor grow arrogant when winning big victories; neither shall we grow complacent and underestimate the enemy.

Thanks to the oneness of mind of our government and people, of our soldiers and civilians, to the unity and dauntlessness of our entire people, to the support of the peoples of democratic countries and of justice-loving personalities in the world,

Our long war of resistance will certainly end in victory!

National reunification and independence will certainly be achieved!

30

POLITICAL REPORT AT THE SECOND NATIONAL CONGRESS OF THE VIET NAM WORKERS' PARTY

February 1951

I. THE INTERNATIONAL SITUATION IN THE PAST FIFTY YEARS

The year 1951 marks the closing of the first half and the opening of the second half of the twentieth century. We are at a moment of great importance in the history of mankind.

Quicker and more important changes have occurred in the past fifty years than in many previous centuries added together.

The cinema, radio, television and atomic energy have been invented or discovered in the course of these fifty years. Mankind has thus made a big stride in harnessing the forces of nature. In this same period, capitalism has passed from free competition to monopoly, to imperialism.

In these fifty years, the imperialists have unleashed two *world wars*, the most terrible wars in history. As a result of these wars, the Russian, German, Italian and Japanese imperialists have been annihilated; the British and French imperialists have gone downhill, while the US capitalists have become the leading imperialists, the leading reactionaries.

Most important of all was the triumph of *the Russian October Revolution*. The Soviet Union, a socialist country, was established, covering one-sixth of the area of the globe. Nearly half of the human race has taken the path of *new democracy*. The oppressed peoples have risen up one after another against imperialism, for independence and freedom. The Chinese Revolution was successful. The workers' movement in the imperialist countries has grown ever stronger.

In the same period, in Viet Nam, *our party* was born twenty-one years ago. Our country regained her *independence* six years ago. Our *protracted war of resistance* has proceeded vigorously and is now in its fifth year.

In a word, many events of great importance have occurred in the first half of the twentieth century, but we can predict that thanks to the efforts of the revolutionaries, even greater and more glorious changes will take place in its second half.

II. THE BIRTH OF OUR PARTY

After World War One (1914–18), to make up for their heavy losses the French colonialists invested more capital in our country in order to intensify their exploitation of our wealth and manpower. On the other hand, the triumph of the Russian Revolution and the revolutionary effervescence in China were exerting deep and extensive influence. As a result, *the Vietnamese working class* matured, grew politically conscious, began to struggle, and needed a vanguard, a general staff, to lead it.

On 6 January 1930 *our party came into being.*[1]

After the success of the Russian October Revolution, the *Communist International* was set up under Lenin's leadership. Since then, the international proletariat and the world revolution have become one great family, and our party is one of its youngest members.

Due to the French colonialists' policy of savage persecution, our party was born in very difficult circumstances. However, immediately after its founding our party led a fierce struggle against the French colonialists, which climaxed in the days of the Nghe An soviets.

This was the first time our people held local power and began to put democratic policies into effect, though only over a small area.

The Nghe An soviets failed, but they had a great influence. Their heroic spirit was kept alive in the hearts of the masses and paved the way for subsequent victories. From 1931 to 1945, always under the leadership of our party, the revolutionary movement in Viet Nam had ups and downs, rising, then ebbing, then rising again. These fifteen years can be divided into three periods:

1. Period from 1931 to 1935;
2. Period from 1936 to 1939; and
3. Period from 1939 to 1945.

III. PERIOD FROM 1931 TO 1935

From 1931 to 1933, the French colonialists pursued a policy of savage terror. Many Party cadres and sympathizers were arrested and killed. Almost all Party and mass organizations were destroyed. As a result, the revolutionary tide temporarily ebbed.

Thanks to the loyalty and devotion of the remaining comrades, the determination of the Central Committee and the assistance of the friendly parties, from 1933 onwards the revolutionary movement again rose gradually.

At that time, the Party strove, on the one hand, to consolidate its underground organizations and, on the other, to combine underground work with legal activity, propaganda and agitation in the press and in the municipal councils, regional councils, etc.

In 1935, the *Party held its First Congress* in Macao. The congress assessed the situation in our country and in the world, reviewed the work done and mapped out a programme for the coming period.

But the policies worked out at the Macao Congress were not in keeping with the revolutionary movement in the world and in our country at that time. (They advocated distribution of land to the agricultural workers, and failed to grasp the anti-fascist task and be aware of the danger of fascist war, etc.)

IV. PERIOD FROM 1936 TO 1939

In 1936, at the Party's first national conference, Comrades Le Hong Phong and Ha Huy Tap rectified these errors and worked out new policies in line with the resolutions of the Seventh Congress of the Communist International (setting up of the Democratic Front; semi-legal activity of the Party).

At that time, in France, the Popular Front was in power. Our party launched a movement for democracy and set up the Indochinese Democratic Front.

The Democratic Front movement was fairly strong and widespread. The people struggled openly. This was a good point. But there were shortcomings. The Party's leadership was not close enough; so in many localities our cadres were affected by narrow-mindedness, legalism, and were intoxicated by partial successes to the extent of neglecting the consolidation of the Party's underground organization. The Party failed to make clear its standpoint on the question of national independence. A number of comrades engaged in unprincipled co-operation with the Trotskyites. When the Popular Front in France collapsed and World War Two broke out, the Democratic Front movement in our country was repressed by the colonialists, and our party was thrown into confusion for a time.

However, this movement left our party and the present National Front invaluable experiences. It taught us that whatever conforms to the people's aspirations will receive support from the masses, who will wholeheartedly struggle for it, and as such is a real mass movement. It also taught us to avoid at all costs subjectiveness, narrow-mindedness, etc.

V. PERIOD FROM 1939 TO 1945

The great changes that occurred in this period in our country and in the world were only ten years back. Many of us witnessed them, many still remember them. I shall recall only some principal ones:

A. IN THE WORLD

In 1939, *World War Two* broke out.

At first, it was an imperialist war between the German, Italian and Japanese fascist imperialists on one side and the British, French and American imperialists on the other.

In June 1941, the German fascists attacked the Soviet Union, the fortress of the world revolution, which had to fight back and to ally itself with the British and Americans against the fascist camp. Thenceforward, the war became one between the democratic camp and the fascist camp.

Owing to the immense forces of the Red Army and the Soviet people, and to Comrade Stalin's correct strategy, in May 1945 Germany was crushed, and in August 1945 Japan surrendered. *The democratic camp had won complete victory*.

In this victory, the *greatest success* in the military field as well as in the political and moral field was that of *the Soviet Union*.

Thanks to the success won by the Soviet Union, the countries of Eastern Europe, which formerly were bases or parts of fascist Germany, have become *new democracies*.

Thanks to the success won by the Soviet Union, semicolonial countries such as China, and colonial countries such as Korea and Viet Nam have driven out or are driving out the aggressive imperialists to wrest back freedom and independence.

Thanks to the success won by the Soviet Union, national liberation movements in other colonies are rising.

The United States was successful in the financial field. While the other countries were pouring their forces into the war and were devastated by it, the United States made big profits.

After the war, the German, Italian and Japanese fascists were annihilated. The British and French imperialists were going downhill. The Soviet Union very quickly recovered, and developed its work of socialist construction. But treading in the steps of Germany, Italy and Japan, the US has now become the ringleader of the fascist imperialists.

B. IN OUR COUNTRY

After the outbreak of World War Two, the Party Central Committee met in November 1939, and worked out these policies: to set up a *united front* against the French colonialists and the imperialist war and to prepare for an insurrection; not to put forward the slogan 'Confiscate the landlords' land for distribution to the tillers' in order to draw the landlord class into the National Front.

After France's capitulation to fascist Germany, Japan encroached upon French power in Indochina and used the French colonialists as agents for repressing the revolution in our country.

In that period, our people launched three uprisings: in Bac Son, Nam Ky and Do Luong.

In May 1941, the *Party Central Committee* held its *Eighth Plenum*. The main question was to regard the present revolution in Viet Nam as one for national liberation; to set up the League for the Independence of Viet Nam (the Viet Minh) with the following slogan: To unite the entire people, oppose the Japanese and the French and wrest back independence; to postpone the agrarian revolution.

The name *Viet Nam Doc Lap Dong Minh* (League for the Independence of Viet Nam) had a very clear and practical meaning, and corresponded to the aspirations of the entire people. Besides, it set forth a simple, practical and comprehensive programme in ten points, as expounded in a propaganda ditty:

> *The programme comprises ten points:*
> *All in the interests of the country and the people.*

These ten points include points common to the whole nation and others dealing with the struggle for the interests of the workers, peasants and various strata of the population.

As a result, the Viet Minh was warmly welcomed by the people, and thanks to the efforts made by the cadres to keep in close touch with the people, it developed very rapidly and vigorously. Hence the Party also expanded. The Party also helped progressive intellectuals to found the Viet Nam Democratic Party in order to attract young intellectuals and civil servants and to accelerate the disintegration of the pro-Japanese Dai Viet.

In the world, the Soviet Union and the Allies scored repeated victories. In our country, the Japanese and the French were in conflict. Under the Party's leadership, the Viet Minh had grown fairly strong. In that context, the Standing Bureau of the Central Committee held an *enlarged session* in March 1945. The main resolution was to *push forward the anti-Japanese movement and to prepare for the general insurrection*. By that time, power had already fallen from the hands of the French colonialists into those of the Japanese fascists.

In May 1945, Germany capitulated. In August, Japan surrendered. The Soviet Union and the Allies had won complete victory.

Early in August, the Party held its *Second National Conference* at Tan Trao to decide on a plan of action and on participation in the *National People's Congress* convened by the Viet Minh, to be held at Tan Trao in the same month.

The National People's Congress approved the plan set forth by the Viet Minh and the order for general insurrection and elected the Central National Liberation Committee which was to become the Provisional government of our country.

Because the Party's policy was correct and was carried out in a timely and flexible way, the August general insurrection was crowned with success.

VI. FROM THE AUGUST REVOLUTION UP TO NOW

The triumph of the August Revolution was due to the clear-sighted and resolute leadership of our party and the unity and fervour of the entire people, both inside and outside the Viet Minh.

Comrades,

Not only our own toiling classes and people but also the toiling classes and oppressed peoples of other countries can be proud of this fact: for the first time in the revolutionary history of colonial and semicolonial peoples, *a party barely fifteen years old has led the revolution to success and seized power throughout the country.*

For our part, we must bear in mind that our success was due to the great victory of the Soviet Red Army over the Japanese fascists, to the friendly assistance of international solidarity, to the close unity of our entire people and to the heroic sacrifices of our revolutionary predecessors.

Our comrades, like Tran Phu, Ngo Gia Tu, Le Hong Phong, Nguyen Thi Minh Khai, Ha Huy Tap, Nguyen Van Cu, Hoang Van Thu and thousands of others, placed the interests of the Party, the revolution, the class and the nation above and before everything else. They had deep confidence in the immense forces and glorious future of the class and the nation. They willingly sacrificed everything, even their lives for the sake of the Party, the class and the nation. They watered with their blood the tree of revolution which has now bloomed and borne fruit.

In order to become truly deserving revolutionaries, all of us must follow these examples of heroism, of utter devotion to the public interest and complete selflessness.

The August Revolution overthrew the centuries-old monarchy, broke the chains of the nearly one hundred years of colonial rule, gave back power to the people and built the basis for an independent, free and happy Democratic Republic of Viet Nam.

This is an extremely great change in the history of our country.

The triumph of the August Revolution has made us a member of the great democratic family in the world.

The August Revolution has exerted a direct and very great influence on two friendly nations: Cambodia and Laos. After the success of the August Revolution, the Cambodian and Lao peoples also rose up against the imperialists and claimed independence.

On 2 September 1945, *the government of the Democratic Republic of Viet Nam* declared to the world the independence of Viet Nam and put into effect democratic freedoms in the country. One fact should be stressed here: At the time of the setting up of the Provisional government some comrades, members of the Central Committee elected by the National People's Congress, should have taken part in the government; yet, of their own accord they withdrew in favour of patriotic personalities who were not members of the Viet Minh. This is a selfless, magnanimous gesture by men who do not care for position, who put the interests of the nation, of the national union, above individual interests. This is a gesture worthy of praise and respect, one that should serve us as an example.

VII. THE DIFFICULTIES ENCOUNTERED BY THE PARTY AND THE GOVERNMENT

As soon as the people's power came into existence it met with great difficulties.

Due to the policy of ruthless exploitation by the Japanese and the French, within only half a year (end of 1944 and beginning of 1945) more than two million people in the North had died of starvation.

Hardly a month after our declaration of independence British troops entered the South. Under the pretence of disarming the Japanese army, they acted as an expeditionary corps helping the French colonialists in their attempts to reoccupy our country.

Chinese Kuomintang troops entered the North, allegedly also to disarm the Japanese, but actually in pursuit of three wicked aims:

- to destroy our party.
- to smash the Viet Minh.
- to help the Vietnamese reactionaries overthrow the people's power and set up a reactionary government at their beck and call.

In the face of that grave and pressing situation, our party had to do everything that was necessary in order to keep itself in existence, work and develop, to give more discreet and effective leadership, and to gain time in order gradually to consolidate the forces of the people's power and strengthen the National United Front.

At that time the Party could not hesitate: hesitation would have meant failure. The Party had to take quick decisions and adopt measures – even painful ones – likely to save the situation.

In spite of many great difficulties, the Party and the government guided our country through dangerous rapids and implemented many points in the programme of the Viet Minh:

- holding general elections to elect the National Assembly and draw up the Constitution;
- building and consolidating the people's power;
- annihilating the Vietnamese reactionaries;
- building and consolidating the people's army and arming the people;
- promulgating labour legislation;
- reducing land rent and interest rates;
- building people's culture;
- broadening and consolidating the National United Front (setting up of the Lien Viet).

Mention should be made here of the *Preliminary Agreement of 6 March 1946*, and the *Modus Vivendi of 14 September 1946*, because they were regarded by a number of people as manifestations of a *rightist policy* and caused some grumbling on their part. But in the opinion of our comrades and compatriots in the South this policy was correct. And correct it was, because our southern comrades and compatriots cleverly availed themselves of this opportunity to build up and develop their forces.

Lenin said that one should make a compromise even with bandits if it was advantageous to the revolution

We needed peace to build our country, and therefore we forced ourselves to make concessions in order to maintain peace. Although the French colonialists broke their word and unleashed war, nearly one year of temporary peace had given us time to build up our basic forces.

When the French deliberately provoked war and we could no longer put up with them, the nationwide war of resistance broke out.

VIII. THE PROTRACTED WAR OF RESISTANCE

The enemy schemed for a *lightning war.* They wanted to attack swiftly and win swiftly. For our part, our party and government set forth the motto: *Protracted war of resistance.* The enemy plotted to sow dissensions among us, so our watchword was: *Unity of the entire people.*

Thus, right from the start, our strategy prevailed over the enemy's.

To wage a protracted war of resistance, there must be an adequate supply of arms and munitions to the army, of food and clothing to the troops and the people. Our country is poor and our technical level low. Cities and towns with some industry are all occupied by the enemy. We must seek to offset our material deficiencies by the enthusiasm of our entire people. So the Party and the government have promoted *patriotic emulation.* Emulation covers all fields but it is aimed at three main objectives: to get rid of famine, liquidate illiteracy and annihilate the foreign invaders.

Our workers have emulated one another in manufacturing weapons for our troops, who have trained hard and scored good results. Our recent victories in battle are proof of this. Our people have ardently emulated one another and recorded satisfactory results. Although our country is economically backward, we have been waging the war of resistance for nearly five years and can keep fighting without suffering too many privations. This is a fact. The majority of our population have been freed from illiteracy. This is a brilliant achievement admired by the world. I suggest that our Congress send cordial thanks and praise to our troops and fellow countrymen.

However, concerning the work of organization and supervision and the exchange and summing up of experiences we are still weak. These are shortcomings. From now on we should strive to overcome them; then the emulation movement will certainly reap more and better results.

Military activity is the keystone in the war of resistance.

When the war of resistance began *our army* was still in its infancy. Though full of heroism, it lacked weapons, experience, officers, everything.

The enemy army was well known in the world. It had land, naval, and air forces. Moreover it was supported by the British and American imperialists, especially the latter.

The discrepancy between our forces and the enemy's was so great that at the time some people likened our war of resistance to a fight between 'a grasshopper and an elephant'.

And such a fight it would be if things were looked at with a narrow mind, solely from the angle of material strength and in their present state. Indeed against the enemy's airplanes and artillery we had only bamboo sticks. But our party is a Marxist-Leninist one. We look not only at the present but also to the future and have firm confidence in the spirit and strength of the masses of the nation. Therefore we resolutely told those wavering and pessimistic people:

> *Yes, it's now grasshopper versus elephant,*
> *But tomorrow the elephant will collapse.*

Facts have shown that the colonialist 'elephant' is getting out of breath while our army has grown up into a powerful tiger.

Although at the beginning, the enemy was so strong and we still so weak, we none the less fought with the greatest energy, scored many successes, and kept firm confidence in our final victory. This is because our cause is just, our troops courageous, our people united and un-daunted, and because we are supported by the French people and the world democratic camp. This is also because our strategy is correct.

Our party and government have estimated that our war of resistance includes three stages:

In the first stage, which went from 23 September 1945, to the end of the Viet Bac campaign in autum–winter 1947, our efforts were aimed at preserving and increasing our main forces.

In the second stage, from the end of the Viet Bac campaign in 1947 up to now, we have actively contended with the enemy and prepared for the general counteroffensive.

The third stage is to be that of the general counteroffensive.

On this last point, because they did not grasp the policy of the Party and the government, a number of comrades got wrong ideas. Some thought that the slogan of 'preparation for general counteroffensive' was premature. Others wanted to know the day and hour of the general counteroffensive. Still others believed that the general counteroffensive would certainly be launched in 1950, etc.

These wrong conceptions were harmful to our work. We must first of all keep in mind that *the war of resistance will be long and hard, but will certainly end in victory*.

The war of resistance must be a protracted one because our population and territory are small and our country is poor. Long and all-round preparations have to be made by our entire people. We must always bear in mind that in relation to us the French invaders are quite strong, and in addition, they are assisted by the British and Americans.

They are like a 'tangerine with a thick rind' and so we must have time to 'sharpen our fingernails' in order to peel it.

We must also understand that each stage is linked up with others: it succeeds the one that precedes it and produces seeds for the one that follows.

Many changes occur in the course of the passage from one stage to another. Each stage also contains changes of its own.

It is possible to determine major stages on the basis of the general situation but it is not possible to separate one stage completely from the other, like slicing a cake. The length of each stage depends on the situation at home and in the world, and on the changes in the enemy's forces and in ours.

We must understand that protracted resistance is closely connected with preparations for a general counteroffensive. As the war of resistance is a long one, long preparations are also needed for a general counter-offensive. Whether the general counteroffensive will come early or late depends on changes in the enemy's forces and in ours, and also on changes in the international situation.

In all circumstances, the more careful and complete the preparations, the more steadily and favourably the general counteroffensive will proceed.

The slogan '*To prepare for a vigorous switch to the general counteroffensive*' was set forth early in 1950.

Did we make preparations during that year?

Yes, we did. The government issued the general mobilization order and launched the movement for patriotic emulation. As is well known, our troops and our people have made active preparations and have obtained good results.

Did we make the move in 1950?

Yes, we did and are still doing it. The great diplomatic successes scored early in 1950 and the great military victories won towards the end of that year were proof of this.

Have we launched the general counteroffensive?

We have been preparing to switch over vigorously to the general counteroffensive, but have not yet actually launched it. We must fully grasp the meaning of the words 'To prepare for a vigorous switch to . . .'

Once *the preparations are fully completed* we will launch the general counteroffensive. The more complete, the more fully complete, the preparations, the sooner the general counteroffensive will come and the more favourable the conditions for its success.

We should avoid precipitation, rashness and impatience.

The troops, the people, the cadres, everybody and every branch must *strive to make fully complete preparations*. When our preparations are completed we will launch the general counteroffensive and then it will certainly be successful.

IX. CORRECTION OF SHORTCOMINGS AND MISTAKES

Our party has recorded many achievements but has also committed *not a few mistakes*. We must sincerely engage in self-criticism in order to correct them. Efforts must be made to correct our mistakes so as to progress.

Before speaking of our shortcomings we must recognize that our party has cadres – especially those in the zones still temporarily under enemy control – who are very heroic and devoted, who, in spite of all hardships and dangers, always keep close to the people, stick to their work without fear or complaint, and are ready to sacrifice even their lives.

They are model fighters of the nation, meritorious sons and daughters of the Party.

It can be said that since the founding of the Party, *its policies on the whole have been correct*. If they were not how could we have recorded such tremendous achievements? But we have also shown major shortcomings and weaknesses:

Doctrinal studies are still inadequate, many Party cadres and members are not yet mature ideologically and their theoretical level is still low. As a result, in the carrying out of the policies of the Party and the government there have occurred erroneous tendencies, either 'leftist', or rightist (as in problems relating to land, the Front, the national minorities, religion, the administration etc.).

Our organizational work is also still weak, and often cannot ensure correct implementation of the policies of the Party and the government.

Therefore, *to study our doctrine, sharpen our ideology, raise our theoretical level and perfect our organization* are urgent tasks for the Party.

Besides, in leading organs at all levels there still exist fairly prevalent and grave mistakes in the style of work measures adopted and manner of guiding. These are *subjectiveness*, *bureaucracy*, *commandism*, *narrow-mindedness* and *arrogance*.

Subjectiveness manifests itself in the belief that the long-term war of resistance can turn out to be a short-term war.

Bureaucracy is evidenced by red tape, divorce from the masses and by failure to conduct investigations and surveys, to engage in control and supervision, and learn from the experiences of the masses.

Commandism reveals itself in reliance on administrative compulsion to get things done, and failure to conduct propaganda and explanatory work to make the people work on their own.

Narrow-mindedness is apparent in judging non-Party people with undue severity, or slighting them and refusing to discuss with them or ask for their opinion.

As for *arrogance*, it is revealed in the following:

– To boast of one's past achievements, extol oneself and consider oneself the 'saviour' of the people and the 'meritorious servant' of the Party. To ask for position and honour. Unable to fulfil major tasks, one is unwilling to accept minor ones. Arrogance is very harmful to solidarity both within and without the Party.

– To rely on one's position as Party member to make light of discipline and hierarchy in mass organizations or government organs.

The comrades affected by this disease do not understand that each Party member must be a model of discipline, not only Party discipline but also that of mass organizations and organs of revolutionary power.

The Central Committee is partly responsible for that disease and others which affect Party members, because it has not paid adequate attention to *control work*. Ideological training has not been given to all, nor in sufficient amount. Inner Party democracy has not been broadly practised. Criticism and self-criticism have not yet become regular habits.

However, these defects are being corrected to a certain extent. The recent critical reviews and the movement for criticism and self-criticism have yielded good results in spite of a few deviations.

Stalin said that a revolutionary party needs criticism and self-criticism just as a human being needs air. He also said that close control can help avoid many grave mistakes.

From now on the Party must try to dispense doctrinal education in order to raise the political standards of its members. *A collective style of work* must be promoted. *Relations between the Party and the masses* must be strengthened. *Observance of discipline, respect of principles and Party spirit* must be heightened in every Party member. The Party must widen the movement for criticism and self-criticism within the Party, the State organs, the mass organizations, in the press and among the people. Criticism and self-criticism must be conducted regularly, in a practical and democratic way, from top to bottom and from the bottom upwards. Lastly there must be close control by the Party.

By so doing, we shall commit fewer errors and make quicker progress.

X. NEW SITUATION AND NEW TASKS

A. NEW SITUATION

As is well known the world is at present divided into two distinct camps:

– The *democratic camp* headed by the Soviet Union and comprising the socialist countries and the new democracies in Europe and in Asia. It also embraces the oppressed nations which are struggling against aggressive imperialism and the democratic organizations and personalities in the capitalist countries.

The democratic camp is a powerful camp which is growing in strength. The following few points are sufficient evidence of this.

Let us look at a map of the world: from Eastern Europe to Eastern Asia the USSR and the new democracies form an immense bloc of 800 million people. In this bloc the nations are united, pursue the same goal and are not divided by any antagonisms. It is the symbol of progress and of the bright future of mankind. It is an extremely powerful force.

At the Second Congress of the Peace Front held in the Polish capital in November 1950, the representatives of 500 million peace fighters in 81 countries pledged their determination to safeguard world peace and to oppose imperialist wars. This is the *United Front* of the peaceful and democratic world. This is a very powerful force whose strength is growing with every passing day.

– The *anti-democratic camp* is headed by the US. Immediately after the end of World War Two, the US became the ringleader of world imperialism and reaction. Britain and France are its right- and left-hand men and the reactionary governments in the East and the West its henchmen.

Aspiring to world hegemony, the US holds out dollars in one hand to entice people and brandishes the atomic bomb in the other to menace the world. The Truman Doctrine, Marshall Plan, NATO Pact, and Programme for Southeast Asia are all US manoeuvres aimed at preparing for a third world war.

But the US ambitions have run into a tremendous obstacle: the immense force of the Soviet Union, the movement for democracy and peace, and the movement for national liberation seething all over the world.

At present, the US policy is as follows:

– In Asia, to assist the reactionaries such as Chiang Kai-shek, Syngman Rhee, Bao Dai, etc.; to help the British imperialists repress the resistance forces in Malaya and the French colonialists crush the Resistance in Viet Nam, while the US itself is waging an aggressive war against Korea and is occupying Taiwan in an attempt to undermine the Chinese revolution.

– In Europe the US has, through the Marshall Plan and NATO, seized control over the Western countries in the military, political and economic fields, and at the same time has been striving to arm them and compel them to supply cannon fodder, as in the plan for setting up seventy divisions in Western Europe under an American commander-in-chief.

However, the US camp has a great many weaknesses:

Besides the strength of the democratic camp, the US camp faces another threat: economic crisis.

There are many contradictions in the US camp. For example: the US wants Western Germany to set up an army of ten divisions but this has been opposed by the French people. Britain covertly opposes the US because the two are contending for oil in the Near East and for influence in the Far East.

The people, especially the toiling sections in countries 'aided' by the US, hate it for encroaching upon their economic interests and the independence of their countries.

The US is too greedy. It schemes to set up bases all over the world. It helps every reactionary group and every reactionary government. Its front extends beyond measure, consequently its forces are spread thin. Clear proof of this is supplied in Korea, where the United States together with forty of its vassals are suffering defeats at the hands of the country they have invaded. The US helped the reactionary clique in China, the Kuomintang headed by Chiang Kai-shek, but Chiang was defeated. The

US helps the French colonialists in Viet Nam, yet the Vietnamese Resistance is winning.

In short, we can foretell that the reactionary imperialist camp will certainly be defeated and the camp of peace and democracy will certainly be victorious.

Viet Nam is a part of the world democratic camp. It is at present a bastion against imperialism, against the anti-democratic camp headed by the US.

Since the beginning of our war of resistance, Britain and the US have helped the French colonialists. And since 1950, the US has openly intervened in our country.

At the end of 1950, Britain and France prepared to set up a 'united' front to join forces against the resistance in Malaya and in Viet Nam.

Thus, the international situation is closely related to our country. Every success of the democratic camp is also ours, and every success won by us is also one for the democratic camp. Therefore, at present our main slogan is: '*To crush the French colonialists and defeat the US interventionists in order to regain unity and complete independence and safeguard world peace.*'

B. NEW TASKS

The comrades of the Central Committee will report on such important questions as the Party's political programme and constitution, the military question, the administration, the National United Front, the economy, etc. This report will only emphasize some main tasks among our new ones:

1. *To bring the war of resistance to complete victory.*
2. *To organize the Viet Nam Workers' Party.*

1. Efforts must be made to develop the strength of the troops and the people in order to win success after success and advance towards the general counteroffensive.

This task aims at these main points:

– *In the building and development of the army*, all-out efforts must be made towards the organization and consolidation of *political and military* work among our troops. Their political consciousness, tactics and techniques, and *self-imposed discipline* must be heightened. Our army must become a genuine *people's* army.

Simultaneously, the *militia and guerrilla units* must be developed and consolidated in organization, training, leadership and combat strength. They must make up a vast and solid steel net spread all over the country so that wherever the enemy goes he will get enmeshed.

– *To enhance patriotism* – Our people are inspired by ardent patriotism. This is an invaluable tradition of ours. At all times, whenever the fatherland is invaded, this patriotism forms an immensely powerful wave sweeping away all dangers and difficulties and drowning all traitors and aggressors.

Many great wars of resistance in our history are proofs of our people's patriotism. We can be proud of the glorious pages of history written by our people in the days of the Trung Sisters, Lady Trieu, Tran Hung Dao, Le Loi, Quang Trung, etc. We must engrave in our minds the achievements of our national heroes because they are the symbols of a heroic nation.

Our fellow countrymen today are worthy of their forefathers. White-haired folk, children, people residing abroad, people living in the areas still under enemy control, in the plains, in the highlands – all are imbued with ardent love for the country and hatred for the aggressor. Fighters at the front go hungry for days on end in order to remain in contact with the enemy and annihilate him. Government employees in the rear go hungry for the sake of the troops. Women urge their husbands to enlist in the army while they themselves help to transport supplies. Combatants' mothers take care of the troops as they would their own children. Workers and peasants of both sexes emulate one another to increase production, shrinking from no hardships in order to contribute their part to the Resistance. Landowners offer their lands to the government. These lofty gestures are all different; yet they are similar for they stem from the same ardent patriotism. Patriotism is like valuable objects. Sometimes these are exhibited in a glass or a crystal vase and are thus clearly visible. But at other times they may be discreetly hidden in a trunk or a suitcase. Our duty is to bring all these hidden valuables into full view. That is, every effort must be made in explanation, propaganda, organization and leadership so that the patriotism of all may find expression in work benefiting the country and the Resistance.

Genuine patriotism is altogether different from the chauvinism of the reactionary imperialists. It is part and parcel of internationalism. It was thanks to their patriotism that the army and the people of the Soviet Union crushed the German and Japanese fascists and safeguarded their socialist fatherland, thereby helping the working class and the oppressed peoples of the world. It was thanks to their patriotism that the Chinese Liberation Army and the Chinese people destroyed the traitorous Chiang Kai-shek clique and drove out the American imperialists. It is thanks to their patriotism that the Korean troops and people, together with the Chinese Volunteers, are routing the American imperialists and their henchmen. It is also thanks to their patriotism that our troops and people have for long years endured untold sufferings and hardships, determined to smash the colonialist aggressors and the Vietnamese traitors, and to build an independent, reunified, democratic, free, and properous Viet Nam, a new democratic Viet Nam.

– *To step up patriotic emulation.* First, let the troops emulate one another to exterminate the enemy and score feats of arms; second, let the people emulate one another to *increase production.* We must devote ourselves heart and soul to these two tasks.

– In the great work of carrying on the war of resistance and engaging in national construction, the *Lien Viet–Viet Minh* Front, the trade unions, the peasants' associations and other mass organizations exert great influence. We must help them develop, strengthen and work vigorously.

– *Concerning the land policy*, in the free zones, we must strictly implement the reduction of land rent and interest rates, confiscate lands belonging to the French and the Vietnamese traitors and temporarily distribute them to the poor peasants and the families of armymen, with a view to improving the livelihood of the peasants, heightening their spirit, and fostering their forces for the Resistance.

– *Concerning the economy and finance*, we must safeguard and develop our economic bases and fight the enemy in the economic field. There must be an equitable and rational tax system. A balance must be achieved in receipts and expenditures in order to ensure supplies for the army and the people.

– *Cultural work* must be speeded up to form the new man and train new cadres for the Resistance and for national construction. All vestiges of colonialism and the enslaving influence of imperialist culture must be systematically rooted out. Simultaneously, we must develop the fine traditions of our national culture and assimilate the new in world progressive culture in order to build a Vietnamese culture with a national, scientific and popular character.

Following our victories, the *areas still under temporary enemy control* will be liberated one after another. Therefore, preparations must be made to consolidate the newly liberated areas in all respects.

– The life and property of *foreign residents* who abide by the Vietnamese law will be protected. *Chinese residents* should be encouraged to take part in the Resistance. If they volunteer to do so they will enjoy every right and fulfil every duty of a Vietnamese citizen.

We are waging our war of resistance, the brotherly Cambodian and Lao nations are also waging theirs. The French colonialists and the American interventionists are the common enemy of our three nations. Consequently, we must strive to help our Cambodian and Lao brothers and their wars of resistance, and proceed to set up a Viet Nam Cambodian Lao Front.

– Our successes in the Resistance are partly due to the sympathy of the *friendly countries* and of the people of the world. Therefore, we must strengthen the friendship between our country and the friendly countries, and that between our people and the people of the other countries in the world.

2. To carry these points into effect, we must have a legal party organized in a way consistent with the situation in the world and at home in order to lead our people's struggle to victory. This party is named the *Viet Nam Workers' Party*.

As regards its *composition*, the Viet Nam Workers' Party will admit the most enthusiastic and most enlightened workers, peasants and intellectuals.

As regards its *doctrine*, it adheres to Marxism-Leninism.

As regards its *organization*, it adopts the system of democratic centralism.

As regards *discipline*, it has an iron discipline which is at the same time a self-imposed one.

As regards its law of *development*, it makes use of criticism and self-criticism to educate its members and the masses.

As regards its *immediate goal*, the Viet Nam Workers' Party unites and leads the entire people to wage the war of resistance, take it to complete victory and win back national unity and complete independence; it leads the entire people to realize new democracy and create conditions for the advance to socialism.

The Viet Nam Workers' Party must be a great party – powerful, firm, pure and thoroughly revolutionary.

The Viet Nam Workers' Party must be the clearsighted, determined and loyal leader of the working class and toiling people, of the Vietnamese people, whose aim is to unite and lead the people in the resistance until complete victory, and to realize new democracy.

In the present stage, the interests of the working class and toiling people and those of the nation are at one. It is precisely because it is the party of the working class and toiling people that the Viet Nam Workers' Party must be the party of the Vietnamese people.

The first task, the most urgent task of our party today, is to *lead the war of resistance to victory*. The other tasks must be subordinated to it.

Our task is immense, our future glorious. But we shall have to experience many more difficulties. The war has its difficulties; victory has its own. For example:

– Ideologically, our cadres, Party members and people are not yet mature enough to cope with all developments at home and abroad.

– The American imperialists may give the French aggressors even greater assistance, causing the latter to act even more rashly.

– We are facing more and more work, but we have not enough cadres and those we have lack ability and experience.

– We must solve economic and financial problems in the most rational way, one that is the most beneficial to the people, etc.

We do not fear difficulties. But we must foresee them, clearly realize them, and be prepared to overcome them.

With the solidarity and unity of mind, the determination and dauntless spirit of our party, government and entire people, we will certainly surmount all difficulties and gain complete victory.

The October Revolution triumphed. The building of socialism in the Soviet Union has been successful. The Chinese revolution was victorious. These great successes have opened the way to success for the revolution in our country and many other countries in the world.

We have a great, powerful party. Its greatness and strength is due to Marxism-Leninism, to the constant efforts of all our Party members, and to the love, confidence and support of our entire army and people.

That is why I am convinced that we will fulfil our heavy but glorious tasks, which are

– to build the Viet Nam Workers' Party into a most powerful one;
– to bring the Resistance to complete victory;
– to build a new democratic Viet Nam; and
– to contribute to the defence of democracy in the world and a lasting peace.

31

THE IMPERIALIST AGGRESSORS CAN NEVER ENSLAVE THE HEROIC VIETNAMESE PEOPLE[1]

January 1952

I avail myself of the short New Year holiday to write these lines.

More fortunate than other peoples, we the Vietnamese people, like our friends the Chinese and the Korean peoples, enjoy two New Year festivals every year. One New Year's Day is celebrated according to the Gregorian calendar and falls on the First of January. On that day, which is the official New Year's Day, only government offices send greetings to one another. Another New Year's Day, the Tet, is observed according to the lunar calendar, and this year falls on a day of the closing week of January. This traditional New Year's Day, celebrated by the people, usually lasts from three to seven days in peacetime.

In our country spring begins in the first days of January. At present, a splendid springtime prevails everywhere. The radiant sunbeams bring with them a merry and healthy life. Like an immense green carpet, the young rice plants cover the fields, heralding a coming bumper harvest. The birds warble merrily in evergreen bushes. Here winter lasts only a few days and rarely the thermometer falls to 10 degrees centigrade above zero. As far as snow is concerned, generally speaking, it is unknown for all our people.

Before during the Tet festival, pictures and greetings written on red paper could be seen stuck at entrance doors of palaces as well as tiny thatched huts. Today these greetings and pictures are replaced by slogans urging struggle and labour, such as 'Intensify the emulation movement for armed struggle, production and economic development!', 'The war of resistance will win!', 'Combat bureaucracy, corruption and waste!', 'The national construction will certainly be crowned with success!'

During the Tet festival, people are clad in their most beautiful garments. In every family the most delicious foods are prepared. Religious services are performed in front of the ancestral altars. Visits are paid between kith and kin to exchange greetings. Grown-ups give gifts to children; civilians send presents to soldiers . . . In short, it can be said that this is a spring festival.

Before telling you the situation of Viet Nam, may I send you and all our comrades my warmest greetings!

COLLUSION BETWEEN THE AGGRESSORS

Let us review Viet Nam's situation in 1951.

After their defeat in the China–Viet Nam border campaign in October 1950, the greatest reverse they had ever suffered in the whole history of their colonial wars, which involved for them the loss of five provinces at one time – Cao Bang, Lang Son, Lao Cat, Thai Nguyen and Hoa Binh – the French colonialists began the year 1951 with the despatch of General de Lattre de Tassigny to Viet Nam.

They resorted to total war. Their manoeuvre was to consolidate the Bao Dai puppet government, organize puppet troops and redouble spying activities. They set up no man's lands of from 5 to 10 kilometres wide around areas under their control and strengthened the Red River delta by a network of 2,300 bunkers. They stepped up mopping-up operations in our rear, applied the policy of annihilation and wholesale destruction of our manpower and potential resources by killing our compatriots, devastating our countryside, burning our ricefields, etc . . . In a word, they followed the policy of 'using Vietnamese to fight Vietnamese and nursing the war by means of warfare'.

It is on orders and with the assistance of their masters, the American interventionists, that the French colonialists performed the above-mentioned deeds.

Among the first Americans now living in Viet Nam (of course in areas under French control) there are a fairly noted spy, Donald Heat, ambassador accredited to the puppet government, and a general, head of the US military mission.

In September 1951, de Lattre de Tassigny went to Washington to make his report and beg for aid.

In October, General Collins, chief of staff of the US army, came to Viet Nam to inspect the French Expeditionary Corps and puppet troops.

In order to show their American masters that US aid is used in a worthwhile manner at present as well as in the future, in November de Lattre de Tassigny attacked the chief town of Hoa Binh province. The result of this 'shooting offensive', which the reactionary press in France and in the world commented on uproariously, was that the Viet Nam People's Army held the overwhelming majority of enemy troops tightly between two prongs and annihilated them. But this did not prevent de Lattre de Tassigny and his henchmen from hullabalooing that they had carried the day!

At the very beginning of the war, the Americans supplied France with money and armaments. To take an example, 85 per cent of weapons, war materials and even canned food captured by our troops were labelled 'made in USA'. This aid had been stepped up all the more rapidly since June 1950 when the US began interfering in Korea. American aid to the French invaders consisted in airplanes, boats, trucks, military outfits, napalm bombs, etc.

Meanwhile, the Americans compelled the French colonialists to step up the organization of four divisions of puppet troops with each party footing half the bill. Of course, this collusion between the French and American aggressors and the puppet clique was fraught with contradictions and contentions.

The French colonialists are now landed in a dilemma: either they receive US aid and be then replaced by their American 'allies', or they receive nothing, and be then defeated by the Vietnamese people. To organize the puppet army by means of pressganging the youth in areas under their control would be tantamount to swallowing a bomb when one is hungry: a day will come when at last the bomb bursts inside. However not to organize the army on this basis would mean instantaneous death for the enemy because even the French strategists have to admit that the French Expeditionary Corps grows thinner and thinner and is on the verge of collapse.

Furthermore, US aid is paid for at a very high price. In the enemy-held areas, French capitalism is swept aside by American capitalism. American concerns like the Petroleum Oil Corporation, the Caltex

Oil Corporation, the Bethlehem Steel Corporation, the Florida Phosphate Mining Corporation and others, monopolize rubber, ores, and other natural resources of our country. US goods swamp the market. The French reactionary press, especially *Le Monde*, is compelled to acknowledge sadly that French capitalism is now giving way to US capitalism.

The US interventionists have nurtured the French aggressors and the Vietnamese puppets, but the Vietnamese people do not let anybody delude and enslave them.

People's China is our close neighbour. Her brilliant example gives us a great impetus. Not long ago the Chinese people defeated the US imperialists and won a historical victory. The execrated Chiang Kai-shek was swept from the Chinese mainland, though he is more cunning than the placeman Bao Dai. Can the US interventionists, who were drummed out of China and are now suffering heavy defeats in Korea, conquer Viet Nam? Of course not!

ATROCIOUS CRIMES OF THE US INTERVENTIONISTS

Defeated on the battlefield, the French colonialists retaliated upon unarmed people and committed abominable crimes. Hereunder are a few examples.

As everywhere in the enemy-controlled areas, on 15 October 1951 at Ha Dong, the French soldiers raided the youths even in the streets and pressganged them into the puppet army. And there as everywhere, the people protested against such acts. Three young girls stood in a line across the street in front of the trucks packed with the captured youngsters to prevent them from being sent to concentration camps. These courageous acts were worthy of heroine Raymonde Dien's. The French colonialists revved the engines and, in a split second, our three young patriots were run over.

In October 1951, the invaders staged a large-scale raid in Thai Binh province. They captured more than 16,000 people – most of whom were old people, women and children – and penned them in a football field surrounded by barbed wire and guarded by soldiers and dogs.

For four days, the captives were exposed in the sun and rain, ankle-deep in mud. They received no food and no drinking water. Over 300 of them died of exhaustion and disease.

The relatives and friends who brought food to the captives were roughly manhandled, and the food was thrown into the mud and trampled underfoot. Mr Phac, a surgeon of seventy, who tried to save the victims' lives, was shot dead on the spot, as also were a number of pregnant women.

Incensed by these barbarous acts, the townsfolk staged a strike and sought ways and means to help the internees. The determination of the population compelled the French colonialists to let the food in, but on order of Colonel Charton of the French Expeditionary Corps, it was declared a donation from the USA.

On 28 October 1951, Le Van Lam, 27, from Ha Coi, a puppet soldier who had been saved from drowning by an old fisherman at Do Son, said after he had come to:

> On 27 October the French embarked me as well as one hundred other wounded men on board a steamer, saying they would send us to Saigon for medical attention. In the night, when the ship was in the offing, they threw us one by one into the water. Fortunately, I managed to snatch at a piece of floating wood and swam landward. I was unconscious when I was saved.

Hereunder is the confession of Chaubert, a French captain captured at Tu Ky on 25 November 1951. 'The French High Command gave us an order to destroy everything in order to transform this region into a desert,' he said.

> This order was observed to the letter. Houses were burnt down. Animals and poultry were killed. Havoc was wrought to gardens and plants and trees hewn down. Ricefields and crops were set afire. Many days on end, black smoke covered the sky and there was not a single soul alive, except the French soldiers. The conflagration lasted until 25 November, when the Viet Nam People's Army unexpectedly attacked and annihilated our unit.

The examples quoted above can be counted by the thousands and are sufficient proof to substantiate the essence of the French colonialists' and US interventionists' 'civilization'.

ACHIEVEMENTS RECORDED BY
THE DEMOCRATIC REPUBLIC OF VIET NAM

In 1951, the Vietnamese people made a big stride forward. In the political field, the founding of the Viet Nam Workers' Party, the amalgamation of the Viet Minh and Lien Viet, the setting up of the Committee of Action for Viet Nam, Cambodia and Laos, greatly consolidated the unity and enhanced the confidence of the Vietnamese people; they strengthened the alliance between the three brother countries in their struggle against the common enemies – the French colonialists and US interventionists – in order to realize their common goal, i.e. national independence.

So we were able to frustrate the enemy's policy of 'divide and rule'.

In the economic field, the National Bank of Viet Nam has been established, our finance is placed under centralized and unified super-vision, and communications have been reorganized.

Formerly we demolished roads to check the enemy's advance; at present we repair them to drive the enemy to an early defeat. Formerly we did our utmost to sabotage roads, now we encounter great difficulties in mending them, but have managed to complete our work quite rapidly. This is a hard job, especially when we lack machines. However, thanks to the enthusiasm and sacrificing spirit of our people, this work was carried through. To avoid enemy air raids, it was done at night by workers even knee deep in water. In the bright torchlight, hundreds of men, women and young people dug the earth to fill the gaps in the roads, broke stones, felled trees and built bridges. As in any other work, here the workers' enthusiasm was roused by emulation drives. I am sure that you would be astonished to see teams of old volunteers from sixty to eighty years competing with teams of young workers.

Here it must be pointed out that in the free zone, most of the work is done at night – children go to school, housewives go to market, and guerrillas go to attack the enemy . . .

Great successes have been achieved in the elaboration of the agri-cultural tax. Formerly the peasants were compelled to pay taxes of various kinds and make many other contributions; nowadays, they have only to pay a uniform tax in kind. Households whose production does not exceed 60 kilograms of paddy per year are exempt from tax. Households who harvest greater quantities have to pay a graduated tax. Generally speaking, the taxes to be paid do not exceed 20 per cent of the total value of the annual production. To collect taxes in time, the

Party, the National United Front and the government have mobilized a great number of cadres to examine the new tax from the political and technical points of view. After their study, these cadres go to the countryside and hold talks and meetings to exchange views with the peasants and explain to them the new taxation policy.

After this preparatory period, the peasants of both sexes appoint a committee composed of representatives of the administration and various people's organizations whose duty it is to estimate the production of each household and fix the rate to be paid after approval by a Congress in which all the peasants take part.

This reform was welcomed by the population who enthusiastically took part in this tax collection.

Agricultural tax has been established simultaneously with the movement for increased production. At present the government possesses adequate stocks of foodstuffs to cater for the soldiers and workers.

So we have thwarted the enemy's cunning plot of blockading us to reduce us to starvation.

As far as mass education is concerned, in 1951 we scored worthwhile results. Though great difficulties were created by the war, such as frequent changes of school site, schooling at night-time, lack of school requisites, the number of schools rose from 2,712 in 1950 to 3,591 in 1951 with an attendance of 293,256 and 411,038 pupils respectively.

In south Viet Nam the situation is all the more ticklish. There, the free zones exist everywhere, but they are not safe. Children go to their classrooms – in fact there are only single classrooms and not schools in the strict meaning of this word – with the same vigilance as their fathers and brothers display in guerrilla fighting. Despite that, at present there are in south Viet Nam 3,332 classrooms attended by 111,700 pupils.

The liquidation of illiteracy is actively undertaken. In the first half of 1951, there were in zone III, zone V and Viet Bac zone, 324,000 people who were freed from illiteracy and 350,000 others who began learning. During the same period illiteracy was wiped out in 53 villages and 3 districts (one district is composed of from 5 to 10 villages).

People's organizations opened 837 classes attended by 9,800 public employees.

The Party, National United Front, government, the General Confederation of Labour and the army have periodically opened short-term political training courses (about one week).

In short, great efforts are being made in mass education.

DEVELOPMENT AND STRENGTHENING
OF INTERNATIONAL RELATIONS

In 1951, the relations between the Vietnamese people and foreign countries were developed and strengthened.

For the first time, in 1951 various delegations of the Vietnamese people visited great People's China and heroic Korea. Through these visits, the age-old friendship between our three countries has been strengthened.

The delegation of the Vietnamese youth to the Youth Festival in Berlin, the delegation of the Viet Nam General Confederation of Labour to the Congress of the World Federation of Trade Unions in Warsaw, and the delegation to the World Peace Conference in Vienna, have returned to Viet Nam, filled with confidence and enthusiasm. At various meetings and in the press, members of these delegations told the Vietnamese people the tremendous progress they had witnessed in the people's democracies and the warm friendship shown by the brother countries to the Vietnamese people who are struggling for national independence and freedom.

Those of the delegates who had the chance of visiting the Soviet Union are overjoyed because they can tell us of the great triumph of socialism and the evergrowing happiness enjoyed by the Soviet people.

Upon returning from the Youth Festival, Truong Thi Xin, a young woman worker, said, 'The youth in the Soviet Union received us most affectionately during our stay in their great country.'

The talks held by these delegates are living lessons most useful for the inculcation of internationalism.

'Peace in Viet Nam!', 'Withdraw foreign troops from Viet Nam!', were the claims formulated in a resolution passed by the plenary session of the World Peace Council held in Vienna, claims which have given great enthusiasm to the Vietnamese people.

THE INTERVENTIONISTS SUFFER DEFEAT AFTER DEFEAT

Last year was a year of brilliant victories for our People's Army, and a year of heavy defeats and losses in men and materials for the invaders. According to incomplete figures and excluding the China–Viet Nam border campaign in October 1950, during which the French army lost more than 7,000 men (annihilated and captured), in 1951 the enemy lost 37,700 officers and men, (POWs included). He will never forget the Vinh Yen – Phuc Yen campaign (north Viet Nam) in January last year during which he received a deadly blow from the Viet Nam People's Army. He will not forget the strategic points of Quang Yen (road number 18), Ninh Binh, Phu Ly and Nghia Lo in north Viet Nam where our valiant fighters crushed him to pieces in March, May, June and September. But the most striking battle was waged in December in the Hoa Binh region which left to the enemy no more than 8,000 men alive. Our heroic militiamen and guerrillas who operate in the north, centre and south of Viet Nam have caused heavy losses to the enemy. From the outbreak of the war of aggression unleashed by the French, their Expeditionary Corps has lost 170,000 men (killed, wounded and captured), while the Vietnamese regular army and guerrilla units have grown stronger and stronger.

Guerrilla warfare is now being intensified and expanded in the enemy-controlled areas, especially in the Red River delta. Our guerrillas are particularly active in the provinces of Bac Giang, Bac Ninh, Ha Nam, Ninh Binh, Ha Dong, Hung Yen and Thai Binh. Hereunder are some facts.

Early in October 1951, 14 enemy regiments carried out a large scale raid in the districts of Duyen Ha, Hung Nhan, and Tien Hung. From 1 October to 4 October our guerrillas waged violent battles. In three points (Cong Ho, An My and An Binh) 500 French soldiers were annihilated. All these victories were due to the heroism of our soldiers and guerrillas and to the sacrifice of the entire Vietnamese people. In each campaign tens of thousands of voluntary workers of both sexes helped the armymen. As a rule they worked in very hard conditions, in pelting rain, on muddy and steep mountain tracks, etc.

Thousands of patriots have left the enemy-controlled areas to take part in the above-mentioned task. It is worth mentioning here that the youth have set up many shock units.

The following example will illustrate the great patriotism and initiative of our people.

In the Hoa Binh campaign, our army had to cross the Lo river. French troops were stationed along the right bank, while their boats continually patrolled the river. In these conditions how could the crossing be made without the enemy noticing it?

But the local population managed to find a way. In a locality some dozen kilometres from the Lo river, they called in a great number of craft and, through roundabout paths, carried them to the spot assigned at the scheduled time. As soon as our troops had crossed the river, the inhabitants carried their craft back so as to keep secrecy and avoid enemy air raids.

Here I wish to speak of the women who sponsor the soldiers. Most of them are old peasants; many have grandchildren. They help our officers and men and nurse the wounded as if they were their own sons. Like 'goddesses protecting our lives' they take care of those of our fighters who work in enemy-controlled areas. Their deeds are highly esteemed and appreciated.

As is said above, the French colonialists are compelled to set up puppet troops in order to offset the losses suffered by the French Expeditionary Corps. But this is a dangerous method for the enemy.

First, everywhere in the enemy-held areas, the population struggles against the enemy raiding and coercing the youth into their army.

Second, the people so mobilized have resorted to actions of sabotage. Take an example. Once, the Quisling governor of Tonking, styling himself 'elder of the youth', paid a visit to the officers' training school of second degree at Nam Dinh. On hearing this news, the cadets prepared in his honour a 'dignified' reception by writing on the school wall the slogans 'Down with Bao Dai!', 'Down with the puppet clique!', while Bao Dai's name was given to the lavatory.

During this visit, the cadets made so much noise that the governor was unable to speak. They put to him such a question as, 'Dear elder! Why do you want to use us as cannon fodder for the French colonialists?' A group of cadets contemplated giving him a thrashing, but he managed to take French leave like a piteous dog.

Many units of the puppet army secretly sent letters to President Ho Chi Minh, saying they were waiting for a propitious occasion to 'pass over to the side of the fatherland' and they were ready to 'carry out any orders issued by the Resistance, despite the danger they might encounter'.

COMPLETE FAILURE OF THE FRENCH COLONIALISTS

As soon as de Lattre de Tassigny set foot in Viet Nam early in 1951, he boasted of the eventual victories of the French troops.

After his defeat and disillusion at the beginning of 1952, he realized that he would soon meet with complete failure.

The fate of the French colonialists' policy brought misgivings to the most reactionary circles in France.

In the paper *Information* issued on 22 October 1951, Daladier, one of the 'criminals' in the Munich affair, wrote:

> Delving into the real reason of our desperate financial situation, we shall see that one of the underlying causes was lack of ripe consideration of our policy over Indochina . . . In 1951, an expenditure of as much as 330,000 million francs was officially reserved for the Indochinese budget. Due to the constant rise in the prices of commodities and increase in the establishments of the French Expeditionary Corps which number 180,000 at present, it should be expected that in 1952 this expenditure will increase by 100,000 million francs. We have the impression that the war in Indochina has caused exceedingly grave danger to our financial as well as military situation . . . It is impossible to foresee a rapid victory in a war which has lasted five years and is in many ways reminiscent of the war unleashed by Napoleon against Spain and the expedition against Mexico during the Second Empire.[2]

In its issue of 13 December 1951, the paper *Intransigeant* wrote,

> France is paralysed by the war in Indochina. We have gradually lost the initiative of operation because our main forces are now pinned down in the plains of north Viet Nam . . . In 1951, 330,000 million francs were earmarked for the military budget of Indochina, while according to the official figures, our expenditure amounted to over 350,000 million. A credit of 380,000 million francs will be allotted to the 1952 budget but in all probability the mark of 500,000 million will be reached. Such is the truth . . . Whenever France tried to take some action, well, she immediately realized that she was paralysed by the war in Indochina.

In its number of 16 December 1951, *Franc Tireur* wrote:

> General Vo Nguyen Giap's battalions, which are said to have been annihilated and to have a shattered morale, are now launching counteroffensives in the Hanoi region . . . It is more and more

obvious that the policy we have followed up to the present time, has failed. Today it is clear that it has met with complete failure.

Hereunder is an excerpt from a letter sent to his colleagues by captain Gazignoff, of the French Expeditionary Corps, captured by us on 7 January 1952 in the Hoa Binh battle:

> Taken prisoner a few days ago, I am very astonished at the kind and correct attitude of the Viet Nam People's army men towards me . . . The Vietnamese troops will certainly win final victory, because they struggle for a noble ideal, a common cause, and are swayed by a self-imposed discipline. It is as clear as daylight that the Viet Nam People's Army will crush the French Expeditionary Corps, but it is ready to receive any of us who will pass over to its side.
>
> French officers, non-commissioned officers and men who want to go over to the Viet Nam People's Army will be considered as friends and will be set free.

THE VIETNAMESE PEOPLE WILL WIN

In 1952, Viet Nam will embark on a programme which includes the following points:

- to buckle down to production work and consolidate the national economy;
- to struggle and annihilate the enemy's forces. To intensify guerrilla warfare;
- to expose by all means the enemy's policy of 'using the Vietnamese to fight the Vietnamese, and nursing the war by means of warfare';
- to link patriotism closely to internationalism;
- energetically to combat bureaucracy, corruption and waste.

The patriotism and heroism of the Vietnamese people allow us to have firm confidence in final victory.

The Vietnamese people's future is as bright as the sun in spring. Over-joyed at the radiance of the sun in spring, we shall struggle for the splendid future of Viet Nam, for the future of democracy, world peace and socialism. We triumph at the present time, we shall triumph in the future, because our path is enlightened by the great Marxist-Leninist doctrine.

32

TO PRACTISE THRIFT AND OPPOSE EMBEZZLEMENT, WASTE AND BUREAUCRACY

1952

Comrades,

The working programme of our government and Party this year is still epitomized in these words: 'Protracted war of resistance, self-reliance.'

For a correct implementation of this programme, the government and the Party have stressed the following main points:

To emulate one another in wiping out enemy forces, increasing production and practising thrift, and

- to oppose embezzlement;
- to oppose waste;
- to oppose bureaucracy.

Concerning the *movement of emulation to wipe out enemy forces and score feats of arms*, the High Command has worked out a comprehensive plan and sent it down to all Party branches and all members of the National Defence Army, regional forces, militia and guerrilla units for them to study, grasp and implement

With regard to the *emulation movement to increase production*, the government has drawn up a comprehensive general plan. On the basis of it, the different branches, localities and families will work out their own particular plans which must be realistic and well-coordinated and strive to fulfil them at all costs.

The comrades in charge will give a clear account of these two matters. Here I will only speak of the *emulation movement to practise thrift and oppose embezzlement, waste and bureaucracy.*

I. THRIFT

First of all, let us ask some questions:

- What is thrift?
- Why must we practise thrift?
- What kind of thrift must be practised?
- Who must practise thrift?

1. To practise thrift does not mean to be stingy, 'to consider a coin as big as a drum', not to do things worth doing, not to spend sums worth spending; to practise thrift does not mean to impose privations on our armymen, cadres and people. On the contrary, to practise thrift is essentially aimed at helping to increase production, and as a result to raise their living standards. Scientifically speaking, to practise thrift is a positive, not a negative act.

2. Our country was plundered by the French for eighty years and then by the Japanese imperialists, that is why our economy is poor and backward. Now we must have a strong economy to wage the war of resistance and reconstruct the country.

To build our economy we must have funds. To get these, the capitalist countries use three means: to raise loans abroad; to pillage their colonies; and to exploit their peasants and workers. We cannot resort to such means. Only by increasing production and practising thrift can we secure more funds for economic construction and development.

3. We must *save time*. For example: by improving organization and raising efficiency, we can finish in one day what used to be done in two.

We must *save labour*. For instance: with better organization and higher efficiency, a job which used to require ten persons can now be done with five.

We must *save money*. For example: by cutting down on manpower, time and raw materials we now spend only 10,000 dong on what used to cost 20,000.

In brief, we must streamline organization so that one person can do the work of two, one day is enough to finish the work of two, and one dong can be as useful as two.

4. Everybody must *practise thrift*. First of all, in public services, the army, and in enterprises. Some people may ask: How can the army practise thrift since it only concerns itself with fighting the enemy and scoring feats of arms and is not a service of production?

In the army, such services as the Commissariat, the Ordnance Corps, the Transport Department, etc., must practise thrift. For instance:

Previously, suppose each fighter used 60 cartridges on an average per enemy soldier killed, now he uses only 10 as a result of diligent training and better marksmanship. Thus, he saves 80 per cent on cartridges, and the raw materials and manpower saved can be used to produce other weapons. Previously, the Transport Department had to use 100 trucks to carry cartridges, now it only needs 20, thus saving on vehicles, petrol and lubricants; and if fewer vehicles are in service, less manpower will be needed to mend the roads, etc.

In the various military campaigns we have captured a lot of booty (ammunition, food, arms). Our armymen take good care of them and use them against the enemy; in this way they also *increase production*.

Some may ask: Besides growing crops and raising livestock for their own use how can the public services (for example the judicial service) practise thrift?

Any public service must and can practise thrift. For example, all public services use envelopes; if every envelope is used twice or three times, each year the government can save tens of tons of paper. If the judicial cadres raise their efficiency, they will help people who have dealings with the judicial service to save time to increase production.

5. *Results from thrift* The above-mentioned examples show that *if we know how to save manpower*, resources and time, with what we have now our production as well as our forces in every field can be increased several times.

In the *Soviet Union*, due to thrift, the funds invested in the Five-Year Plan (1946–50) increased by 26,000 million roubles, that is, by one-third.

For example, in 1948, a garment shop in Moscow saved more than 34,000 metres of fabric, enough to make 20,000 more shirts.

Time is saved when efficiency is raised. Formerly it took 20,000 work-hours to make a big airplane, now only 12,700 hours are needed;

formerly 8,000 work-hours were necessary to make a big tank, now only 3,700 hours.

In *China* in 1951, due to increased output and thrift the people of the North-East produced 14 million more tons of foodstuffs. This year, the workers and the population of this zone have promised Chairman Mao Tse-tung that they would save 22 million tons.

Thanks to thrift the North-West has got an increase of one million tons of foodstuffs, 600,000 metric quintals of cotton, 350,000 head of buffaloes and oxen, etc.; the other zones have achieved similar results.

Time saving and higher productivity go hand in hand. Previously a weaver had to make more than 5,200 steps in two hours. Now, after the popularization of the *Xich Kien Tu* method, only 2,300 steps are needed. Fatigue is lessened, while output is raised. *Xich Kien Tu*, the author of this method of rationalization, is a girl weaver of seventeen.

Thanks to emulation in both production and *thrift*, only five years after World War Two the economy of the Soviet Union has made prodigious leaps. While in the capitalist countries, the cost of living is rising, and the people have to suffer ever more privations, in the Soviet Union prices have been cut four times, and the people are getting happier and happier.

The triumph of the Chinese revolution dates back only a few years but thanks to increased production and thrift, the economy has been developed, finances unified, prices stabilized, and the people's living standards improved very rapidly.

We are waging a war of resistance, our conditions are more difficult. But if we are determined to increase production and practise thrift we shall certainly succeed in doing so.

II. TO WIPE OUT EMBEZZLEMENT, WASTE AND BUREAUCRACY

To have a good crop we must weed the field, otherwise the rice will grow badly in spite of careful ploughing and abundant manuring. To be successful in increasing production and practising thrift, we must also weed the field, that is, root out embezzlement, waste and bureaucracy. Otherwise they will harm our work.

A. WHAT IS EMBEZZLEMENT?

For the cadres, embezzlement means:

To rob public property, to extort money from the people, to pick and steal from army funds, to falsify expenditure reports. To abuse public property and government funds, and divert them to the benefit of one's locality or one's unit is also embezzlement.

On the side of the people, embezzlement means:

To rob the people's property; to make collective fraudulent reports.

B. WHAT IS WASTE?

Waste takes on many forms:

Waste of labour   Because of lack of the sense of responsibility or bad organization, a large number of people are assigned to a job which can be done by a few.

This shortcoming exists in the army, public services and enterprises. For example, owing to defective organization there is much waste in the use of civilian manpower in the repair of roads and bridges, and in serving military campaigns.

Waste of time   Several days are spent for a job which can be done in one day or even half a day. For instance: meetings may last three or five days instead of only one, because the cadre in charge has not prepared the programme carefully and because those who attend the meeting have not reflected upon the matter to be debated.

Waste of public property   It assumes many forms, of which here are but a few examples:

- Waste of materials by public services.
- Bad use of machines and raw materials in enterprises.
- The Transport Department does not take good enough care of its vehicles, and does not save enough on petrol and lubricants.
- Granaries under the Department of Storehouses are not carefully built; the keepers have a poor sense of responsibility, and so the paddy is damp and damaged.
- The State Trading Department is not careful in its arrangements and calculations, thus suffering damage and losses.
- Armymen do not take good care of their weapons, equipment and the booty captured.

- Money is badly managed by the Bank and does not help increase production.
- Plans worked out by economic organs are not practical and in harmony with the situation, thus causing losses to the revolution.
- People let their lands lie fallow, burn votive offerings to the spirits, pawn their buffaloes and sell their fields for costly weddings and funerals, etc.

Embezzlement is robbery and pillage. Waste is not, but its consequences are none the less ruinous to the people and the government, sometimes even more ruinous than embezzlement.

Embezzlement and waste stem from bureaucracy, from the fact that leading individuals and organs at all levels fail to get down to brass tacks, to supervise and educate the cadres, and to get in close touch with the masses. They pay undue attention to matters of form and fail to tackle their jobs in detail and in depth. They only like to convene meetings, write instructions and read reports, but *control nothing thoroughly*.

In short, leading individuals and organs affected with bureaucracy have eyes, but do not see clearly, ears, but do not hear distinctly; regulations and discipline are not observed, and as a result, bad elements and irresponsible cadres are given free rein to indulge in embezzlement and waste.

Thus bureaucracy fosters, tolerates and protects embezzlement and waste. Hence to wipe out embezzlement and waste, one must first and foremost eliminate bureaucracy.

III. EMBEZZLEMENT AND WASTE
ARE ENEMIES OF THE PEOPLE

A. EBEZZLEMENT, WASTE AND BUREAUCRACY ARE ENEMIES OF THE PEOPLE, THE ARMY AND THE GOVERNMENT.

They are quite dangerous enemies because they wield no swords and guns, but lie in our own organizations to spoil our work.

Whether they are committed deliberately or not, embezzlement, waste and bureaucracy are allied with colonialism and feudalism because they hamper our war of resistance and our national reconstruction. They spoil the integrity of our cadres and their determination to overcome difficulties. They undermine our revolutionary virtues: industry, thrift, integrity and uprightness.

To contribute to the success of the war of resistance and of national construction, our fighters have shed their blood, and our compatriots their sweat. But those who commit embezzlement, waste and bureaucracy sap the spirit, waste the strength and squander the wealth of the government and the people; this is a crime as serious as that committed by traitors and spies.

For these reasons, the struggle against embezzlement, waste and bureaucracy is as important and urgent as the fight on the front! This is the ideological and political front.

As on other fronts, to succeed on this one, we must have plans, organization, leadership and activists.

B. TO OPPOSE EMBEZZLEMENT, WASTE AND BUREAUCRACY ARE REVOLUTIONARY ACTS.

To wage a revolution is to destroy the bad, and build the good. Our revolution aims at destroying the colonial and feudal regime and building a new democracy.

If after the colonialists and feudalists have been annihilated, the evils left by them (embezzlement, waste, bureaucracy) still subsist, our revolutionary work is not yet completed, because these evils still undermine and sabotage the constructive work of the revolution.

There are people who are enthusiastic and faithful in struggle; they fear neither dangers, hardships, nor the enemy, thus they have *served the revolution well*; but as soon as they hold some authority, they grow arrogant and luxurious, indulge in embezzlement, waste and unconscious bureaucracy, thus *becoming guilty in the eyes of the revolution*. We must save them, help them recover their revolutionary virtues. Others, while pretending to serve the fatherland and the people, indulge in embezzlement and waste and harm the fatherland and the people. We must educate them, and lead them to the revolutionary path.

Embezzlement, waste and bureaucracy are evils left by the old society. They spring from self-interest and selfishness. They are begotten by the regime of 'exploitation of man by man'.

We want to build a new society, a free society where all men are equal, a society where industry, thrift, integrity and uprightness prevail, hence we must wipe out all bad habits of the old society.

C. TO OPPOSE EMBEZZLEMENT AND WASTE IS DEMOCRACY.

Our armymen unstintingly shed their blood and our compatriots their sweat to save the country. Our fighters entrust their lives, our compatriots their labour and wealth to the government and the Party to wage the war of resistance and reconstruct the country. This is a form of *democratic centralism.*

The government and the Party give the cadres authority to command the army, and use money and resources in the war of resistance and national reconstruction. The duty of the cadres is to love and take care of every fighter and to value and save every cent, every bowl of rice, every workhour of their compatriots. Our fighters and compatriots have the right to demand that the cadres fulfil this task, and to *criticize* those who do not.

Democracy means to rely on the masses, correctly to follow the mass line. Hence, to be successful, the movement against embezzlement, waste and bureaucracy must *rely on the masses.*

By the masses we mean all armymen, all workers in the factories, all civil servants in the public services etc., and the entire people. As in any other work, only by *mobilizing the masses, implementing democracy*, making the masses understand and enthusiastically participate in this movement, can we be certain of success. The greater the participation of the masses, the more complete and rapid the achievements.

The *task of the masses* is to participate enthusiastically in the movement against embezzlement, waste and bureaucracy. The fighters contribute their exploits and the people their wealth to fight the enemy and save the country. Embezzlement, waste and bureaucracy are a kind of 'internal enemy'. If our fighters and people, while striving to oppose *the enemy from outside*, forget to fight the enemy from inside, they will not have fulfilled their task. Therefore they must zealously participate in this movement.

At all echelons, we must act as one man and join forces in this struggle. Success will help us strengthen our solidarity and raise productivity even further. It will help our cadres remould themselves ideologically, heighten their political consciousness, become imbued with revolutionary virtues, and wholeheartedly serve the army and the people. It will help purify our administration and make it worthy of our fighters' and compatriots' confidence and sacrifices. It will help us fulfil the plan of the government and the Party for increased production and thrift and complete our preparations for the general counteroffensive.

33

INSTRUCTIONS GIVEN AT A CONFERENCE ON GUERRILLA WARFARE

July 1952

I. All of you here have to various degrees made efforts, scored achievements, endured hardships. For this you deserve praise. However you should remember that *these accomplishments belong not to any one individual but to all our army and compatriots*. Without their assistance your talents would have been of no avail.

II. Since the Hoa Binh Campaign, guerrilla warfare behind enemy lines has greatly developed compared with last year; in particular, *our compatriots and cadres are confident that they can by themselves defeat the enemy*. This is a correct assessment and a very good change.

You must know that *our war of resistance is a long and hard, but surely victorious, one*. It is long because it will last till the enemy is defeated, till he 'quits'. The eighty-year-long oppression by the French imperialists is like a chronic disease that cannot be cured in one day or one year. Don't be hasty, don't ask for an immediate victory: this is subjectiveness. A long resistance implies hardships, but will end in victory.

This long and hard war of resistance *calls for self-reliance*. This is especially true when operating behind enemy lines. The assistance of friendly countries is of course important, but we should not be dependent on it and stay idle. A nation which does not rely on its own strength but merely looks for help from other peoples does not deserve to be independent.

In this long resistance what should the guerrillas behind enemy lines do? What is their task? *Guerrilla warfare, too, is protracted warfare. The present task is to foil the enemy's scheme of 'feeding war with war, and using Vietnamese to fight Vietnamese'*. The enemy, being unable to grab manpower and material resources in the free zones, is trying to do so in the zones to his rear. We must frustrate this scheme. By so doing, we shall effectively contribute to the preparation for a general counteroffensive. The enemy will be gradually weakened and finally defeated.

III. Operating behind enemy lines, you have shown many good qualities: perseverance, courage and solidarity. I shall not expatiate on your strong points. Let me only stress a few shortcomings that should be redressed.

1. *The cadres of the army, mass organizations, administration and Party have not studied with sufficient care, in sufficient detail and in sufficient depth the orders and directives from the Party Central Committee and the government.* This is a serious shortcoming. The Central Committee and the government see far and wide. Their directives are the results of careful study of situations and experiences all over the country. The cadres of the army, mass organizations, administration and Party must carefully study these directives so as to apply them to the concrete situation of each locality. Individual regions have only a limited range of vision; they can only see the tree but not the forest, they can grasp only part of the situation, not the whole of it. And so a job deemed a success by a given region may turn out to be a failure when viewed in the general context. This is due to inadequate study of directives from the government and the Party Central Committee.

2. *The regular, regional and guerrilla forces should not content themselves with fighting the enemy*. To fight the enemy is a good thing; but *to confine oneself to fighting him* without paying due attention to politics, economics, propaganda and education of the people is to know only one aspect of things, for fighting cannot be dissociated from politics and economics. If we only think of fighting without caring for economics, we won't be able to fight when we run short of rice. So, let us fight of course, but fighting alone will not do, other things must also be thought of.

3. Another shortcoming lies in the fact that *the regular, regional and guerrilla forces are all eager to fight big battles and win great victories* while failing to conduct a careful study of the situation and a detailed assessment of our own possibilities as well as those of the enemy so as to determine appropriate targets and combat methods. As a result, hitches have developed in practice. Wherever you may be, attack only when you

are sure of winning, do not engage the enemy when you are not, especially when you are surrounded by enemy forces.

4. *Army cadres concern themselves solely with military affairs, government cadres with administrative jobs, Party cadres with Party business.* They are like men standing on one leg. It is wrong for a cadre to be acquainted only with one field. He will not be truly proficient because army, mass, government and party work forms a whole which would not be strong and complete should one of its components go missing. Party and government cadres seem to rely entirely on the army for fighting the enemy, unaware that the Party should exercise overall leadership and that, in combat, victory can come only if there is close co-ordination of all elements.

5. As regards Party cadres in particular, partly because of unfavourable conditions but mostly because they do not grasp the main link, i.e. the basis of the Party organization, the Party bases in the areas still under temporary enemy control are not yet very strong. It should be known that if the Party is strong, everything will get along well.

6. *Security* measures are not yet satisfactorily carried out, state secrets not yet well kept.

7. *Propaganda and agitation work among puppet troops* has recorded some achievements but has not yielded steady results. Good work is done in places where the cadres show resourcefulness; but things slacken wherever they lack initiative. The enemy has rigged up units of village guards and security forces. These brambles should be got rid of. You should exchange experiences and step up this political work among puppet troops.

8. As regards *propaganda behind enemy lines*, let us remember that before the August Revolution, in spite of the presence of the Japanese, the French and the Vietnamese traitors, we succeeded in carrying out propaganda work among the people. This was due to our resourcefulness; besides verbal propaganda, we also used press publications. At present the Central Committee and the government are trying to send such papers as *Cuu Quoc* (National Salvation) and *Nhan Dan* (The People) into enemy-occupied zones. But this is not enough and we have met with difficulties. Behind enemy lines we must circulate papers printed from lithographic stone or clay which need neither be of large size nor be issued every day; the main purpose being to popularize the government's line and policies and carry out a *practical propaganda* among the people about our successes as well as the enemy's crimes and failures. There lies the educational work of the Party.

IV. Now about the jobs to be done:

1. First of all, there must be close internal unity, i.e. our army, people, government and party must be closely united. For whatever we do, there should be careful study and discussion, unity of thought and action, mutual help and sincere criticism and self-criticism with a view to common progress.

2. The orders and directives from the Central Committee and the government must be carefully studied, correctly applied and thoroughly carried out.

3. What matters the most is that our armed forces, be they regulars, regionals or guerrillas, must hold fast to the people; divorce from the latter will surely lead to defeat. To cling to the people means to win their hearts, gain their confidence and affection. This will allow us to overcome any difficulty and achieve sure success. To this end, we must protect, assist and educate the people. Educating the people does not mean to thrust books into their hands and compel them to learn; if we act in this way, we shall go counter to their interests and those of the revolution. This is bureaucratic commandism. We must persuade the people so that they will do things of their own accord; coercion would only produce temporary results but no lasting effects.

4. Regular forces operating behind enemy lines must assist regional and guerrilla forces in organization and training; they should assist them, not do things in their place. Furthermore they must help the people; some units have managed to do so, but others have not. As goes a saying of ours: 'One should curl up when inside a sphere and stretch out when inside a tube.' When fighting in an enemy-occupied area, we must use guerrilla tactics, not fight regular warfare as in the free zones. We must absolutely not go in for large-scale battles and big victories, unless we are 100 per cent certain of success.

5. The aim of guerrilla warfare is not to wage large-scale battles and win big victories, but to nibble at the enemy, harass him in such a way that he can neither eat nor sleep in peace, to give him no respite, to wear him out physically and mentally, and finally to annihilate him. Wherever he goes, he should be attacked by our guerrillas, stumble on land mines or be greeted by sniper fire. Here is what French soldiers say in their letters: 'In Viet Nam, death is lying in wait for us in every cave, every bush, every pond . . .'

If you manage to redress your shortcomings and do as I said, you will surely gain successes. However, you should bear in mind that so long as a single enemy soldier remains on our land, our victory is not yet complete. The failures of the enemy forces, in spite of their better equipment and greater experience, have been due to their subjectivity. So, if you guard against subjectivity and are careful not to underrate the enemy, you will win.

Back in your home localities, you must urge people to emulate one another in all fields: to fight the enemy and accomplish deeds, to organize propaganda and agitation work among the enemy troops and their puppets, to increase production and practise thrift. A saying goes: 'Adequate food, strong army.' We shall not have enough food for our war of resistance if we do not boost production and practise economy. Can you promise to do as I told you? (*All said yes in a loud voice.*) You have made a pledge; you must fulfil it at all costs.

Another point: you must report our troops' and our compatriots' accomplishments to the Central Committee and the government for commendation and reward which is also a means of education and exhortation. Those commended will be encouraged while the others will actively emulate them. So far, the local authorities have sent but very few reports; from now on, you must make up for it.

Lastly, I ask you to transmit my best wishes and those of the Central Committee and the government to our compatriots, our cadres and fighters, particularly to our elderly guerrillas, women guerrillas and children of the resistance. The Central Committee, the government and I myself are glad and confident that our army and compatriots behind enemy lines will correctly implement the line and policies of the resistance so as to achieve quick victory.

34

REPORT TO THE THIRD SESSION OF THE NATIONAL ASSEMBLY

I December 1953

(. . .)

LAND REFORM

Concerning this problem, I only wish to stress the following points:

The significance of land reform:

Our revolution is a people's democratic national revolution against aggressive imperialism and its prop, feudalism.

Our slogan during the war of resistance is 'All for the front, all for victory!' The more the war of resistance develops, the more manpower and wealth it requires. Our peasants have contributed the greatest part of this manpower and wealth to the resistance. We must liberate them from the feudal yoke and foster their strength in order fully to mobilize this huge force for the resistance and win victory.

The key to victory for the resistance lies in consolidating and enlarging the National United Front, consolidating the worker–peasant alliance and the people's power, strengthening and developing the army, consolidating the Party and strengthening its leadership in all respects. Only by mobilizing the masses for land reform can we carry out these tasks in favourable conditions.

The enemy actively seeks to use Vietnamese to fight Vietnamese and to feed war with war. They are doing their utmost to deceive, divide and exploit our people. Land reform will exert an influence on our peasant compatriots behind enemy lines and will encourage them to struggle even more vigorously against him in order to liberate themselves, and to give even more enthusiastic support to the democratic government of the resistance; at the same time it will have an impact on the puppet armed forces and cause their disintegration because the absolute majority of the puppet soldiers are peasants in enemy-occupied areas.

The overwhelming majority of our people are peasants.

Over these last years, it is thanks to their forces that the war of resistance has been going on successfully. It is also thanks to the peasant forces that it will gain complete victory and our country will be successfully rebuilt.

Our peasants account for almost 90 per cent of the population but they own only 30 per cent of the arable land; they have to work hard all the year round and suffer poverty all their lives.

The feudal landlord class accounts for less than 5 per cent of the population but they and the colonialists occupy about 70 per cent of the arable land and live in clover. This situation is most unjust. Because of it our country has been invaded and our people are backward and poor. During the years of resistance, the government has decreed the reduction of land rent, the refunding of excess land rent and the temporary distribution of land belonging to the French and the Vietnamese traitors and that of communal land to the peasants in the free areas. But the key problem remains unsolved: the peasant masses have no land or lack land. This affects the forces of the resistance and the production work of the peasants.

Only by carrying out land reform, giving land to the tillers, liberating the productive forces in the countryside from the yoke of the feudal landlord class can we do away with poverty and backwardness and strongly mobilize the huge forces of the peasants in order to develop production and push the war of resistance forward to complete victory.

The goal set for land reform is to wipe out the feudal system of land ownership, distribute land to the tillers, liberate the productive forces in the countryside, develop production and push forward the war of resistance.

The general line and policy is to rely entirely on the landless and poor peasants, closely unite with the middle peasants, enter into alliance with the rich peasants, wipe out feudal exploitation step by step and with discrimination, develop production, and push forward the war of resistance.

To meet the requirements of the resistance and the National United Front, which consist in satisfying the land demands of the peasants while consolidating and developing the National United Front in the interests of the resistance and production, in the course of land reform we must apply different kinds of treatment to the landlords according to their individual political attitudes. This means that depending on individual cases we shall order confiscation or requisition with or without compensation, but not wholesale confiscation or wholesale requisition without compensation.

The *guiding principle for land reform* is boldly to mobilize the peasants, rely on the masses, correctly follow the mass line, organize, educate and lead the peasants to struggle according to plan, step by step, with good discipline and under close leadership.

The dispersion of land by landlords after the promulgation of the land rent reduction decree (14 July 1949) is illegal (except for particular cases mentioned in the circular issued by the Prime Minister's Office on 1 June 1953).

The land confiscated or requisitioned with or without compensation is to be definitvely allotted to the peasants who have no or not enough land. These peasants will have the right of ownership over the land thus distributed.

The *guiding principle for land distribution* is to take the village as unit, to allot land in priority to those who have been tilling it, to take into consideration the area, quality and location of the land, so as to give a fair share to everyone; especial consideration must be given to the peasants who have previously tilled the land to be distributed. As for the diehard elements bent on sabotaging land reform, the traitors, reactionaries and local despots, those among them who are sentenced to five years' imprisonment and more will not receive any land.

The mass mobilization launched this year gives experience in preparation for the land reform drive to be carried out next year. From this experience we have drawn a number of lessons. In general, in those localities where the Party and government policies have been firmly grasped and the mass line correctly followed (in spite of mistakes and deviations by some cadres in some places), satisfactory results have been recorded.

But failures have happened wherever the movement has been launched hurriedly by hot-headed local cadres before the decision had been taken by the central authorities.

Land reform is a policy to be applied throughout the country, but it must be carried out step by step, in accordance with local conditions.

After the land reform law has been approved by the National Assembly, the government will, next year, fix the dates and the places in the free zone for land reform to be carried out.

The government will later on take decisions concerning the regions inhabited by national minorities, the Fifth Interzone, Nam Bo and the guerrilla bases. In guerrilla and enemy-occupied areas, land reform will be carried out after their liberation.

In those localities where mass mobilization has not yet been launched for radical land rent reduction, the latter must be completed before land reform is undertaken. This is in order to organize the peasants, raise their political consciousness, build up their political supremacy in the villages and at the same time to train cadres, adjust organization and prepare the political conditions for land reform.

No locality is a allowed to start mass mobilization for land reform without authorization by the government.

Land reform is a peasant revolution, a class struggle in the countryside; it is a large-scale, hard and complex struggle which requires careful preparations, clearly mapped-out plans, close leadership, judicious choice of places, strict timetable and correct implementation. These are conditions for success.

The experience gained in other countries shows that a successful land reform will help overcome many difficulties and solve many problems.

In the *military field*, our peasant compatriots will join the resistance even more enthusiastically, hence it will be easier to build up the army and recruit voluntary civilian manpower. Our soldiers, with their minds at peace about their families, will fight even more resolutely.

In the *political field*, political and economic power in the countryside will be in the hands of the peasants, the people's democratic dictatorship will be truly carried into effect, the worker–peasant alliance will be consolidated, the National United Front will include more than 90 per cent of the people in the countryside and will become prodigiously great and strong.

In the *economic field*, liberated from feudal landlordism, the peasants will enthusiastically carry out production and practise thrift, their purchasing power will increase, industry and commerce will develop and the national economy as a whole will expand.

Thanks to the development of production, the livelihood of the peasants, workers, soldiers and cadres will be improved more rapidly.

In the *cultural and social field*, the large majority of the people, now having enough food and clothing, will study even harder, in accordance with the saying: 'One must have enough to eat before one could practise the good doctrine.' Good customs and habits will develop. The experience drawn from localities where mass mobilization has been launched shows that our compatriots are very fond of study and that there are good opportunities for the intellectuals to serve the people.

As said above, land reform is an immense, complex and hard class struggle. It is all the more complex and all the harder because we are conducting a war of resistance. But it is precisely because we want to push the resistance forward to victory that we must be determined to make land reform a success.

Because it is a complex and hard struggle, a number of cadres, whether they are Party members or not, might commit mistakes and deviations in their thoughts and deeds while implementing it. To prevent and set right these shortcomings and mistakes, we must firmly grasp the policies of the Party and the government, completely rely on the masses, and correctly follow the mass line.

The government and the Party call on all cadres and Party members to abide by the policies of the government and the Party, keep discipline, side entirely with the peasants, lead them in struggle. Whenever their own private interests or those of their families run counter to the interests of the resistance and those of the peasant masses, they must sacrifice the former to the latter.

We must mobilize the entire Party, the entire army and the entire people to ensure the implementation of land reform, to fulfil this great task.

For the Party members and the cadres, for the democratic parties and the patriotic personalities, this is a tremendous trial. All of us must win this trial, just as we are winning this other immense trial: the war of resistance against aggressive imperialism.

So our two central tasks in the next year will be: to fight the enemy and to carry out land reform.

We must fight the enemy on all fronts, annihilate as much of his force as possible, and smash his new military schemes.

We must mobilize the masses to carry out land reform in the regions fixed by the government.

To carry out land reform is aimed at securing victory for the war of resistance.

To fight the enemy and to annihilate his forces is aimed at securing success for land reform.

All other undertakings must be focused on those two central tasks and serve them. In 1954, we must pay particular attention to three great tasks, combining them with land reform:

To strengthen the armed forces (the regular army, the regional forces, the militia and guerrilla units) in all respects: organization, training, raising of their political consciousness, technical level and combat strength.

To train cadres and raise their ideological level, promote them to appropriate posts, reorganize the Party bases in the countryside.

To develop agricultural production; to meet the requirements of the resistance and supply food to the people; to push forward the national economy.

The full implementation of these two central undertakings and three great tasks will create more favourable conditions for the carrying out of other duties: firmly to maintain and develop the struggle behind enemy lines, to consolidate the people's democratic power in the villages, to reorganize the security service, to develop and consolidate the National United Front, to collect agricultural taxes, to develop our economy and finances, to intensify propaganda and education and to promote work in the cultural and social fields.

Our strength lies in the tens of millions of our peasant compatriots who are ready to organize themselves under the leadership of the government and the Party and to rise up and smash the feudal and colonial yoke. With skilful organization and leadership, these forces will shake heaven and earth and sweep away all colonialists and feudalists. We can conclude that under the firm and correct leadership of the government and the Party and with the wholehearted assistance of the National Assembly and the Front, the successful completion of land reform will take us a long way towards victory for the resistance and success for national construction.

35

REPORT TO THE SIXTH PLENUM OF THE VIET NAM WORKERS' PARTY CENTRAL COMMITTEE

15 July 1954

(. . .)

II. NEW TASKS

The new situation has set new tasks, new guidelines and new tactics. Over nearly nine years of resistance, under the leadership of our Party and government, our people and army have overcome difficulties, fought heroically, and won glorious victories. Our forces have made headway in all respects. Thanks to the correct policy of our Party and government, we have recorded good achievements.

At present the situation has changed; so have our tasks and consequently so should our policy and slogans. Up to now we have concentrated our efforts on wiping out the forces of the French imperialist aggressors. But now the French are having talks with us while the American imperialists are becoming our main and direct enemy; so our spearhead must be directed at the latter. Until peace is restored, we shall keep fighting the French; but the brunt of our attack and that of the world's peoples should be focused on the United States. US policy is to expand and internationalize the Indochina war. Ours is to struggle for peace and oppose the US war policy. For some nine years now, our Party has made clear its programme: complete independence for Viet Nam, Cambodia and Laos, which must be freed from the French yoke; to refuse to recognize the French Union, drive out all French troops from Indochina, destroy the puppet administration and armed forces, confiscate all properties of the imperialists and the traitors, launch a drive for the reduction of land rents and interest rates as a step towards agrarian reform, bring democracy to the whole nation, and carry our war of resistance through to final victory. This programme has won many successes. It is a correct one.

However, in the new situation we cannot maintain the old programme. Our previous motto was 'Resistance to the end'. At present, we must put forward a new one: 'Peace, unity, independence, democracy'. We must take firm hold of the banner of peace to oppose the US imperialists' policy of direct interference in, and prolongation and expansion of, the war in Indochina. Our policy must change in consequence: formerly we confiscated the French imperialists' properties; now, as negotiations are going on, we may, in accordance with the principle of equality and mutual benefit, allow French economic and cultural interests to be preserved in Indochina. Negotiations entail reasonable mutual concessions. Formerly we said we would drive out and wipe out all French aggressive forces; now, in the talks held, we have demanded, and the French have accepted, that a date be set for the withdrawal of their troops. In the past, our aim was to wipe out the puppet administration and army with a view to national reunification; now we practise a policy of leniency and seek reunification of the country through nationwide elections.

Peace calls for an end to the war: and to end the war one must agree on a ceasefire. A ceasefire requires regrouping zones, that is, enemy troops should be regrouped in a zone with a view to their gradual withdrawal, and ours in another. We must secure a vast area where we would have ample means for building, consolidating and developing our forces so as to exert influence over other regions and thereby advance towards reunification. The setting up of regrouping zones does not mean partition of the country; it is a temporary measure leading to reunification. Owing to the delimitation and exchange of zones, some previously free areas will be temporarily occupied by the enemy; their inhabitants will be dissatisfied; some people might fall prey to discouragement and to enemy deception. We should make it clear to our compatriots that the trials they are going to endure for the sake of the interests of the whole country, for the sake of our long-range interests, will be a cause for glory and will earn them the gratitude of the whole nation. We should keep everyone free from pessimism and negativism and urge all to continue a vigorous struggle for the complete withdrawal of French forces and for independence.

To set up regrouping zones as a step towards peace, to hold nation-wide elections to achieve national reunification, such is our policy. The aims of our war of resistance are independence, unity, democracy and peace. The very restoration of peace is aimed at serving the cause of reunification, independence and democracy. The new situation requires a new policy for securing new successes.

At any juncture, peace or war, we must firmly hold the initiative, show foresight and be in full readiness.

To secure peace is not an easy task; it is a long, hard and complex struggle; with advantageous conditions but also with difficulties. The advantageous conditions: the friendly countries support us, so do the world's people; our people are full of spirit and confidence in our party and government, under whose wise leadership they will certainly unite and struggle in peace as in war. The difficulties: the United States is trying its hardest to sabotage the restoration of peace in Indochina, the partisans of peace in France have not completely freed themselves from American influence.

The new situation is not only a difficult but also a complex one. Here are some instances: we should apply different policies to the old free areas and the newly liberated areas; to our own free zone and to the zone temporarily reserved for regrouped enemy troops; in the past we only worked in the countryside, at present we must have a policy for cities. The present policy with regard to France should be different from the past. Policies are not the same with respect to the pro-American traitors and the pro-French traitors. In the past we only had to care about home affairs and relations with friendly countries; now we have extended our foreign relations to other countries.

We should make a distinction between immediate and future interests, between local interests and overall interests.

The situation is undergoing great changes; furthermore difficulties and complications have cropped up; as a result, changes are also happening in the minds of the people and cadres. Failing good preparations and timely leadership, confusion might be thrown into thought and action.

The following ideological errors may be committed: *Leftist deviation*. Some people, intoxicated with our repeated victories, want to fight on at all costs, to a finish; they see only the trees, not the whole forest; with their attention focused on the withdrawal of the French they fail to detect their schemes; they see the French but not the Americans; they are partial to military action and make light of diplomacy. They are unaware that we are struggling in international conferences as well as on the battlefields in order to attain our goal. They will oppose the new slogans, which they deem to be rightist manifestations and to imply too many concessions. They set forth excessive conditions unacceptable to the enemy. They want quick results, unaware that the struggle for peace is a hard and complex one. Leftist deviation will cause one to be isolated, alienated from one's own people and those of the world, and suffer setbacks. *Rightist deviation* will lead to pessimism, inaction and unprincipled concessions. It causes one to lack confidence in the people's strength and to blunt their combative spirit; to lose the power to endure hardships and to aspire only to a quiet and easy life.

Leftist and rightist tendencies are both wrong. They will be exploited by the enemy; they will benefit them and harm us.

TASKS AND WORK

The new situation has set us three new responsibilities:

1. To secure and consolidate peace; to achieve unity, independence and democracy for the whole country.
2. To strengthen the people's armed forces and build up a mighty people's army capable of meeting the requirements of the new situation.
3. To keep implementing the slogan: land to the tiller. To strive to restore production and to prepare for national reconstruction.

These three responsibilities entail ten tasks:

1. To create unity of mind in the whole Party and among the entire people as regards the new situation and the new tasks.
2. To strengthen leadership in diplomatic struggle.
3. To strengthen the people's army.

4. To take over the newly liberated zones; especial attention to be paid to the taking over and management of the cities.
5. To give a new orientation to work in the zone temporarily reserved for regrouped enemy forces.
6. To keep consolidating the former free zones.
7. To mobilize the masses vigorously for land reform.
8. To improve economic and financial work and prepare conditions for the reconstruction of the country.
9. To assist the Pathet Lao and Khmer forces.
10. To continue the work of reorganization and ideological rectification of the Party in the newly liberated areas.

These ten tasks are under the leadership of the Central Committee. Each locality and each branch will not necessarily have to carry out all ten but each will be assigned a certain number of tasks.

Of the above ten tasks, ideological leadership is the most important. For both members and non-members of the Party, only a clear grasp of the new situation and the new tasks can bring about unity of mind, which will lead to unity of action. If all of us, both inside and outside the Party and at all levels, are at one in thought and action, we will successfully carry out our tasks, however difficult and complex.

At present, the US imperialists are the main enemy of the world's people and the main and direct enemy of the Indochinese people and so all our actions must be directed against them. Any person or country that is not pro-American can (even temporarily) join us in a united front. Our unalterable goal is peace, independence, unity and democracy. We must unswervingly stick to principles but show flexibility in tactics. All our activities should be interrelated and well co-ordinated, each part being integrated into the whole. Each task should be done in accordance with the concrete situation in each locality at a given moment.

Thanks to the correct leadership of our party and government, the unity and efforts of all our cadres and people, the sympathy and support of the people of the friendly countries and peace-loving people all over the world we will surely fulfil the above three responsibilities and ten tasks.

36

TO THE NATION

6 July 1956

Dear fellow countrymen,

For nearly a century, our people heroically struggled against the colonialists. The result was the triumph of the August Revolution and the founding of the Democratic Republic of Viet Nam.

But the perfidious colonialists provoked war in an attempt to re-conquer our country. After nearly nine years of extremely heroic and hard struggle by our entire people, the resistance was victorious. The Geneva Agreements restored peace, recognized Viet Nam's independence, sovereignty, unity and territorial integrity and stipulated that free general elections be held throughout the country in July 1956 to reunify the country.

Strictly implementing the Geneva Agreements, the government of the Democratic Republic of Viet Nam has repeatedly proposed to the South Viet Nam authorities the holding of a consultative conference with a view to organizing free general elections to reunify the country.

But the US imperialists and the pro-American authorities in South Viet Nam, scheming to divide our country permanently, have prevented the holding of free general elections at the time prescribed by the Geneva Agreements. They are acting against the interests of our fatherland and our people's wishes.

Faced with this situation, our sacred *duty* is to continue to struggle with determination for the implementation of the Geneva Agreements, the reunification of our country by peaceful means on the basis of independence and democracy, and for the completion of the glorious task of national liberation.

Our present line is closely and broadly to unite the entire people from North to South within the Viet Nam Fatherland Front, endeavour to consolidate the North and make it a strong base for the struggle for national reunification.

All honest Vietnamese can only approve of and support this noble aim. That is why we advocate a broad union of all Vietnamese at home and abroad who love their fatherland and stand for peace and unity. On the strength of this unity, we will make continuous efforts to bring the North and the South ever closer to each other, and will struggle with determination to consolidate peace, achieve reunification, and bring independence and democracy to the whole country.

Our present political struggle is a long, hard and complex one, but it will certainly be victorious. Victory is certain because our cause is just, our people are closely united and of one mind, our fellow countrymen in both South and North are struggling with heroism, the peoples of the world are supporting us, and the world peace movement is growing stronger every day, while the imperialists' warlike schemes have suffered ever more serious failures.

To meet our people's ardent wishes, which are to consolidate peace and achieve national reunification on the basis of the Geneva Agreements, the government of the Democratic Republic of Viet Nam proposes these practical measures:

1. *To restore normal relations* and free movement between the two zones; to create the required conditions for contacts between political, economic, cultural and social organizations of the North and of the South.
2. *To hold a consultative conference* between representatives of the two zones in order to discuss the question of free general elections to reunify the country on the basis of the Geneva Agreements.

Dear fellow countrymen at home and abroad,

Viet Nam will certainly be reunified. Our people of South and North will certainly be reunited. Let all unite closely and broadly on the basis of the Programme of the Viet Nam Fatherland Front, participate wholeheartedly in the patriotic emulation movement, endeavour to consolidate the North and struggle with determination and perseverance for a peaceful, reunified, independent democratic and prosperous Viet Nam.

Reunification is our people's road to salvation. Broad unity is an invincible force. Thanks to broad unity, our revolution has triumphed, our resistance has been victorious. With broad unity, our political struggle will certainly win, our country will certainly be reunified.

37

INSTRUCTIONS GIVEN AT THE CONFERENCE REVIEWING THE MASS EDUCATION IN THE FIRST HALF OF 1956[1]

16 July 1956

On behalf of the Party and government, I inquire after your health – cadres and mass education fighters – and congratulate the mass education service on its achievements during the first six months of the year. Over the past six months, 2,100,000 persons attended classes. This is a great achievement. Formerly, in the imperialist and feudal days, over 90 per cent of our population were illiterate. Later, the late Mr Nguyen Van To and a number of progressive people worked for the popularization of the national script. They made great efforts but only 5,000 persons per year went to classes. In the first six months of this year, there were over two million pupils. This is a great achievement, but we should not consider it as sufficient, we should make further efforts and avoid self-conceit and complacency.

After seven days of discussion and exchange of experiences, you are now probably more experienced than I am. But I would like to contribute a number of my own experiences.

1. In order to wipe out illiteracy among the great masses, where the overwhelming majority are peasants, the education movement should be a mass movement. We should stand close to the masses, discuss with them, apply forms and methods suitable to their life, and rely upon them to promote the movement.

Formerly, a number of other cadres and I carried out clandestine revolutionary activities in Cao Bang. The majority of our compatriots there were Nung, Man and Tho [*national minorities*], who knew little Vietnamese, lived scattered in the mountains far from one another, and were busy with their work; both teaching and studying had to be done in secret. We carried out mass education in these difficult conditions, but we succeeded. The cadres drafted a plan, in consultation with our compatriots, and the latter told them what to do. The literate taught the illiterate, those who knew much taught those who knew little.

Classes were run in caves; each village sent a person to study for a few days, then he went back and taught his co-villagers. When his knowledge was exhausted he returned to the class and learned some more. While teaching others, the teachers also learned for themselves. Such was the method we adopted for the mass education work and for its development into a movement.

At that time, in spite of the enemy restrictions and continuous persecutions, our compatriots were very studious, women and children being more studious than men. At present, on my visits to the classes, I also find that women and children are more numerous than men. Many men have not attended classes yet. There were no classes or schools then; people who went weeding or gathering vegetables appointed a place and went there to teach one another. Buffalo boys gathered at a certain spot and learned from one another. Cadres going to the fields to work were often stopped by the villagers and asked to hear them recite lessons; if the lessons were wrongly read out, the cadres would correct them; if they had been well learned, the cadres would be asked to give a new lesson.

Workers and peasants have a lot of work to do. If the method of teaching is not suitable to the learners, to their work and mode of life, if we expect classes provided with tables and benches, we cannot be successful. The organization of teaching should be in accordance with the living conditions of the learners, then the movement will last and bear good results. Our compatriots are still poor and cannot afford paper and pens; therefore a small pocket exercise-book is enough for each person. Reading and writing exercises can be done anywhere, using charcoal, the ground or banana leaves as pens and paper. Clandestine cadres were to teach and make one person literate every three months. At that time, there was no assistance from the government, no ministry or department in charge of educational problems, but in such precarious conditions, the movement kept developing, like oil spreading, the literate teaching the illiterate.

In studying like in teaching, the youth is the main force of the mass education movement. Everywhere, we should make the youth understand this task. In teaching as well as in studying the youth must always be in the van.

2. Mass education work is also teaching work, but not in schools or classes provided with lamps and books as in general schools. It is a wide, complicated and self-sufficient movement. General schools are divided into first, second, third and fourth forms, but in mass education, there are students of all kinds, the young, the old, some know much, others just a little, some assimilate quickly, others slowly; therefore this is a hard task which requires much patience and effort. The fear of difficulties and hardships is not admissible in mass education. Sometimes, we have to come and teach a mother of many children at her own house. With those aged people who are reluctant to attend classes, we should patiently convince them to do so or sometimes come and teach them in their own houses. In order to wipe out illiteracy from among the people, industriousness is indispensable, bureaucratism and ordering about are impossible.

The work is inconvenient and hard, and gives no fame at all. In the resistance war, if we succeeded in killing many of the enemy we could become model fighters or heroes; working in factories, if we make many innovations or surpass the production target, we become also outstanding workers or labour heroes. Mass education work, though not giving us fame, or being a well-sounding job, is however very glorious. We should not stand in one place and wish for another one; we should not nourish the wrong intention of giving up mass education work and entering a technical school, or teaching in a general school or taking another profession.

In social life there are many professions; a division of work is therefore inevitable. I do one work, you take up another. Mass education work is an important one, having a great bearing on the nation and society, and also on the building of our fatherland. Although not a well-sounding, famous or outstanding job which makes one become a hero, it is really a very important one. A person who is now a mass education worker should refrain from the desire of assuming another profession.

3. Mass education work is also placed under leadership. We have the ministry, the department, the zonal and the provincial services. To lead is not to sit and write office notes at the desk. In the Resistance time, there were cadres who could draft a good programme for secondary education

but were unable to take charge of a mass education class because they were always in the office. The leaders should closely unite with and assist the cadres to overcome difficulties; bureaucratism and ordering about are to be avoided. In any work, close connection with the people is essential; mass education services at all levels should correct their own mistakes if any, and learn from the experience of others.

4. Formerly, being poor, workers and peasants could not send their children to school; only a small number of children could attend classes, and the majority of these were from well-to-do families which had enough food to eat. In the countryside, only the children of landlords and rich peasants could go to school. Some cadres put the question as to whether the children of landlords and rich peasants should be allowed to teach in a mass education class. This is posing the question incorrectly. Any youth, male or female, is given this job if he or she is good, otherwise the work will not be entrusted to them. A worthy young person who does not approve his or her parents' exploitations and does not side with them to act against the people, will be accepted as a teacher in a mass education class. If he or she has committed serious faults, the job will not be given to them, either in mass education work or any other work. If a certain young person whose parents are guilty landlords does not follow his or her parents, he or she is not guilty and can maintain citizenship rights like other young people. He or she can attend classes or take part in public work or join people's organizations. This point should be well understood and correctly applied by you who live in the countryside.

5. Mass education work, though apparently not heroic, can be of a very great service to the nation if it can wipe out illiteracy among the people in three years. Our country would be proud of having rapidly eliminated illiteracy. In so-called civilized countries such as the USA, Great Britain and France, there are still some illiterate people. To wipe out illiteracy in two or three years is a very great victory. We should realize this and make further efforts. By so doing, it will not be this young man or that young woman who becomes a hero, but all cadres and teachers working for mass education will be heroes; and collective heroes are all the better.

If illiteracy is wiped out in three years, new tasks are set for the government, the Ministry of Education, and the Ministry of Culture; you too, you will be faced with new tasks. It does not mean when everybody knows how to read and write, you will have fulfilled your tasks and you may rest or take up another work.

Illiterate people should learn to become literate. When they have learned to read, they should push further in their studies. Literate people will fall into illiteracy again if they have no reading materials. The government and the Ministry of Education have therefore the task of furnishing books and newspapers suited to the standards of these readers.

You have the task of helping our illiterate compatriots to become literate, then to push forward their studies. So you yourselves should push forward your studies in order to be able to teach at a higher level. Our nation goes forward, the cadres should also go forward. They should march in the lead in order to ensure the continuous progress of the nation.

To conclude, the Party and the government will reward such communes as wipe out illiteracy first in a district, such districts as can do so in a province, and such provinces as can do so in the whole country.

If you want to be rewarded, you should make efforts. Making efforts does not mean issuing orders and compelling people to come and study, or to force them to study beyond their capacities; you should be industrious, and make efforts in accordance with the mass line.

Our compatriots are very studious, we have experiences of this. If our cadres endeavour to enrich their experiences, exchange their views, and discuss matters with one another, the work will certainly be successful.

I present you with fifteen remembrance insignia as rewards to those cadres who have obtained good achievements.

38

CONSOLIDATION AND DEVELOPMENT OF IDEOLOGICAL UNITY AMONG MARXIST-LENINIST PARTIES[1]

3 August 1956

The Twentieth Congress of the Communist Party of the Soviet Union was warmly greeted in the Democratic Republic of Viet Nam as in all other countries and considered as an extremely important historical event. The new measures taken following the congress in the home and foreign policies of the Soviet Union, the development of the revolutionary energy of the masses pointed out by the congress, show that the significance of the congress to builders of communism cannot be fully appraised. It is beyond question that the great programme translated into the targets of the Sixth Five-Year Plan, the raising of all political, economic and social forces of the country as put forth in the congress, the checking of the personality cult and its consequences, are brilliant successes recorded by the Soviet Union, which allow us to look forward to new great achievements of the Soviet Union in the near future.

The important theoretical principles set forth by the Twentieth Congress of the Communist Party of the Soviet Union on peaceful coexistence between countries with different social systems, on the possibility of preventing war in the present phase, on the multiform character of the transitional period towards socialism in various countries, all these principles have contributed to the consolidation of the forces of peace, democracy and socialism throughout the world.

The congress also revealed new possibilities and opened new prospects to the working class movement for socialism and to all peoples who are defending their national independence.

The effective struggle against the personality cult as unanimously approved by the Twentieth Congress of the Communist Party of the Soviet Union exerts a great influence over the whole communist movement. The 30 June 1956 resolution of the Central Committee helps us understand more deeply the question of the personality cult, and that of overcoming its consequences.

Speaking about the conditions required for the admission of various parties into the Communist International, V.I. Lenin pointed out that:

> In the present phase, that of fierce internal war, the Central Committee can fulfil its task only if it is organized in the most centralized way, if there is inner-Party iron discipline, almost as rigorous as military discipline, and if the central organ of the Party is influential and enjoys the general esteem of all its members.

Obviously, Lenin meant that the stage of fierce civil war and the restriction of democracy imposed on the Soviet people were only provisional and had to be abolished as soon as the new regime was consolidated.

However, our enemies hoped to undermine the socialist camp from inside. They made a big error in thinking that their hopes could come true, mistaking the development of socialist democracy for a beginning of disorder and utter loss of spirit of organization and inner-Party discipline among Marxist-Leninist parties.

It is crystal clear that once victorious, socialism can never tolerate the personality cult and its harmful consequences. The energetic measures taken by the Central Committee of the Communist Party of the Soviet Union to do away with the personality cult, and its consequences, set a brilliant example of unprecedented political boldness in history. The strict implementation of these measures in no way weakens but consolidates ideological solidarity among builders of communism, centred around the leading nucleus faithful to Lenin. The absolute prestige of the Communist Party of the Soviet Union is more and more enhanced and consolidated. Starting from Lenin's position regarding the question of criticism and self-criticism, the Central Committee of the Communist Party of the Soviet Union clearly stated that it had more concern with the necessity to correct mistakes and educate the party of the working class and of the masses of people, than with the question of 'what would the reactionaries say'. Lenin held it as the criterion of a correct and serious Party which is clearly aware of its responsibility and grasps the fact that the future interests of the movement should always come before everything.

Such a policy certainly enhances now as in the future the prestige of the CPSU in the socialist camp, as well as among the toiling masses of the capitalist countries and dependent countries.

An uproarious campaign of slander, launched by our enemies on the Communist Party of the Soviet Union for having worked out measures to liquidate the consequences of the personality cult, proves that they were blind politically; history will confirm it before long. The CPSU again demonstrates that the most important aspect of self-criticism is to practically and effectively correct one's errors. The scientific analysis of the conditions engendering errors has the effect of preventing their recurrence. All fraternal parties can draw valuable lessons from the documents of the Twentieth Congress, and its high level of further development of Marxist-Leninism. It is beyond question that the resolutions of the Twentieth Congress will help brother parties correct their errors and improve their work.

In the struggle to build a peaceful, unified, independent, democratic, prosperous and strong Viet Nam, the Viet Nam Workers' Party has always grasped the identity between the interests of the struggle for the liberation of all peoples from the imperialist yoke and those of the struggle for the liberation of the toiling masses from exploiting capitalism. Therefore, it has been able to lay the foundation for a solid friendship between the Vietnamese people and other peoples such as the Cambodian, Laotian and French peoples. In a wider meaning, in the struggle for national reunification, the Viet Nam Workers' Party has never isolated itself from the fraternal parties; in its whole practice, it has proved that genuine patriotism can never be separated from proletarian internationalism, and that the fraternal alliance between all fighters for a common cause – liberation of mankind, building of a classless society, peaceful coexistence and lasting peace – is unshakeable.

While the imperialists increased their organization and set up international aggressive blocs such as the SEATO, NATO and the Baghdad Pact, the Viet Nam Workers' Party has never departed from its policy of cementing relations with the brother parties.

The Viet Nam Workers' Party is aware that international reaction is hatching big schemes, especially in South Viet Nam and in the whole 'Pacific area' (Taiwan, South Korea . . .). It is also aware that through these plots, international reaction is spearheading its forces at the national liberation movement, at the working class and peasants in Asia; that while carrying out these schemes, imperialism is seeking every means to weaken the ideological unity and fraternal solidarity between the Marxist-Leninist parties of the working class in various countries.

In the present international conjuncture, national features and conditions peculiar to each country become a more and more important factor in the elaboration of the policies of every communist and workers' party. At the same time, Marxism-Leninism remains the unshakeable basis of the common struggle of all parties, exchange of experiences on this struggle keeps its full meaning, and questions arising for this or that party is in no way this or that party's 'own concern', but have vital connection with the international proletariat as a whole.

For example, we Vietnamese people not only have to define our own methods and measures in the struggle against the US imperialists' and South Viet Nam administration's schemes to perpetuate the division of our country, and in our struggle to gradually advance to socialism – this is obvious – but our party also clearly understands that our activities now and in the coming period cannot be confined within the mere national limit, that these activities are connected by thousands of ties with the general struggle waged by the progressive world, and that the genuine solidarity shown by the socialist camp and the peace-loving peoples throughout the world is as necessary to us as it was formerly, during the Vietnamese people's resistance war for national salvation.

The Ninth plenary session of the Central Committee of our party, held from 19 to 24 April 1956, made a deep study of the documents of the Twentieth Congress of the CPSU. Participating in the work of the session were members of the Central Committee, secretaries of the Party committees of zones, provinces and important towns, and a number of responsible cadres in central organs.

The Viet Nam Workers' Party has recorded big results in the creative application of Marxism-Leninism to the Vietnamese reality. Our people scored great victories during and after the war, in the consolidation of the completely liberated North, and in the political, economic and social spheres. Besides, the Party could unite in the Viet Nam Fatherland Front all patriots struggling for independence and national reunification through peaceful means.

The resolutions of the Ninth plenary session of the Central Committee of the Viet Nam Workers' Party also emphasized the great significance of the principles of collective leadership in the building and consolidating of the Party, the importance of which was emphasized at the Twentieth Congress of the CPSU. In general, our party has carried out the principle of collective leadership. However, a profound study of it has spotlighted many shortcomings.

We must admit that the personality cult has also existed to some degree in Viet Nam, both inside and outside the Party. Though it has not led to serious errors, yet it has limited the initiative and fighting spirit of the active elements and of the people. We have found manifestations of the personality cult both in leading central and local organs; to overcome these shortcomings, we have decided to improve ideological work in the Party and among the people.

In a recent session, the Council of Ministers highlighted the great achievements made in the carrying out of land reform and in economic rehabilitation, in raising the people's living standards and in the political consolidation of our people's democratic state. The congress also pointed out many shortcomings and errors in the implementation of the policy of alliance against feudal influence in the countryside, in methods of struggle against the enemy of the working class, in the implementation of the finance policy and in the readjustment of organization.

In the press and at Party meetings, we have constantly called on all Party members to strengthen their ties with the masses and take into account the situation in the South while putting forth and carrying out the Party policies. Our struggle is not yet over. We still have to overcome many difficulties, especially those arising from the partition of our country and the wrong execution of correct policies. We are firmly convinced that these difficulties can be overcome and that we shall be victorious, because our party enjoys the confidence of the people, the support of the socialist countries and the sympathy of progressive forces all over the world.

By severely criticizing Stalin's errors and by launching a resolute struggle against the personality cult, the Twentieth Congress of the CPSU has set us a brilliant example of political boldness and deep confidence in the people. The Viet Nam Workers' Party considers the cricitism of the personality cult as an eloquent proof of strength, and a great victory of the CPSU and of the world revolutionary movement.

Our enemy has attempted to make use of the criticism of personality cult to mitigate the influence of the great achievements recorded by the Soviet Union and to blemish the revolutionary movement which is ceaselessly gaining more victories. They try to sow confusion among the communist and workers' parties and to split the ranks of the toiling people. But their efforts will be set at naught. Like other brother parties, the Viet Nam Workers' Party is clearly aware that the struggle of the CPSU and its fraternal aid has a very great significance for the liberation of all peoples. All manoeuvres of the enemy of communism to blemish the Soviet Union and its Communist Party will certainly fail.

We are clearly aware that our common enemy's clamours only betray their fear in face of new forces and new victories. Faced with the ever more perfidious schemes of the imperialist reactionary influence, now more than ever we must strengthen and develop ideological unity, solidarity among communist and workers' parties, and tirelessly struggle to defend the purity of Marxism-Leninism, which is our common treasury; study and apply correctly the theoretical principles of Marxism-Leninism to the realities of each country. We are confident that under the banner of Marxism-Leninism, victory will certainly be ours.

39

ON REVOLUTIONARY MORALITY

1958

Ever since the beginning of its existence mankind has had to *struggle* against nature – wild beasts, the weather, etc. – in order to survive. To succeed in this struggle each individual must rely on the force of large numbers of people, on the collective, on *society*. Alone, he cannot get the better of nature and subsist.

In order to survive, man must also *produce* to get food and clothing. Production, too, must rely on the collective, on society. Alone, the individual cannot produce.

Our era being a civilized, revolutionary era, one must rely all the more on the force of the collective, of society, in all undertakings. More than ever the individual cannot stand apart but must join the collective, join society.

Therefore, *individualism* goes counter to *collectivism*; collectivism and socialism will certainly prevail while individualism will surely disappear.

The mode and forces of production ceaselessly develop and change; so do, therefore, man's thinking, social systems, etc. All of us know that from the past to the present, the mode of production has evolved from the use of tree branches and stone axes to that of machines, electricity and nuclear energy. Social systems have also developed from primitive communism through slave ownership and feudalism to capitalism, and today nearly half of mankind is progressing to socialism and communism.

No one can stop this development and progress.

With the coming into being of private ownership, society has been divided into *classes* – exploiting classes and exploited ones – hence the emergence of social *contradictions* and class *struggle*. Any person necessarily belongs to one class or another and no one can stand outside the classes. At the same time, each individual represents the *ideology* of his own class.

In the old society, the feudal landlords, capitalists and imperialists mercilessly oppressed and exploited the other social strata, especially the workers and peasants. They plundered the common property produced by society, turned it into their own private property and lived in clover. But they kept ranting about 'virtue', 'freedom', 'democracy' . . .

Refusing to endure this oppression and exploitation for ever, the workers, peasants and other toiling people have risen up and made the *revolution* in order to liberate themselves and transform the wicked old society into a fine new one, in which all labouring people would live happily, and from which the exploitation of man by man would be banned.

To succeed, the revolution must be *led by the working class* – the most advanced, conscious, resolute, disciplined and best-organized class – with the proletarian party as its staff. This has been incontestably borne out by the revolution in the Soviet Union and in the other socialist countries.

To make the revolution, to transform the old society into a new one is a very glorious, but also an extremely heavy task, a complex, protracted and hard struggle. Only a strong man can travel a long distance with a heavy load on his back. A revolutionary must have a solid foundation of *revolutionary morality* in order to fulfil his glorious revolutionary task.

Born and brought up in the old society, we all carry within ourselves, to varying extent, traces of that society in our thinking and habits. The worst and most dangerous vestige of the old society is *individualism*. Individualism runs counter to revolutionary morality. The least remaining trace of it will develop at the first opportunity, smother revolutionary virtues and prevent us from wholeheartedly struggling for the revolutionary cause.

Individualism is something very deceitful and perfidious; it skilfully induces one to backslide. And everybody knows that it is easier to backslide than to progress. That is why it is very dangerous.

To shake off the bad vestiges of the old society and to cultivate revolutionary virtues, we must study hard, and educate and reform ourselves in order to progress continuously. Otherwise we shall retrogress and lag behind, and shall eventually be rejected by the forward-moving society.

It is not only by going to school or attending training courses that we can study and educate and reform ourselves. In every revolutionary activity, we can and must do it. Underground revolutionary activities, the general insurrection, the war of resistance, the present building of socialism in the North and the struggle for national reunification are very good schools where we can acquire revolutionary virtues.

People with revolutionary virtues fear neither difficulties, hardships nor failures; they neither waver nor step back. For the sake of the interests of the Party, the revolution, the class, the nation and mankind, they never hesitate to sacrifice their own interests, and if need be, even their own lives. This is a very clear and lofty expression of revolutionary morality.

In our party, Comrades Tran Phu, Ngo Gia Tu, Le Hong Phong, Nguyen Van Cu, Hoang Van Thu, Nguyen Thi Minh Khai and many others have laid down their lives for the sake of the people and the Party, thus setting brilliant examples of total dedication to the public interest and complete selflessness.

People with revolutionary virtues remain simple, modest and ready to face more hardships, even when meeting with favourable conditions and winning successes. 'Worry about work before the others, think of enjoyment after them.' We must think of how best to fulfil our task, not of how to get the greatest reward. We must avoid boasting about past achievements and claiming special prerogatives, or indulging in bureaucratism, conceit and depravation. This also is an expression of revolutionary morality.

In brief, revolutionary morality consists of the following:

To devote one's life to struggling for the Party and the revolution. This is the most essential point.

To work hard for the Party, observe Party discipline, and implement Party lines and policies.

To put the interests of the Party and the labouring people before and above one's own interests. To serve the people wholeheartedly. To struggle selflessly for the Party and the people and to be exemplary in every respect.

To endeavour to study Marxism-Leninism and constantly use self-criticism and criticism to heighten one's ideological standard, improve one's work and progress together with one's comrades.

Each revolutionary must deeply realize that our Party is the most advanced and close-knit organization of the working class, the leader of the latter and the labouring people at large. At present, our working class, though still not very numerous, is developing with every passing day. In future, agricultural co-operatives will be organized everywhere, machines will be widely used in the countryside, and peasants will become workers. The intellectuals will become well acquainted with manual labour, and the difference between brain and manual workers will be gradually wiped out. Our country's industry will develop day by day. Hence, the workers will be ever more numerous, their strength will grow, and the future of the working class is great and glorious. It will reform the world and itself as well.

The revolutionary must clearly realize this and firmly stick to the *stand* of the working class so as to struggle wholeheartedly for socialism and communism, for the working class and all the labouring people. *Revolutionary morality consists in absolute loyalty to the Party and the people.*

Our party pursues no other interests than those of the working class and the toiling people. Therefore, its immediate objective is to struggle for the gradual building of socialism in the North and the reunification of the country.

Under the Party's leadership our people have fought heroically, overthrown the colonial and feudal domination, and completely liberated the North of our country. This was a great success. But the revolution is not yet totally victorious, and the present aim of the Party is to struggle for national reunification in order to build a peaceful, reunified, independent, democratic and prosperous Viet Nam, to eliminate exploitation of man by man all over the country and build a new society with happiness and abundance for all.

However, our industry is still backward. Thanks to the devoted help of the fraternal countries, first of all the Soviet Union and China, it is developing. For our effort to succeed, our workers must emulate one another and strive to produce ever more, faster, better and more economically, observe labour discipline and actively participate in the management of their enterprises: we must oppose waste and embezzlement, and our cadres must be truly industrious, thrifty, honest and upright and join the workers in labour.

Land has been allotted to our peasants, whose life has been partially improved. But the mode of production is still scattered and backward; hence the yields have not yet increased much and living conditions have improved but slightly. The movement for setting up work-exchange teams and co-operatives in our countryside must be extensively and firmly pushed forward in order to bring about a firm increase in production; only then can our peasants escape poverty and see their condition improved.

Therefore, *revolutionary morality consists in striving to achieve the Party's objective*, faithfully serving the working class and the toiling people, and never wavering.

Most members of the Party and the Working Youth Union and most cadres have done so, but some have not. They wrongly think that now that the colonialists and feudalists have been got rid of in the North, the revolution has been successfully completed. That is why they let individualism develop within themselves, demand enjoyment and rest, and want to pick their own work instead of fulfilling the tasks entrusted to them by their organization. They want high positions but shirk responsibilities. Their combativeness and energy gradually weaken, and so do their revolutionary courage and noble virtues. They forget that the prime criterion of a revolutionary *is his resolve to struggle all his life for the Party and the revolution.*

We must realize that the successes recorded by us so far are only the first steps on a thousand-league road. We must advance further, the revolution must make further progress. Otherwise, we shall regress, and the successes we have gained cannot be consolidated and developed.

To advance to socialism, we must wage a long and hard struggle. We must have revolutionaries for there still exist *enemies*, who oppose the revolution.

There are three kinds of enemies:

Capitalism and imperialism are very dangerous ones.

Backward habits and traditions are also big enemies: they insidiously hinder the progress of the revolution. However, we cannot repress them, but must seek to correct them with caution, perseverance and over a long period of time.

The third enemy is *individualism*, the petty-bourgeois mentality which still lurks in each of us. It is waiting for an opportunity – either failure or success – to rear its head. It is the ally of the two above-mentioned categories.

Therefore *revolutionary morality* consists, in whatever circumstances, in resolutely struggling against all enemies, maintaining one's vigilance, standing ready to fight, and refusing to submit, to bow one's head. Only by so doing can we defeat the enemy, and fulfil our revolutionary tasks.

It is due to its correct policy and unified leadership that our party can lead the working class and the entire people to socialism. This unified leadership springs from the unity of thought and action of all its members.

Without this unity we would be like 'an orchestra in which the drums play one way and the horns another'. It would not be possible for us to lead the masses and make revolution.

The Party members' words and deeds have a great bearing on the revolution for they exert great influence on the masses. For instance: the present policy of our party and government is broadly and closely to organize *work-exchange teams and co-operatives*, to carry out agricultural co-operation. But a number of Party and Working Youth Union members do not join them or, having joined them, do not actively contribute to their building and consolidation. It is *individualism* which has led those comrades to do as they please and to go counter to the Party's organization and discipline. Wittingly or unwittingly, their actions impair the prestige of the Party, hinder its work and impede the advance of the revolution.

All the Party's policies and resolutions aim at serving the people's interests. Therefore, for a Party member, revolutionary morality consists in *resolutely implementing them*, whatever the difficulties, and setting an example for the masses. Each Party member must heighten his sense of responsibility to the people and the Party. He must guard against and resolutely oppose individualism.

Our party represents the *common interests* of the working class and the entire labouring people, not the private interests of any group or individual. This everyone knows.

The working class struggle not only to free themselves, but also to liberate mankind from oppression and exploitation. Therefore, their interests and those of the people are at one.

The Party member, in the name of the Party, represents the interests of the working class and the labouring people. That is why his own interests lie within, not without, those of the Party and the class. Success and victory for the Party and the class mean success and victory for the militant. Separated from the Party and the class, no individual, however talented, can achieve anything.

Revolutionary morality, for a Party member, consists in *putting the Party's interests above everything else*, in all circumstances. If the Party's interests are in contradiction with those of the individual, the latter must absolutely give way to the former.

Having not cleansed themselves of individualism some Party members still boast of 'their services to the Party', for which they claim the Party's 'gratitude'. They want to enjoy favour, honour, rank and privilege. If their desires are not satisfied they bear resentment against the Party, complaining that they have 'no future' and are 'sacrificed'. They gradually drift away from the Party; worse still, they sabotage its policies and discipline.

Many cadres and fighters in the period of underground struggle and the war of resistance heroically laid down their lives; many labour heroes and elite workers have done their utmost to increase production. Those comrades have never asked for rank and honour, never demanded thanks from the Party.

Our party has a mass character, and hundreds of thousands of members. Owing to the situation in our country the bulk of Party members spring from the petty bourgeoisie. There is nothing surprising in it. In the beginning, under the influence of bourgeois ideology the stand of some Party members may lack firmness, their outlook may be confused and their thinking not quite correct, but owing to the fact that they have been tempered in the revolution and the war of resistance, our Party members are by and large good militants, faithful to the Party and the revolution.

Those comrades know that those Party members who commit errors will lead the masses into error; therefore, they stand ready to correct any mistake they may make, and this in a timely way, and do not allow small errors to accumulate into big ones. They sincerely practise criticism and self-criticism, which makes it possible for them to progress together.

This conforms to revolutionary morality. During its many years of underground activity, our party, although harshly repressed by the colonialists and meeting with numerous difficulties and dangers, developed and grew stronger with every passing day, and then led the revolution and the war of resistance to victory. This is due to its effective use of this sharp weapon: *criticism and self-criticism.*

However, there still remain some Party members who, unable to shake off individualism, become arrogant and conceited and keep flaunting their merits. While criticizing others, they do not like being criticized; they avoid self-criticism or practise it without sincerity and seriousness. They are afraid they might lose face and prestige. They pay no attention to the opinion of the masses, and make light of non-Party cadres. They do not realize that it is difficult not to commit any errors in one's work. We are not afraid of possible mistakes, but of failure to correct them resolutely. To redress them, we must listen to criticism by the masses and practise sincere self-criticism. Otherwise we shall lag behind and regress, which will lead to our being cast aside by the masses. This is the inevitable consequence of individualism.

The forces of the working class and the labouring people are immense, boundless. But they must be led by the Party if they are to win. At the same time the Party must stay close to the masses, and skilfully organize and lead them, if the revolution is to triumph.

Revolutionary morality consists in uniting with the masses in one body, trusting them and paying attention to their opinion. By their words and deeds. Party and Working Youth Union members and cadres win the people's confidence, respect and love, closely unite them around the Party, organize, educate and mobilize them so that they will enthusiastically implement the Party's policies and resolutions.

That is what we have done during the revolution and the war of resistance.

But at present, individualism is haunting a number of our comrades. Claiming to be clever in everything they stray from the masses, refuse to learn from them and want only to be their teachers. They are reluctant to engage in organization, propaganda and education work among the masses. They become infected with bureaucratism and commandism. As a result, the masses neither trust nor respect them, much less love them. Eventually, they can do nothing good.

The North of our country is advancing to socialism. This is the urgent aspiration of millions of labouring people. This is the collective under-taking of the toiling masses under our party's leadership. Individualism is a big obstacle to the building of socialism. Therefore, *the success of socialism cannot be separated from that of the struggle for the elimination of individualism.*

To struggle against individualism is not 'to trample on individual interests'. Each person has his own character, his fortes, his private life and that of his family. There is no harm when the interests of the individual do not go counter to those of the collective. But one must realize that only under the socialist regime can each person improve his private life and develop his personality and his strong points.

No system equals socialism and communism in showing respect for man, paying due attention to his legitimate individual interests and ensuring that they be satisfied. In a society ruled by the exploiting class only the individual interests of a few people belonging to this class are met, whereas those of the toiling masses are trampled underfoot. But in the socialist and communist systems, of which the labouring people are the masters, each man is a part of the collective, plays a definite role in it and contributes his part to society. That is why the interests of the individual lie within those of the collective and are part of them. Only when the latter are secured can the former be satisfied.

The interests of the individual are closely tied to those of the collective. If there is any contradiction between them, revolutionary morality demands that the former yield to the latter.

The revolution unceasingly progresses. So does the Party. And so must the revolutionary.

The revolutionary movement involves hundreds of millions of people. Revolutionary work involves thousands of extremely complex and difficult tasks. In order to be able to assess all complex situations, clearly see the contradictions, and correctly solve the various problems, we must *strive to study Marxism-Leninism.*

Only by so doing can we consolidate our revolutionary morality, firmly maintain our stand, raise our theoretical and political level, and fulfil the tasks entrusted to us by the Party.

To study Marxism-Leninism is to learn the spirit in which one should deal with things, with other people and with oneself. It means to study the universal Marxist-Leninist truths in order to apply them creatively to the practical conditions of our country. We must study with a view to action. Theory must go hand in hand with practice.

But some comrades only learn by heart a few books on Marxism-Leninism. They think they understand Marxism-Leninism better than anyone else. Yet, when faced with practical problems, they either act in a mechanical way or are thrown into confusion. Their deeds do not match their words. They study books on Marxism-Leninism but do not seek to acquire the Marxist-Leninist spirit. They only want to show off their knowledge, not to apply it to revolutionary action. This is also *individualism.*

Individualism spawns hundreds of dangerous diseases: bureaucratism, commandism, sectarianism, subjectiveness, corruption, waste . . . It ties up and blindfolds its victims whose every action is guided by their desire for honour and position, not by concern for the interests of the class and the people.

Individualism is a cruel enemy of socialism. The revolutionary must do away with it.

At present, the task of our party and people is to endeavour to increase production and practise thrift in order to build up the North, gradually take it to socialism, and turn it into a strong base for the reunification of the country. This is an extremely glorious task. Let all members of the Party and the Working Youth Union, let all cadres within and without the Party be resolved to devote all their lives to serving the Party and the people. This is the noble virtue of the revolutionary, this is revolutionary morality, the Party and class spirit, which ensures victory for the Party, the class and the people.

Revolutionary morality does not fall from the sky. It is developed and consolidated through persevering daily struggle and effort. Like jade, the more it is polished the more it shines. Like gold, it grows ever purer as it goes into the melting pot.

What can be a greater source of happiness and glory than to cultivate one's revolutionary morality so as to bring a worthy contribution to the building of socialism and the liberation of mankind!

I earnestly hope that all members of the Party and the Working Youth Union and all cadres within and without the Party will strive hard and progress.

40

REPORT ON THE DRAFT AMENDED CONSTITUTION[1]

18 December 1959

Members of the Presidium,

Deputies,

At its Sixth session, the National Assembly decided to amend the 1946 constitution and to set up a committee entrusted with preparing a draft amended constitution and submitting that draft to its approval.

The drafting of the amended constitution has been a long process of careful preparation and study. Following completion of the first draft in July 1958, we submitted it to discussion by high- and middle-ranking cadres in the army, mass organizations, administrative departments and Party offices. The draft was then improved and, on 1 April 1959, was made public for the entire people to discuss it and contribute constructive suggestions. These discussions lasted four consecutive months. Everywhere, in government offices, factories, schools and other people's organizations, in both town and countryside, the study and discussion of the draft constitution proceeded in an enthusiastic atmosphere and became a broad mass movement with the participation of all sections of the people. In the press, the discussions were also lively and fruitful. The Committee for the Amendment of the Constitution received many letters carrying the views of individual people and groups, including letters from our dear compatriots in the South and Vietnamese nationals residing abroad.

The views contributed by the people have been carefully studied and debated by the Committee for the Amendment of the Constitution and, on that basis, we have again improved the draft.

On behalf of the Committee for the Amendment of the Constitution,

I am presenting to the National Assembly this report on the draft constitution.

I IMPORTANT SIGNIFICANCE
OF THE AMENDED CONSTITUTION

Viet Nam, our fatherland, has been built in the course of thousands of years of industrious labour and heroic struggle of our people.

In the middle of the nineteenth century, the French imperialists began to invade our country. The feudal kings and mandarins surrendered to the aggressors and sold out our country to the French imperialists. For nearly a century the latter colluded with the local feudal class to rule over our country in an extremely cruel manner. Right in the beginning, our people had risen up to fight the French imperialists in order to win back national independence. Thanks to their spirit of selfless struggle, the movement for national liberation developed unceasingly. However, after nearly half a century of struggle, the imperialist and feudal domination was not yet overthrown and our country was not yet independent.

It was then that the Russian October Revolution broke out and won glorious victory. The Union of Soviet Socialist Republics was founded. The colonial system of imperialism began to collapse. The Soviet Union brought to the oppressed peoples a model of equal relationships between the nations.

The oppressed peoples of the world saw that only by relying on socialist revolution and following the line of the working class was it possible to overthrow the imperialists, win back complete national independence and realize genuine equality among the nations. The Russian October Revolution welded the socialist revolutionary movement and the revolutionary movement for national liberation into an anti-imperialist front.

In Viet Nam, following World War One, the national bourgeoisie and the petty bourgeoisie were unable to lead the movement for national liberation to success. The Vietnamese working class, in the light of the October Revolution, charted the course of the Vietnamese revolution. In 1930, the Indochinese Communist Party, the political party of the working class, was founded and showed that the Vietnamese revolution should go through two stages: the national democratic revolution and the socialist revolution. For the first time, the Vietnamese revolution was provided with a comprehensive political programme worked out by the party of the working class. And ever since then, under the unified leadership of the working class and its political party, it has developed rapidly and steadily.

The 1930 Nghe Tinh Soviets and the 1936–39 democratic action movement gave a strong impetus to the Vietnamese revolution and strengthened even more the ties between the working class and its party on the one hand and the peasants and other sections of the people on the other.

In 1939, World War Two broke out. The French imperialists and Japanese militarists worked hand in glove to rule over our country. Under the leadership of the Party, our people rose up to fight the aggressive imperialists in a most heroic manner. The Bac Son and Nam Ky uprisings were the harbingers of a widespread revolutionary movement. In 1941, the Party established the Viet Minh with the task of 'driving out the Japanese and the French in order to make the country fully independent and build the Democratic Republic of Viet Nam'.

In 1945, the Soviet Union and the democratic forces of the world defeated the fascists and World War Two came to an end. Seizing this opportunity, the Party led the August Revolution to victory. The imperialist and feudal yoke was thrown off. The people's power was established throughout the country. On 2 September 1945, the Democratic Republic of Viet Nam was founded. The independence of our country was solemnly proclaimed before the peoples of the world. After nearly a century of slavery, our fatherland was liberated and our people emancipated. An extremely glorious chapter began in the history of our nation.

After the victorious August Revolution, our people began building the nation in order to consolidate and develop the fruits of the revolution. On 6 January 1946, in free nationwide general elections, our people elected our first-ever National Assembly. On 9 November 1946, the National Assembly adopted the first constitution of our country.

The preamble to the 1946 constitution pointed out:

> The task of our people in this stage is to preserve territorial integrity, win complete independence and build the country on a democratic basis. The Vietnamese Constitution must record the glorious achieve-

ments of the Revolution and must be built on the principle of unity of the entire people; it must guarantee democratic freedoms and set up a strong people's power.

The regime instituted by the 1946 constitution guaranteed national independence and broad democracy for the people. Right after its establishment under the leadership of the Party, the people's power promulgated labour legislation, reduced land rent, confiscated land belonging to the French colonialists and the Vietnamese traitors and distributed it to the peasants. The right of the people to vote and stand for elections and to participate in the affairs of the state was guaranteed, and democratic freedoms were carried into effect. This was the regime of new democracy.

However, the French imperialists provoked war in an attempt to reconquer our country. Our people, closely united around the Party and the government, waged a long and hard war of resistance, and resolutely smashed the enslaving schemes of the imperialists and the traitors, their henchmen. In 1953, while our people were waging the war of resistance, the National Assembly adopted the law on land reform in pursuance of the principle 'Land to the tillers.'

The Dien Bien Phu victory and the success of the Geneva Conference brought the extremely heroic resistance of our people to a glorious end; North Viet Nam was completely liberated.

For the first time in history, an oppressed nation defeated the aggression of a mighty imperialist power, won back national independence, brought land to the tillers and genuine democratic rights to the people. This victory was due to the ardent patriotism and valiant struggle of our army and people, the close unity of our entire people within the National United Front, the reliance of our people's power on the worker–peasant alliance led by the working class and the Party, and the support of the fraternal countries in the socialist camp and the forces of peace and democracy throughout the world.

The victory of the August Revolution and the great war of resistance proves that even a small and weak nation can most certainly defeat the imperialist aggressors, if it is closely united under the leadership of the working class and its Party and correctly follows the Marxist-Leninist line.

Following the victory of the war of resistance and the restoration of peace, the Vietnamese revolution moved on to a new stage. Under the people's democratic regime, North Viet Nam, completely liberated, entered a period of transition to socialism. But South Viet Nam is still under the imperialist and feudal yoke and our people must carry on the national democratic revolution in the new conditions of our country.

In North Viet Nam, following its complete liberation, rapid progress has been achieved in all fields.

In the three years from 1955 to 1957, we healed the wounds of war and rehabilitated our economy.

In 1958, we began a three-year economic plan aimed at developing and transforming the national economy along the socialist line.

The fourteenth plenum of the Central Committee of the Viet Nam Workers' Party pointed out that 'the socialist forces in North Viet Nam have now become definitely stronger than the capitalist forces'.

In the economic and cultural fields, we have achieved great progress. For instance:

– From 1955 to 1959, in agriculture, paddy output increased from 3.6 million tons to 5.2 million tons. In industry, starting with only 17 factories in 1955, we have 107 state factories in 1959.

– Agricultural co-operatives of the lower level now embrace 43.9 per cent of peasant households and most of the rest have joined work-exchange teams.

– 53 per cent of craftsmen have joined co-operative organizations.

– In culture, we have basically eliminated illiteracy. Compared with 1955, the number of students has increased twofold in general education schools, sixfold in secondary vocational schools, and sevenfold in colleges and universities. The number of medical doctors has increased by 80 per cent, etc.

We are advancing to a socialist economy. Along with these successes, class relations in North Viet Nam have changed. The feudal landlord class has been overthrown. The working class is growing day by day and is strengthening its leadership over the state. The peasantry has taken the co-operative path. The worker–peasant alliance has been further strengthened. The revolutionary intellectuals are contributing an active part to national construction. The national bourgeoisie, generally speaking, accept socialist transformation. The various sections of our people are united ever more closely within the National United Front. Compared with 1946, when the first constitution of our country was adopted, the situation in present-day North Viet Nam has undergone very important and favourable changes.

While the North has been advancing to socialism, in the South the US imperialists and their henchmen have undermined the Geneva Agreements and refused to hold the consultative conference on general elections to reunify the country. They are enforcing an extremely cruel and autocratic policy, robbing the people of their property, and repressing and persecuting them in the most barbarous manner. They seek to perpetuate the division of our country and turn the South into a colony and a military base of the US imperialists, with a view to a new war in Indochina.

But our compatriots in the South have shown great heroism and the struggle there has been carried on and expanded. They demand improved living conditions, the development of the national economy, democratic freedoms, peace and national reunification; they oppose oppression, exploitation and American 'aid', terror and massacre, military build-up and war preparations.

North Viet Nam's advance to socialism powerfully stimulates the patriotic movement in South Viet Nam. The thoughts of our southern compatriots are constantly turned to the North and to our government, and their confidence in national reunification is all the more strengthened.

In short, the Vietnamese revolution has moved on to a new stage. We have new tasks to perform. Conditions both at home and in the world are favourable.

The 1946 constitution – the first democratic constitution of our country – conformed to the situation and the revolutionary tasks of that period. It has completed its mission. It is no longer compatible with the new situation and the new revolutionary tasks. That is why we must amend it.

The draft amended constitution clearly records the great successes of our people in the past years and clearly outlines the new revolutionary tasks in the new historical period.

II THE MAIN POINTS IN
THE DRAFT AMENDED CONSTITUTION

I present below a summary of the main points in the draft amended constitution:

I. CHARACTER OF THE DEMOCRATIC REPUBLIC OF VIET NAM.

The character of the state is the fundamental question in the constitution. This is the question of the class content of state power. In whose hands is power and whose rights and interests does it serve? This question determines the whole content of the constitution.

The Vietnamese state established after the August Revolution was already a people's democratic state, led by the working class. The preamble of the draft amended constitution points out: 'Our state is a people's democratic state based on the worker–peasant alliance and led by the working class.' In order to build socialism and struggle for the country's reunification, we must unceasingly strengthen the leadership of the working class over the people's democratic state.

The worker–peasant alliance is the foundation of the Democratic Republic of Viet Nam. The peasantry constitutes a very big productive force and at the same time a very great revolutionary force. In the people's democratic national revolution, the peasants have energetically followed the Party and have risen up side by side with the working class to overthrow imperialism and feudalism. At present they are enthusiastically joining the agricultural co-operation movement. This is due to their own active revolutionary spirit and the patient and ceaseless education by the Party and the working class. Therefore, in building socialism, our state strives to help the peasantry and consolidate the worker–peasant alliance.

The working class unites with craftsmen and small traders because they are working people; they willingly take the path of co-operation, approve of and support the socialist revolution.

The socialist revolution is intimately linked with the scientific and technical development and the cultural development of the people. Our intellectuals contributed a valuable part to the resistance. They have been constantly assisted by the Party, which has allowed them to progress. That is why they are for socialism. The working class closely unites with the intelligentsia to help them serve the revolution and socialism.

Under the leadership of the working class, the Vietnamese national bourgeoisie have supported the people's democratic national revolution. Since the restoration of peace they have contributed their part to economic rehabilitation. At present we have the conditions to transform them along socialist lines. In the northern part of our country, the socialist economic forces have grown definitely superior to the capitalist economic forces. We have the people's power. The revolutionary struggle of the working masses is becoming ever more powerful. The national bourgeoisie are ready to accept transformation to contribute to national construction and the building of socialism.

Our country is a united multinational country. All nationalities living on Vietnamese territory are equal in rights and duties.

All the nationalities in our country are fraternally bound together; they share a common territory and in the course of our long history have worked and fought side by side in order to build our beautiful fatherland.

Imperialism and feudalism deliberately sought to undermine the solidarity and equality between the nationalities and to sow discord among them and carried out a 'divide-and-rule' policy. Our party and government have constantly called on the nationalities to forget all enmities caused by imperialism and feudalism and to unite closely on the basis of equality in rights and duties. The minority nationalities have, side by side with their brothers of the majority nationality, fought against their common enemies, and brought the August Revolution and the war of resistance to success. Since the restoration of peace, our state has helped the brotherly nationalities to achieve further progress in the economic, cultural and social fields. The Viet Bac and the Thai Meo Autonomous Regions have been established. Closely united under the leadership of the Party and the state, the nationalities are enthusiastically taking part in the emulation movement for national construction.

Our nationalities policy is aimed at achieving equality and mutual assistance between the nationalities so as to allow them to advance together to socialism. Autonomous regions may be established in areas where minority nationalities live in dense communities.

2. GENERAL LINE OF ADVANCE TO SOCIALISM

For nearly a century, Viet Nam was a colonial and semi-feudal country. The economy was very backward and heterogeneous; production was little-developed and the people's material and cultural living standards were low. To get out of this situation of poverty, North Viet Nam must advance to socialism.

Article 9 of the draft amended constitution points out the line of advance to socialism:

The Democratic Republic of Viet Nam will advance step by step from people's democracy to socialism by developing and transforming the national economy along socialist lines, transforming its backward economy into a socialist economy with modern industry and agriculture and advanced science and technology. The economic policy of the Democratic Republic of Viet Nam is continuously to develop production with the aim of constantly raising the material and cultural standards of the people.

At present in our country these are the main forms of ownership of the means of production:

– Ownership by the state, that is, ownership by the entire people;
– Ownership by the co-operatives, that is, collective ownership by the working people;
– Ownership by individual working people; and
– Ownership of a few means of production by the capitalists.

The aim of our regime is to eliminate the forms of non-socialist ownership, to turn the present heterogeneous economy into a homogeneous one based on the system of ownership by the entire people and collective ownership.

Under article 12 of the draft amended constitution, the state economic sector is owned by the whole people; it leads the national economy, and the state must give priority to its development.

Under article 13, the sector of co-operative economy is collectively owned by the working people; the state is to provide encouragement, guidance and assistance for its development.

We must develop the state economic sector to create the material foundation for socialism and stimulate socialist transformation.

– Agricultural co-operation is the prime mover of socialist transformation in the North. Past experiences have shown that agricultural co-operation in our country must pass through the forms of work-exchange teams and agricultural producers' co-operatives. This is very necessary. If we steadily develop step by step the work-exchange teams and the co-operatives, agricultural co-operation will certainly be successful.

– As regards craftsmen and other individual workers the state protects their right to ownership of their means of production, actively guides and helps them to improve their trades, and encourages them to organize producers' co-operatives in accordance with the principle of voluntariness.

– As regards bourgeois traders and industrialists, the state does not cancel their right to ownership of their means of production and other property but actively guides their activities to keep them in line with the interests of the state and the people's welfare and the state economic plan. At the same time the state encourages and helps them to transform themselves along socialist lines through joint state–private ownership and other forms of transformation.

Under article 10 of the draft amended constitution, the state leads the economic activities according to a unified plan. It uses state organs and relies on trade unions, co-operatives and other organizations of the working people to map out and execute its economic plan.

Following the restoration of peace and the start of economic restoration, we gradually took the economy in the North along the path of planned development. We had a three-year programme for economic rehabilitation (1955–57). At present we are carrying out a three-year plan for initial economic and cultural development and paving the way for our first five-year plan. The three-year plan aims particularly at promoting the socialist transformation of the individual economy of the peasants, craftsmen and other individual working people and the private capitalist sector; at the same time it enlarges and reinforces the state economic sector and stimulates economic development along socialist lines.

3. ORGANIZATION OF THE STATE IN THE DEMOCRATIC REPUBLIC OF VIET NAM

In order to fulfil its revolutionary tasks, our state must develop the democratic rights and political activities of the entire people so as to promote their ardour and creativeness and cause all citizens of Viet Nam to take effective part in managing state affairs, endeavour to build socialism and struggle for national reunification.

Our revolutionary regime has been established for nearly fifteen years. The 1946 constitution set up the People's Parliament and People's Councils at various levels. The National Assembly is the People's Council of the entire country. There are People's Councils at the local level. The National Assembly and the People's Councils are composed of representatives elected by the people through universal suffrage. The

National Assembly decides the most important affairs of the state. The People's Councils decide the most important affairs of the localities.

During the resistance, the National Assembly and the government united and guided our people, and brought the patriotic and anti-imperialist war to glorious victory. The National Assembly adopted the law on land reform aimed at completing the anti-feudalist revolution. In the localities the People's Councils contributed to the mobilization of the people in the anti-imperialist and anti-feudalist revolution.

Since the restoration of peace, the National Assembly has adopted the three-year programme for economic rehabilitation, the three-year plan for initial economic and cultural development, the policies on economic development and transformation along the socialist lines, the laws on democratic freedoms, etc. These are most important problems relating to the national interest and the people's welfare.

Under article 4 of the draft amended constitution, all powers in the Democratic Republic of Viet Nam belong to the people. The people exercise their authority through the National Assembly and the People's Councils at various levels, which are elected by the people and responsible to the people.

Our electoral system is democratic and at the same time realizes unity among the entire people. All citizens from the age of 18 upward have the right to vote, and from the age of 21 upward have the right to stand for election. Elections will be held on the principle of universal, equal, direct and secret suffrage.

The people have the right to dismiss deputies to the National Assembly and to the People's Councils, should the latter show themselves unworthy of their trust. This principle guarantees the people's right of control over their representatives.

Article 6 of the draft amended constitution stipulates that it is the duty of all organs of the state to rely upon the people, keep close contact with them, carefully listen to their opinions and submit to their supervision.

The National Assembly is the supreme organ of state power. The People's Councils are organs of state power in the localities.

The National Assembly elects the president of the country, the Standing Committee of the National Assembly and the government Council. The government Council is the organ entrusted with enforcing the laws and decisions of the National Assembly and the highest administrative organ of the state. It is responsible to the National Assembly and reports to it on its work. In the period between two sessions of the National Assembly the government Council is responsible and reports to the National Assembly Standing Committee.

The National Assembly is the only organ having legislative power. The most important affairs of the state on a national scale are decided by the National Assembly.

The People's Councils elect the administrative committees at various levels. These are executive organs of the People's Councils. They are responsible to the People's Councils and report to them on their work. At the same time they are placed under the direct leadership of the administrative committees of higher levels and the unified leadership of the government Council.

The most important local affairs are decided by the People's Councils.

Our economic and social system aims at fully realizing the democratic rights of the people on the basis of the increasing development of the socialist economy, the gradual elimination of capitalist exploitation, and the improvement of the material and cultural standards of the people. Thus all conditions are gathered for our people to take effective part in the management of the state.

Article 4 of the draft amended constitution clearly stipulates that the principle governing the organization of our state is democratic centralism. The National Assembly, the People's Councils, the central government and other state organs all follow the principle of democratic centralism.

Our state ensures the fullest development of democracy, because it is a people's state. Only through the fullest development of democracy can all forces of the people be mobilized to take the revolution forward. At the same time the highest centralism must be ensured to lead the people in building socialism.

4. BASIC RIGHTS AND DUTIES OF THE CITIZEN

The draft amended constitution clearly stipulates the basic rights and duties of the citizens of our country. These stipulations demonstrate the genuinely democratic character of our regime.

The capitalists often boast that their constitutions guarantee the rights of the individual, democratic liberties and the interests of all citizens. But in reality, only the bourgeoisie enjoy the rights recorded in these constitutions. The working people do not really enjoy democratic freedoms; they are exploited all their life and have to bear heavy burdens in the service of the exploiting class.

The capitalists often circulate the slander that our socialist regime does not respect the personal interests of the citizen. But in reality, only our regime really serves the interests of the people, first and foremost the working people, safeguards all interests of the people and develops democracy to enable the people to take effective part in the management of the state. That is why our people devote all their energies to their duties as the masters of the country, in order to build socialism and make our country strong and our people prosperous.

The draft amended constitution clearly points out that the citizens of the Democratic Republic of Viet Nam have:

- the right to work;
- the right to rest;
- the right to study;
- the right to personal liberty;
- freedoms of opinion, of the press, of assembly, of association; the right to hold demonstrations;
- freedom of religious belief, to adhere or not to adhere to any religion;
- the right to elect and stand for election, etc.

All citizens are equal before the law. Women enjoy equal rights with men in every respect: political, economic, cultural, social and familial. The state pays particular attention to the moral, intellectual and physical education of the youth.

By virtue of the character of our state and our economic and social system, the state not only recognizes the interests of the citizens but also guarantees the necessary material conditions for them to enjoy these interests effectively.

The state guarantees democratic freedoms to the citizens but strictly prohibits any misuse of these freedoms to infringe the interests of the state and the people, as clearly stipulated in article 38 of the draft amended constitution.

In our regime the interests of the state, the collective and the individual are basically at one. Therefore, while enjoying rights brought to them by the state and the collective, all citizens must consciously fulfil their duties to the state and the collective.

The citizens have the duty to respect the constitution, the law, labour discipline, public order and the rules of social life. The citizens have the duty to respect public property, pay taxes according to the law, do military service and defend the fatherland.

Only in a socialist system are the interests of the individual, the state and the collective at one. That is why only a socialist constitution can encourage the citizens to fulfil enthusiastically their duties to the society and the fatherland.

. . .

Deputies,

Fourteen years ago our people joyfully welcomed the first constitution of our country. Today our people have again enthusiastically discussed the draft amended constitution.

In the process of these discussions, they have clearly assessed the difficulties overcome, and have found great inspiration in the successes achieved: the North of our country has been completely liberated, our people hold effective power, the socialist economy is developing at a rapid rate. Our people's material and cultural standards have been improved. Revolutionary morality among our people has been gradually elevated; solidarity among them has been strengthened day by day. The practice of democracy has been developed to a high degree; the people are really the masters of the country.

People of all walks of life in the North and in the South alike warmly welcome the draft amended constitution. Our entire people are firmly convinced that the North and the South will be united in the great family of the reunified Vietnamese fatherland.

The constitution will fill our southern brothers with enthusiasm; they will keep their minds turned towards the National Assembly and the government and will struggle even more vigorously for the reunification of the fatherland.

All our people are aware that the present draft amended constitution is due to the Party – the organizer and leader of the past glorious victories and the guarantor for future great achievements – and to the unity of our entire people and the valiant struggle waged by them for national construction along the Party line.

Since the day our committee was entrusted by the National Assembly with the task of drafting the amended constitution, we have worked uninterruptedly and held twenty-seven meetings. The draft has been completed; today our committee presents it to the National Assembly. We have worked to the best of our ability but cannot claim perfection. We hope that you will debate it and contribute further improvements and that it will be adopted by the National Assembly.

After adoption by the National Assembly, this draft constitution will become the new constitution of our country.

This constitution will further stimulate our people's patriotism and their love of socialism; it will encourage them to unite even more closely and emulate one another even more enthusiastically to build a peaceful, reunified, independent, democratic and prosperous Viet Nam.

41

THIRTY YEARS OF
ACTIVITY OF THE PARTY[1]

1960

Our party is celebrating its thirtieth anniversary. For thirty years, it has waged heroic struggles and reaped glorious successes. On the occasion of this anniversary, we would like to look back at the road travelled and to draw precious lessons in order correctly to determine the revolutionary tasks of the present stage and of the immediate future, and to win still greater, more resounding victories.

Just as the changes that have taken place in our country are inseparable from international developments, so the maturation of our party is inseparable from the growth of the fraternal parties.

The triumph of the Russian October Revolution, which destroyed part of the forces of capitalism, opened to the proletariat and the oppressed peoples all over the world the way to liberation. In 1919, under Lenin's leadership, genuine revolutionaries of all countries founded the Third International. Since then communist parties have been formed in France, China and many other countries. At the beginning, it was due to the direct help of the communist parties of China and France that Marxism-Leninism and the influence of the October Revolution penetrated the iron curtain of French colonialism and reached Viet Nam.

From 1924 on, the revolutionary movement in our country surged up; our workers waged repeated struggles, advancing from economic actions to political ones.

The union of Marxist-Leninist theory with the workers' movement and the patriotic movement led to the formation, early in 1930, of the *Indochinese Communist Party*.

This event, which marked an extremely important turning point in the history of the Vietnamese revolution, showed that our working class had matured and was capable of leading the revolutionary struggle.

Broadly speaking, our party has passed through the following stages:

- underground activity;
- leading the August Revolution to victory;
- leading the war of resistance to victory; and
- the present stage of leading the socialist revolution in the North, and the struggle for reunifying the country and completing the national democratic revolution throughout the land.

At the beginning, for almost fifteen years our party had to work underground. It faced ceaseless and savage persecution by the French colonialists. The jails of Poulo-Condor, Lao Bao and Son La were filled with communists. Many Party cadres and members died the death of the brave in the struggle. But we firmly believed in the ultimate victory of the Party and the revolution, and our ranks continued to grow and gain in strength.

Right at its inception the Party held aloft the banner of the national democratic revolution and led the national liberation movement. At that time the feudal class had capitulated to the imperialists, while the weak bourgeoisie sought to come to terms with imperialism in order to survive. Despite their fervour the petty bourgeois strata were in an ideological impasse. Alone, the *working class*, the most courageous and revolutionary class, kept up the struggle against the colonialist imperialists. Equipped with advanced revolutionary theory and the experience of the international proletarian movement, it proved to be the most able and trustworthy leader of the Vietnamese people.

Imbued with the spirit of Marxism-Leninism, the Party set forth a correct revolutionary line. As early as 1930, in its programme on the bourgeois democratic revolution, it enunciated the task of *struggling against the imperialists and feudalists* for national independence and the realization of the watchword 'Land to the tillers'. This programme fully answered the aspirations of the peasants, who made up the majority of our people. In this way our party succeeded in uniting large revolutionary forces around the working class, while the parties of the other classes either met with failure or found themselves isolated. The leading role of our party, the party of the working class, was thus ceaselessly consolidated and strengthened.

Shortly after its formation the Party organized and led a mass movement of unprecedented magnitude in our country: that for the setting up of *soviets in Nghe An and Ha Tinh provinces*. The workers and peasants in these provinces rose up and threw off the imperialist and feudal yoke, established worker–peasant–soldier rule, and proclaimed democratic liberties for the working people.

Although the movement was drowned by the imperialists in a sea of blood, it testified to the heroism and revolutionary power of the Vietnamese working masses. In spite of its failure, it forged the forces which were to ensure the triumph of the August Revolution.

When, in 1936, the menace of fascism and the threat of a world war became obvious, our party allied itself with the world anti-fascist democratic front and the Popular Front in France, and initiated a broad mass movement for the formation of a *Democratic Front against fascism and colonial reaction in Indochina*. It led mass actions claiming democratic liberties and better living conditions. This involvement embraced millions of people and awakened their political consciousness. The prestige of the Party mounted and struck deep roots among the working people.

Shortly after the outbreak of World War Two, Viet Nam was occupied by the Japanese aggressors, who sought to dominate the country in collusion with the French colonialists. The Party changed its tactics in time. The *Viet Minh* (League for the Independence of Viet Nam) and *mass organizations for national salvation* were established in 1941 with a view to rallying all patriotic forces in a single anti-fascist and anti-colonial front. The Party temporarily withdrew its slogan for agrarian revolution, and confined itself to advocating lower rents and lower interest rates, the confiscation of land belonging to the imperialists and traitors and its transfer to the peasants. In this way it sought to unite all forces in the struggle against the imperialists and their stooges, win over patriotic elements among the landowning class and extend the National Front for the Salvation of the Country.

The Party's correct policy furthered the growth of the revolutionary movement. Resistance bases were set up, and the first units of the Vietnamese Army of Liberation formed. The Party started *guerrilla warfare against the Japanese invaders*, in co-ordination with the international anti-fascist struggle.

This made it possible in the autumn of 1945, immediately after the Soviet Red Army had smashed fascism, to launch *a national uprising for the conquest of power*. The August Revolution of 1945 triumphed. The Democratic Republic of Viet Nam was born.

In 1945 our party, which had been formed from a few groups of militants and tempered in hard struggles, had only about 5,000 members, a number of whom were in prison. But it was able to unite the people and lead their uprising to victory. This was a great victory for the Vietnamese people and also the first victory won by Marxism-Leninism in a colony.

Soon after the August Revolution the French government violated the agreements it had signed with us and unleashed an aggressive war.

At that time the country was in dire straits. We had not yet recovered from the terrible famine caused by French imperialism and Japanese fascism. The enemy had considerable land, sea and air forces equipped with modern weapons. We had only small, newly formed infantry forces, poorly equipped and with little combat experience. But the Party resolutely decided to organize the resistance, simultaneously leading the patriotic struggle and fostering the people's strength. At the beginning, it carried on the policy of reducing land rents and interest rates. When the resistance became widespread, and the need was felt to increase further the forces of the people, mainly the peasantry, we resolutely mobilized the people *for land reform and the full implementation of the slogan 'Land to the tillers'*. Thanks to this correct policy, the resistance forces grew rapidly and won repeated victories.

Our people had been cruelly exploited and oppressed by the French colonialists for nearly eighty years. In the beginning of the patriotic war some units of our army were only armed with bamboo sticks. But we were tempered by nine years of resistance. Our people united into an ironlike bloc. Our regular units, regional detachments and people's militia expanded into an army of heroes, determined to fight and win.

The close unity and heroic sacrifices of our army and people led to the historic victory of Dien Bien Phu in the summer of 1954. The French colonialist troops were shattered, and had to agree to a ceasefire. The agreements signed in Geneva restored peace on the basis of the recognition of the independence, sovereignty and territorial integrity of the peoples of Indochina.

For the first time in history a small colony had defeated a big colonial power. This was a victory not only of our people but also of the world forces of peace, democracy and socialism.

Once again Marxism-Leninism lit the path for the Vietnamese working class and people, and led them to triumph in their struggle to save their country and safeguard their revolutionary gains.

Since the restoration of peace Viet Nam faces a new situation: the country is temporarily divided into two parts. Socialism is being built in the North, now completely liberated, while the imperialists and their underlings now are ruling over the South and trying to turn it into an American colony and military base with the object of rekindling the war. They are savagely repressing patriots in the South, brazenly violating the Geneva Agreements, and stubbornly preventing the convening of a consultative conference to arrange for free elections and the peaceful reunification of the country. They are the most ferocious enemies of our people.

In view of this situation, *two tasks* confront the Vietnamese revolution at present: first, the construction of socialism in the North, and, second, the completion of the national democratic revolution in the South. These tasks have a common aim: to strengthen peace and pave the way to reunification on the basis of independence, and democracy.

This is how the Fifteenth Session of the Central Committee of the Viet Nam Workers' Party defined the tasks facing our entire people:

> Consolidating national unity, vigorously struggling for the reunification of the country on the basis of independence and democracy, completing the national democratic revolution in the whole country; strengthening the North and leading it to socialism; building a peaceful, reunified, independent, democratic and prosperous state; actively contributing to the defence of peace in Indochina, in Southeast Asia and throughout the world.

North Viet Nam is bound to advance to socialism. *The outstanding feature of the transitional period in Viet Nam* is for our economically backward agrarian country to advance *direct* to socialism, bypassing the stage of capitalist development.

The French imperialists left us an economy in a bad state. Small peasant farming with very backward techniques prevailed in the countryside. There were only tiny and scattered industrial undertakings. Fifteen years of war further ruined the economy. The situation was worsened by the economic sabotage carried out by the colonialists before they withdrew from North Viet Nam.

In these conditions our cardinal task is to build the *material and technical basis of socialism*, gradually to take the North to socialism, and to provide it with modern industry and agriculture and advanced culture and science. In this process of socialist revolution we must transform the old economy and create a new one, and constructive labour is the essential task over a long period.

The period between 1955 and 1957 was one of economic rehabilitation. The main task was to restore agriculture and industry in order to heal the wounds of war, stabilize the economy and take the initial steps in improving the people's living standards.

Thanks to the efforts of our entire party and people and the warm-hearted aid accorded us by the brotherly countries, this task was completed in the main by the end of 1957. The level of industrial and agricultural output was approximately that of 1939. Impressive results were achieved in raising food crops. North Viet Nam, which in 1939 produced less than 2,500,000 tons of paddy, harvested over 4,000,000 tons in 1956.

This period also witnessed radical changes in the *relations of production*. New relations of production gradually replaced the old ones. The agrarian reform abolished the system of feudal landownership and released the productive forces in the countryside. The cherished dream of ten-odd million peasants came true: land was distributed to them. The economic monopoly of the imperialists was liquidated. Our state took control of the economic levers, built a state-run economy of a socialist character, and gave leadership to the whole national economy. Thanks to generous and disinterested aid from the socialist states, primarily the Soviet Union and China, twenty-nine old industrial enterprises were rehabilitated and fifty-five new ones built.

In many regions the peasants set up work-exchange teams, an embryonic form of socialism. A number of experimental agricultural co-operatives were formed, and about 10.7 per cent of the craftsmen joined production groups.

Private capitalist industry and trade began to switch over to state capitalism in low or medium forms: working on government orders, using raw materials provided by the state, retailing goods from state-owned wholesale trading organizations, etc.

After the completion of rehabilitation work, the Party led the people for the fulfilment of the three-year plan (1958–60). This plan aims at the socialist transformation of agriculture, handicrafts and private capitalist industry and trade, the main link being the transformation and development of agriculture, which will create conditions for the industrialization of the country. Industry and foreign trade can expand only on the basis of a prospering socialist agriculture. In the three-year plan, socialist transformation is the key problem. When completed as a result of our concentrated efforts, it will create favourable conditions for the rapid building of socialism. The Party's policy for the socialist transformation of agriculture is gradually to take the individual peasants from the work-exchange teams (an embryonic form of socialism) to agricultural co-operatives of the lower (semi-socialist) type and, eventually to co-operatives of the higher (socialist) type.

Densely populated, the North Vietnamese countryside is small in area; farming implements are antiquated, and labour productivity is low. Simply by reorganizing, and improving technique and management, we can already get a higher productivity than the individual farmers. Our peasants are aware of this. They have, besides, revolutionary traditions and great confidence in the Party, and are ready to respond to its calls. That is why they are enthusiastically joining the work-exchange teams and the agricultural co-operatives and taking the socialist path. The co-operatives now account for more than 40 per cent of the peasant households.

The consolidation of socialist relations of production will undoubtedly ensure the advance of agriculture and this, in turn, will further industrial development without which the countryside cannot get the means it needs for water conservation, fertilizers, improved farming implements, agricultural machinery and electric power.

Another task of paramount importance is the *peaceful socialist transformation of the national bourgeoisie*. In the economic field, our policy is to *redeem*, not to confiscate its means of production. In the political sphere the national bourgeoisie is accorded reasonable rights and a place in the Fatherland Front.

In the past, due to the colonial status of our country, our already small and weak national bourgeoisie was bullied by the imperialists and the feudalists and could not develop. For this reason a considerable number of its members joined the working people's anti-imperialist and anti-feudal struggle and took part in the patriotic war. This is its positive side.

However, due to its class nature the national bourgeoisie is reluctant to give up exploitation and still nurtures hopes of development along capitalist lines. But our advance to socialism rules out this possibility. The national bourgeoisie realizes that it can retain its place in the great national family only by agreeing to socialist transformation. Most of its members are aware that sincere acceptance of this transformation will allow them to participate in national reconstruction and socialist building by the side of the working people. This is the only honourable path for them.

Our achievements in the sphere of education are appreciable. Whereas over 95 per cent of our population was illiterate under French rule, illiteracy has now in the main been wiped out in North Viet Nam.

Below are a few figures on school enrolment:

	1939 Whole of Indochina	1959–60 North Viet Nam alone
Universities	582	8,518
Technical schools	438	18,100
General education schools	540,000	1,522,200

The following data relate to health work:

	1939 North and Central Viet Nam	1959 North Viet Nam alone
Hospitals	54	138
Village health centres	138	1,500
Doctors	86	292
Nurses	968	6,020
Public health personnel in the countryside		169,000

In simple terms, the aim of socialism is to free the working people from poverty, provide them with employment, make them happy and prosperous. It is the duty of the Party and the people to increase production and practise thrift, to exert every effort to produce more, faster, better and more economically. Then state plans will surely be fulfilled and the people's life will certainly be ceaselessly improved.

On the basis of the progress made, we must get ready for future long-term plans.

The above successes are due to the following factors:

1. *Our party, which has always taken a firm proletarian class stand and shown absolute loyalty to the interests of the class and the people*, has correctly applied Marxist-Leninist theory to Vietnamese conditions and worked out correct lines and policies. It has ceaselessly combated the reformist tendencies of the bourgeoisie and the political adventurism of the petty bourgeois elements in the national movement, the 'left' phraseology of the Trotskyites in the workers' movement, and the right and 'left' deviations in the Party, in both the elaboration and execution of various revolutionary strategies and tactics at each stage. Marxism-Leninism has helped us to face those trials successfully. This has enabled our party not only to win leadership of the revolution in the whole country, but also to maintain this leadership in all fields and to frustrate all attempts by the bourgeoisie to contend with us for the leading role.

2. Guided by Marxist-Leninist theory, we have realized that in a backward agrarian country such as Viet Nam the national question is at bottom the peasant question, that the national revolution is, basically, a peasant revolution carried out under the leadership of the working class, and that people's power is essentially worker–peasant power. At each stage, our party has firmly grasped and *correctly solved the peasant question and strengthened the worker–peasant alliance*. It has combated the right and 'left' deviations which underestimate the role of the peasants in the revolution, unaware that they are the main force of the revolution, the chief and most trustworthy ally of the proletariat, and the fundamental force which, together with the proletariat, will build socialism. The Party's revolutionary experience shows that in every case when its cadres took correct decisions which satisfied the deep aspirations of the peasants and conformed to the principle of alliance between the working class and the peasantry, the revolution made vigorous progress.

3. The Party has succeeded in assembling all patriotic and progressive forces in the *National United Front* and realizing national unity with a view to the anti-imperialist and anti-feudal struggle. The workers and peasants being the main force in the national union, their alliance forms the basis of the National United Front. In the formation, consolidation and development of the National United Front, the Party has always

combated both sectarianism and isolationism on the one hand and unprincipled compromise on the other. Thirty years of experience in uniting the national forces show that only by waging this twofold struggle against these tendencies can we ensure the Party's leading role in the National United Front, reinforce its worker–peasant base, and broaden its ranks.

4. Our party has matured and developed in the favourable international conditions created by the victory of the Russian Socialist October Revolution. All achievements of our party and people are inseparable from the fraternal support of the Soviet Union, People's China and the other socialist countries, the international communist and workers' movement and the national-liberation movement and the peace movement in the world. If we have been able to surmount all difficulties and lead our working class and people to the present glorious victories this is because the *Party has co-ordinated the revolutionary movement in our country with the revolutionary movement of the world working class and the oppressed peoples.*

We are sincerely grateful to the communist parties of the Soviet Union and China, which have helped us to mould ourselves into a new-type party of the working class. We shall always remember the generous support given to our party and people in their revolutionary struggle by the communist parties of the Soviet Union, China and France.

From now on, while advancing towards new successes in building socialism in North Viet Nam and fighting for the reunification of the country, our party will continue its efforts to strengthen the international solidarity of the working class, increase the might of the socialist camp headed by the Soviet Union, educate our people in the spirit of socialist internationalism, which is inseparable from genuine patriotism, and extend the contacts between the revolutionary movement in our country and the struggles waged by the working masses and the oppressed peoples of the world for peace, democracy, national independence and socialism.

In the past thirty years, tremendous changes have happened in the world. Great changes have also happened concerning our party and our people.

Thirty years ago, our people were crushed under the colonial yoke. Our party was just born, a heroic party but still young and weak. The Soviet Union, the only existing socialist country, was surrounded by imperialism on all sides.

The Chinese Communist Party and Red Army were subjected to fierce attacks by the reactionary Kuomintang. The other fraternal parties were only in their beginnings. Imperialism was ruling the roost over five-sixths of the world and was taking the road to fascism.

In short, most of mankind was then smothered in capitalist oppression.

But now the situation has changed and the world is facing much brighter perspectives.

The Soviet Union, one of the greatest powers on earth, is building communism; it is also the most solid bastion of world peace.

Socialism has become a powerful world system extending from Europe to Asia and comprising more than a billion people. There exist at present 85 communist and workers' parties with 35 million members resolutely struggling for peace, socialism and communism.

Many former colonial countries have become independent states. The national liberation movement is surging up everywhere, in Asia, Africa and Latin America. Imperialism is sinking ever more deeply in a quagmire.

The North of our country has been entirely liberated and the Democratic Republic of Viet Nam is proud to be a member of the great socialist family headed by the Soviet Union. Our party, now comprising hundreds of thousands of members, is organizing and mobilizing our people in building socialism in the North and struggling for the reunification of the country. It is in the van of the revolutionary struggle of our entire people. Raising high the standard of patriotism and socialism, it resolutely leads our people in the struggle to build a peaceful, reunified, independent, democratic and prosperous Viet Nam, thus contributing to the defence of peace in Southeast Asia and the world.

In order to fulfil this difficult but very glorious task, the Party must raise its ideological level and strengthen its organization and *ensure the growth of its ranks* in a cautious, steady and broad fashion among the masses, first and foremost the working class, with the object of strengthening its proletarian core.

All Party members should strive to *study Marxism-Leninism*, strengthen their proletarian class stand, grasp the laws of development of the Vietnamese revolution, *elevate their revolutionary morality, vigorously combat individualism, foster proletarian collectivism*, be industrious and thrifty in the work for national construction, build close contacts with the labouring masses, and struggle wholeheartedly for the interests of the revolution and the fatherland.

Socialist construction in North Viet Nam demands that our party have a good grasp of science and technology; therefore Party members should strive *to raise their cultural, scientific and technological level*.

The Party should strengthen its *leadership* in all spheres of activity.

The *Working Youth Union* should be the Party's right hand in organizing and educating the young generation in the spirit of absolute fidelity to the cause of building socialism and communism.

The *trade unions* should be a true school of state administration, economic management and cultural guidance for the working class.

The *Women's Union* should be a powerful force helping the Party to mobilize, organize and lead the women in the advance to socialism.

Under the leadership of the Party the *agricultural co-operatives* should become powerful armies grouping more than ten million peasants and fighting to increase production, raise living standards, elevate socialist consciousness and build a prosperous countryside.

It is the duty of our *People's Army* to work assiduously to raise its political and technical level, build itself up into an ever more powerful force and stand ready to defend our country and the peaceful labour of our people.

Under the banner of Marxism-Leninism, let our party, with the seething spirit of an invincible army, unite even more closely, and lead our working people boldly forward to new victories in the struggle for socialist construction in the North and for the reunification of the country.

Long live the Viet Nam Workers' Party!

Long live peaceful, reunified, independent, democratic and prosperous Viet Nam!

Long live socialism!

Long live world peace!

42

THE PATH WHICH
LED ME TO LENINISM[1]

April 1960

After World War One, I made my living in Paris, at one time as an employee at a photographer's, at another as painter of 'Chinese antiques' (turned out by a French shop). I often distributed leaflets denouncing the crimes committed by the French colonialists in Viet Nam.

At that time, I supported the October Revolution only spontaneously. I did not yet grasp all its historic importance. I loved and respected Lenin because he was a great patriot who had liberated his fellow countrymen; until then, I had read none of his books.

The reason for my joining the French Socialist Party was because those 'ladies and gentlemen' – so I called my comrades in those days – had shown their sympathy with me, with the struggle of the oppressed peoples. But I had no understanding as yet of what a party, a trade union, socialism and communism were.

Heated discussions were then taking place in the cells of the Socialist Party, about whether one should remain in the Second International, found a 'Second-and-a-half' International or join Lenin's Third International. I attended the meetings regularly, two or three times a week, and attentively listened to the speakers. At first, I did not understand everything. Why should the discussions be so heated? Whether with the Second, Second-and-a-half or Third International, the revolution could be waged. Why squabble? And what about the First International? What had become of it?

What I wanted most to know – and what was not debated in the meetings – was: which International sided with the peoples of the colonial countries?

I raised this question – the most important for me – at a meeting. Some comrades answered: it was the Third, not the Second International. One gave me to read Lenin's 'Theses on the national and colonial questions' printed in *L'Humanité*.

In those theses, there were political terms that were difficult to understand. But by reading them again and again finally I was able to grasp the essential part. What emotion, enthusiasm, enlightenment and confidence they communicated to me! I wept for joy. Sitting by myself in my room, I would shout as if I were addressing large crowds: 'Dear martyr compatriots! This is what we need, this is our path to liberation!'

Since then, I had entire confidence in Lenin, in the Third International.

Formerly, during the cell meetings, I had only listened to the discussions. I had a vague feeling that what each speaker was saying had some logic in it, and I was not able to make out who were right and who were wrong. But from then on, I also plunged into the debates and participated with fervour in the discussions. Though my French was still too weak to express all my thoughts, I hit hard at the allegations attacking Lenin and the Third International. My only argument was: 'If you do not condemn colonialism, if you do not side with the colonial peoples, what kind of revolution are you then waging?'

Not only did I take part in the meetings of my own cell, I also went to other Party cells to defend 'my' position. Here I must again say that comrades Marcel Cachin, Vaillant-Couturier, Monmousseau and many others helped me to broaden my knowledge. Eventually, at the Tours Congress, I voted with them for our joining the Third International.

At first, it was patriotism, not yet communism which led me to have confidence in Lenin, in the Third International. Step by step, during the course of the struggle, by studying Marxism-Leninism while engaging in practical activities, I gradually understood that only socialism and communism can liberate the oppressed nations and the working people throughout the world from slavery.

There is a legend, in our country as well as in China, about the magic 'Brocade Bag'. When facing great difficulties, one opens it and finds a way out. For us Vietnamese revolutionaries and people, Leninism is not only a miraculous 'Brocade Bag', a compass, but also a radiant sun illuminating our path to final victory, to socialism and communism.

43

THE CHINESE REVOLUTION AND THE VIETNAMESE REVOLUTION[1]

I July I96I

The triumph of the Russian October Revolution shook the whole world.

Marxism-Leninism began to propagate to China, one of the world's largest countries, which the imperialists contemptuously called 'the sleeping lion'.

On 1 July 1921, in a small room in the luxurious city of Shanghai, twelve revolutionaries (among whom was Comrade Mao Tse-tung) held a meeting and founded the Chinese Communist Party, which comprised 50 members (and which now has a membership of over 17 million). From then on, the destiny of China began to change.

After twenty-eight years of extremely heroic struggle under the leadership of the Communist Party headed by Comrade Mao Tse-tung, the Liberation Army wiped out over eight million US-equipped Chiang Kai-shek troops and drove the US imperialists out of China; and the People's Republic of China was established (1949).

During twelve years of national construction, the Communist Party has led the 650 million Chinese people in selfless work emulation, turning China from a backward agricultural country, impoverished and illiterate, into a powerful socialist country.

Forty years of glory – forty years of victory. Many comrades have written about the great history of the fraternal Chinese Communist Party. I shall here say only a few things.

Viet Nam and China are two *neighbouring countries* which have had close relations with each other for many centuries. Naturally, the ties between the Chinese revolution and the Vietnamese revolution are also especially close. For instance:

– The influence of the Russian October Revolution and the Marxist-Leninist theory came to Viet Nam mostly through China.

– The Viet Nam Young Revolutionary Comrades' Association (1925), the conference to unify Vietnamese communist groups into a Marxist-Leninist party (1930), the first Congress of the Indochinese Communist Party (1935), were all organized in China and enjoyed the wholehearted assistance of Chinese comrades.

– The Soviet crushing blow at the Japanese militarists in the Northeast helped China to win the war. China's victorious war of resistance created favourable conditions for the success of the Vietnamese August Revolution.

– From 1946 onward, the Chinese Communist Party had to carry on an unceasing fight against the US-supported troops of Chiang Kai-shek (as the civil war started, the 4,300,000-strong Chiang army was equipped with modern weapons supplied by the US, plus those taken from one million Japanese troops). In 1947, the Chiang clique attacked and seized Yenan. In such difficult conditions, the Communist Party and people of China continued their wholehearted support to our people's war of resistance till complete victory.

– Today, along with the Soviet Union and other brotherly countries, China gives us unreserved assistance in the building of socialism in the North, a solid foundation for the peaceful reunification of the country.

Thus, the relationship between the Chinese revolution and the Vietnamese revolution is made up of

A thousand ties of gratitude, attachment and love,

A glorious friendship that will last for ever!

As for myself, on two occasions I had the honour to work in the Chinese Communist Party.

During my stay in Canton in 1924–27, I kept a close watch on the revolutionary movement in our country while performing tasks entrusted by the Chinese Communist Party. The worker–peasant movement was surging up in China. From May 1925 onward, political strikes occurred in virtually all big cities. The biggest was the strike in protest against the British imperialists in Hong Kong, in which more than 250,000 workers participated and which lasted sixteen months. The peasant movement also began to spread, especially in Hunan (where it was led by Comrade Mao Tse-tung) and in Kwangtung (where it was led by Comrade Peng Bai). To push the peasant movement forward, Comrade Mao organized the Peasant Mobilization, Instruction and Training Office to train cadres for the peasant movement in nineteen provinces.

I took part in the translation of materials for internal use and in 'external propaganda', namely by contributing articles on the worker–peasant movement to an English-language newspaper.

The second time I came to China (late in 1938) was during the anti-Japanese war of resistance. As a private in the Eighth Route Army, I was club manager for a unit in Kwelin. Afterwards, I was elected secretary of the Party cell (and was entrusted with radio monitoring) of a unit in Hengyang.

(Thus I managed to acquire some experience in Party building when I was in the Soviet Union, some experience in the struggle against capitalism when in France, and some experience in fighting against colonialism and feudalism when in China). In the meantime, the Chinese comrades tried hard to help me get in touch with my comrades in our country. Our party's Central Committee sent Comrade X to Longzhou to look for me. Unfortunately X was robbed of his purse by a 'friend' and had to leave for home before I reached Longzhou.

Later on, however, the Chinese comrades managed to help me to communicate with home and return to the country.

In short: as they share a lofty aim, communists all over the world unite closely on the basis of Marxism-Leninism and proletarian internationalism while showing mutual sympathy and love like brothers of the same family.

I take this opportunity to convey, on behalf of our party, government and people, to the great Chinese Communist Party headed by beloved Comrade Mao Tse-tung, my most cordial and warmest congratulations.

44

ADDRESS TO THE SIXTH SESSION OF THE SECOND NATIONAL ASSEMBLY OF THE DEMOCRATIC REPUBLIC OF VIET NAM

8 May 1963

Comrade Deputies,

I am deeply moved and happy at the news I have just received that the National Assembly intends to award me the Gold Star Order, the highest decoration in our country. I wish to express my gratitude to the National Assembly.

But I should like to request the Assembly to allow me to put off accepting this decoration. The reason is that decorations are to be awarded to men of merit; for my part I don't think I deserve as yet this high award of the National Assembly.

Our fatherland is temporarily divided in two. The US imperialists are intensifying their aggressive war in South Viet Nam. Our southern compatriots are being trampled upon by the brutal US–Diem regime. Not a day passes without the US–Diemists terrorizing, mopping up and killing people, burning down villages, spraying poisonous chemicals, destroying crops, forcing people into concentration camps, those hells on earth which they call 'strategic hamlets'.

In such conditions of blood and fire, our southern compatriots are daily and hourly sacrificing their lives, struggling heroically, and resolutely opposing the aggressors and traitors, to win back freedom and the right to live.

Uniting closely around the South Viet Nam National Front for Liberation, our southern compatriots – whether they are men or women, old or young, intellectuals, peasants, workers or tradesmen, whether they are majority people or highlanders – all are of one mind, resolved to overcome all difficulties and hardships, and to fight till final victory.

While the North is engaged in emulation to build socialism so as to support our southern compatriots, the latter are heroically fighting to defend the peaceful construction in the North. That is why the northern people think of their southern compatriots every hour, every minute.

For nearly twenty long years struggling against the French colonialists then against the US–Diemists, our southern compatriots are truly heroic sons and daughters of the heroic Vietnamese people. The South fully deserves the title 'Brass Wall of the fatherland' and the highest decoration.

For those reasons, I beg the Assembly to agree to this.

We shall wait till the day the South is completely liberated, the country peacefully reunified, North and South reunited into one family – then the National Assembly will allow our southern compatriots to hand me this high decoration. Thus all our people will be happy and elated.

I take this opportunity to dare President Kennedy to answer the following questions:

– Viet Nam is thousands of miles away from the United States. The Vietnamese and American peoples have no quarrel with each other. For what reason have you launched an aggressive war in South Viet Nam and wasted billions of dollars of the American people to support a corrupt and dictatorial administration, spat upon by the South Vietnamese people? What right do you have to force tens of thousands of young Americans to come and kill innocent South Vietnamese, then to get killed in this unjust, dirty war?

– In 1954, as a member of the US Congress, you criticized President Eisenhower in these words:

> To pour money, weapons and men into the Indochinese jungle without a remote hope of victory might be a dangerous and useless thing, an act of suicide. I am frankly of the belief that no amount of American military assistance in Indochina can conquer an enemy that

> seems to be everywhere and at the same time nowhere, an enemy . . .
> which has the sympathy and covert support of the people . . .

So why has President Kennedy committed a blind act of suicide, against which Senator Kennedy had clearsightedly warned?

– The American people's just opinion, which American personalities pointed out in their letter to their president (1 March 1963) is this: American military intervention in South Viet Nam must be ended, and an international conference must be convened to work out a peaceful solution. Will President Kennedy act upon this just opinion of the American people or will he not?

President Kennedy should know history. History has proved that when a people are of one mind and united in the struggle for independence and freedom (as his own forefathers were in the past and the South Vietnamese people are at present), they are bound to win victory. Therefore it is certain that:

Our southern compatriots will win;

North and South will be reunited in one family; and our beloved fatherland will be peacefully reunified.

Once again, I express my thanks to the National Assembly.

45

APPEAL TO COMPATRIOTS AND FIGHTERS THROUGHOUT THE COUNTRY

17 July 1966

The barbarous US imperialists have unleashed a war of aggression in an attempt to conquer our country, but they are sustaining heavy defeats.

They have rushed an expeditionary force of nearly 300,000 men into the South of our country. They have fostered a puppet administration and puppet troops as instruments of their aggressive policy. They have resorted to extremely savage means of warfare – toxic chemicals, napalm bombs, etc. – and applied a 'burn all, kill all and destroy all' policy. By committing such crimes, they hope to subdue our southern compatriots.

But under the resolute and skilful leadership of the National Front for Liberation, the South Vietnamese armed forces and people, closely united and fighting heroically, have scored splendid victories, and are determined to fight on until complete victory in order to liberate the South, defend the North, and proceed towards national reunification.

The US aggressors have cynically launched air attacks on the North of our country in the hope of getting out of their disastrous situation in the South and compelling us to 'negotiate' on their terms.

However, North Viet Nam has not flinched in the least. Our army and people have eagerly emulated one another in production and fighting. So far, we have downed over 1,200 enemy aircraft. We are determined to frustrate the enemy's war of destruction and at the same time extend all-out support to our kinsfolk in the South.

Of late, the frenzied US aggressors have taken a very serious step in their escalation by starting air strikes on the suburbs of Hanoi and

Haiphong. That is a desperate act, the death throes of a mortally wounded wild beast.

Johnson and his clique should realize this: they may bring in half a million, a million or even more troops to step up their war of aggression in South Viet Nam. They may use thousands of aircraft for intensified attacks against North Viet Nam. But never will they be able to break the iron will of the heroic Vietnamese people, their determination to fight against American aggression, for national salvation. The more truculent they grow, the more serious their crimes. The war may last five, ten, twenty or more years; Hanoi, Haiphong and other cities and enterprises may be destroyed; but the Vietnamese people will not be intimidated! *Nothing is more precious than independence and freedom.* Once victory is won, our people will rebuild their country and make it even more prosperous and beautiful.

It is common knowledge that each time they are about to step up their criminal war, the US aggressors will resort to their 'peace talks' humbug in an attempt to fool world opinion and lay the blame on Viet Nam for unwillingness to engage in 'peace negotiations'.

President Johnson, answer these questions publicly, before the American people and the peoples of the world: Who has sabotaged the Geneva Agreements which guarantee the sovereignty, independence, unity and territorial integrity of Viet Nam? Have Vietnamese troops invaded the United States and massacred Americans? Or isn't it the US government which, on the contrary, has sent US troops to invade Viet Nam and massacre the Vietnamese people?

Let the United States end its war of aggression in Viet Nam, withdraw all American and satellite troops from this country, and peace will be restored immediately. The stand taken by Viet Nam is clear: it is the four points of the government of the Democratic Republic of Viet Nam and the five points of the South Viet Nam National Front for Liberation.[1] There is no other alternative.

The Vietnamese people cherish peace, genuine peace, peace in independence and freedom, not sham peace, not 'American peace'.

To safeguard the independence of our fatherland, to fulfil our duties to all peoples struggling against US imperialism, our people and army, united as one man and fearless of sacrifices and hardships, will resolutely fight on until they gain complete victory. In the past we defeated the Japanese fascists and the French colonialists in much more difficult circumstances. Now that conditions at home and abroad are more favourable, our people's struggle against US aggression, for national salvation, will all the more certainly end in complete victory.

Dear compatriots and fighters,

Our cause is just; our people are united from North to South; we have a tradition of undaunted struggle and the great sympathy and support of the fraternal socialist countries and progressive people all over world. We shall win!

At this new juncture, we are one in our determination to go through all hardships and sacrifices to accomplish the glorious historic task of our people: to defeat the US aggressors.

On behalf of the Vietnamese people, I take this opportunity to express heartfelt thanks to the peoples of the socialist countries and progressive people in the world, including the American people, for their whole-hearted support and assistance. In face of the US imperialists' new criminal scheme I am firmly confident that the peoples and governments of the fraternal socialist countries and of peace- and justice-loving countries in the world will support and help the Vietnamese people still more vigorously until they win complete victory in their struggle against US aggression, for national salvation.

The Vietnamese people will surely win!

The US aggressors will surely be defeated!

Long live a peaceful, reunified, independent, democratic and prosperous Viet Nam!

Compatriots and fighters throughout the country, march valiantly forward!

46

TALK TO DISTRICT CADRES ATTENDING A TRAINING CLASS

18 January 1967

Dear Comrades,

I am very glad today, for seldom have I had an occasion to meet such a large number of district cadres.

How many people are attending this course?

(*'Uncle, we are 288 in all, and 131 of us are working at district level.'*)

And how many women?

(*'Sixteen, Uncle.'*)

The women are too few and this is a shortcoming. The comrades in charge of this course have not paid enough attention to the training of women cadres. This is also a common shortcoming in our party. Many still underestimate the women's abilities, because of their prejudices and narrow-mindedness. This is utterly wrong. At present, many women are holding responsible posts at basic level. Many are doing a very good job. There are women managers of large farming co-ops who are not only zealous but also efficient. Women co-op members generally have many good qualities: they are less liable to commit embezzlement and waste, indulge in revelry and display domineering behaviour than some of their male counterparts. Am I right? If what I say is not true, please correct me.

(*'You're right, Uncle.'*)

I hope that you will seriously correct your biased and narrow-minded attitude towards women. And the women, especially you who work at district level, must fight hard against this attitude. For if you don't fight, the men who hold prejudices against women will not readily mend their ways.

This course is designed to help you understand better the Party lines in our anti-US resistance for national salvation, in the building of socialism in the North, the people's war, the course of agricultural development, Party work and work among the masses in the present situation, so that when you are back home you can do better in fighting and productive work, in organizing the people's life, and in building organizations at basic level, thus turning your district committees into 'four-good' ones.

The aims and contents of this course are very practical in the present situation. Members of the Party Central Committee have given you lectures. Did you understand? Did you really grasp what they said?

(*'Yes, we did.'*)

Speaking of study, I should like to tell you a favourite story of mine.

During the anti-French resistance, I once met several comrades who were having a rest in the shade of a large banian. I asked them, 'Where have you been?' – 'We are back from a political class,' they answered. 'What did you study?' – 'We studied Karl Marx.' – 'Was it interesting?' – 'Very interesting!' – 'Did you understand?' – Now they answered falteringly, 'Uncle, there were so many difficult points we could not understand.'

Such studies were not practical.

Let me tell you another story. Before the August Revolution, a house of culture was set up in the Tan Trao liberated area. One day, two cadres, one man and one woman, came and gave lectures. They spoke with great enthusiasm. I was there. I turned to my neighbour and asked him whether he understood anything of what was being said. He shook his head, saying he did not understand a whit. This was easy to explain. The cadres were talking about too many things and using too many scholarly words. The general educational level was quite low then, so people could not understand such words as 'subjective', 'objective', 'positive', 'negative', etc.

Those stories are for your entertainment and also to remind you that now we must learn things that are practical and will help you to do your work better. And when you go back home and organize training courses for Party members and cadres in the villages, you should try to do it in the same spirit.

Now your course is drawing to an end. I want to give you a few recommendations:

1. You must firmly grasp the Party's lines and policies and keep close contact with the base and the co-ops so as to be well informed of the state of affairs in production, the people's life, Party cells and mass organizations. This will allow you to take correct and timely steps.

This point you probably know already. But I want to stress the necessity to keep in close touch with the basic level, to live among the masses in order to lead them. You should not get into touch with the base the way dragonflies skim over the water. This seems quite easy, but it is still not being done well. At present, a number of district committee members have not really been in close touch with the grassroots; they flinch from difficulties and hardships and don't know the real state of affairs in the area in their charge.

At present, each district committee is made up of 15 to 20 members. You must divide the job among yourselves, each watching one commune or two. You must be fully informed not only about the co-ops, but also about the individual families, their living conditions, housing, education and health problems, etc. If you fail to do so, how can you correctly apply the Party's lines and policies and the provincial directives to your districts?

2. You must devote your energies to building the co-ops, Party cells, youth and women's organizations into truly good ones.

The cells are the basic units of the Party. If they are good, everything will go well. Therefore you must strive to build the cells into 'four-good' ones. You must get practical results, avoid formalism and abstain from sending misleading reports to higher authorities.

To build a good cell, Party members must first of all set good examples in carrying out Party policies; they must truly *respect the people's right to be the collective master* and listen to the masses. Only then will the people trust, respect and love them. And if they do, any difficulties can be overcome.

Members of the Working Youth Union and young volunteers' brigades should act as an arm to the Party cell, taking the lead in productive work and fighting. *The co-op management committees should practise democracy and oppose embezzlement and waste.* Embezzlement is still prevalent in some co-ops. Who are responsible for this state of affairs? Should the district committee be held responsible? Are any district cadres guilty of corruption and commandism? You must check up and conduct severe control.

3. Party members and cadres must unite closely, practise democracy and observe discipline within the Party. All Party members, whether of long standing or newly admitted, old and young, men and women, must love and help each other so as to advance together.

At present, there are both veterans and young cadres in the Party. The veterans are a valuable asset to the Party; they have gained experience in leadership and have been tempered and tested in actual struggle. But there are some veteran cadres who stop at a certain point and cannot make any further progress. They cling to the old and are not sensible of the new. On the other hand, the young cadres, though they haven't yet acquired some of the qualities of the old cadres, are zealous, aware of the new and eager to learn. As a result, they can make rapid progress.

Our party should closely associate veteran and young cadres.

Young cadres should not be looked down upon. Some veteran cadres are puffed-up and have too high an opinion of their past records. They are haughty towards young cadres and Party members, and often ignore their suggestions, reproaching them for trying to 'teach Grandma to suck eggs'. Ours is a seething epoch. Society and the world are making great strides. So it is wrong for veterans to look down their noses at young cadres. On the other hand, the young cadres must not be pretentious; they must humbly learn from their older and more experienced comrades.

All cadres and members of the Party must zealously work for the Party and the people. They must painstakingly study politics, economics, science and technique so as to improve their abilities and help develop the economy, win victories in fighting and better the people's life.

When I speak of studying science and technique, some people think that these goals are too remote. But viewed from a popular and simple angle, they are by no means out of reach. For example, how to grow azolla for green manure, or to ferment compost is a problem of science and technique. That's what science and technique are about. You should study them if you are to provide guidance to production work and raise the yields of the crops.

4. You must rely on the masses to promote all movements, either in production or fighting. You must inspire the masses with enthusiasm and confidence.

In everything you must get the participation of the masses. Nothing can be done without the masses. Recently the *Nhan Dan* newspaper carried a story about air defence. Some village officials were discussing the question of air raid defence. This meant digging trenches and building air raid shelters, which would necessitate tens of thousands of bricks, thousands of bamboos and hundreds of dong. The costs were quite great. How to meet them? A young woman engineer suggested that the issue be put before the masses. People were invited to a meeting and were told about the wanton bombing by enemy aircraft and the need for air raid shelters. They were quite co-operative: some offered wooden planks, others bricks or bamboos, etc. The shelters were completed within two days. In Quang Binh and Vinh Linh, it is thanks to the mass line that thousands of kilometres of trenches and tens of thousands of shelters have been dug. It follows that with the participation of the masses, the most difficult tasks become easier and can be successfully undertaken. The comrades in Quang Binh have aptly put it this way:

> *Even an easy task cannot be done without the people,*
> *While the most difficult ones can be fulfilled with their help.*

In Thai Binh, Quang Binh and some other places, a campaign is being conducted on 'reporting and rating one's services'. Thanks to this campaign, everyone knows what is being well done, not done or poorly done. This is real democracy, a very good form of criticism and self-criticism. By so doing, the masses educate themselves and also help educate the cadres, for while there are good cadres who work hard and match their words with deeds, there are others who only like to give orders. So the campaign is also a good way of selecting people, educating them, bringing them into the Party and making cadres of them. In this way we shall never lack cadres. This is a very good way of building the Party.

Do you think this a good way to act?

(*'Yes, we do, Uncle.'*)

Can you do it?

(*'Yes, we can, Uncle.'*)

But some comrades have not acted this way. In some places, the people have not spoken, or have not dared to speak, their mind, fearing 'reprisals' or 'labels' stuck on them by the cadres. Cadres who have committed mistakes often fear that the people will speak out. But if they are sincere in admitting their mistakes and apologize to the people, the latter will be pleased and will forgive them. Our people are very kind, they love the Party and love the cadres. If we frankly admit our mistakes, the people far from showing dislike or contempt, will feel even greater love, respect and confidence in us.

5. The winter–spring production drive is an urgent and immediate task. Cultivation must be done in time. Buffaloes and oxen must be well looked after. They must be well fed and given good shelter; they should not be left out in the cold. People should be urged to practise economy. Don't indulge in revelry. Illicit distillation of rice wine, slaughter of pigs and oxen and wasteful feasts are forbidden. District officials must go to the villages to have a look and check up everything. They must not indulge in a bureaucratic style of work and be content with forwarding provincial circulars to the villages. Circulars cannot protect buffaloes and oxen from the cold. And if buffaloes and oxen grow thin and weak from hunger and cold, production will be very badly affected.

Buffaloes and oxen should be well tended with a view to production work, not feasts and revelry! The New Year is drawing near, so economy should be emphasized. The central administration often reminds every-one that we must strive to promote production and practise economy. This has been correctly carried out in many places. But in others, the letters in the circulars seem to have blurred and *'tiet kiem'* (thrift, economy) has somehow been read as meaning *'tiet canh'* (a dish)!

I can give you ample evidence of this. Let me read this passage from the *Hai Phong* newspaper:

> As the cadres fail to set good examples, illegal slaughter of pigs still often occurs in My Phuc commune. Two pigs were killed to inaugurate the pumping station. Four pigs were killed to greet the annual assembly of the co-op. Then the collective feast of a produc-tion team entailed the slaughter of one more.

And so on, and so forth.

Listen to this: Doan Ket and Ngo Quyen communes in Thanh Mien district have illegally killed many pigs and buffaloes for their feasts.

Cadres and Party members who did those things were setting bad examples.

This has happened because of the lack of democracy. The Party's rank and file dare not speak out, the people dare not speak out. How can the co-op members not feel irritated? How can the co-op progress in such conditions? While the people work day and night, a few seize upon the least occasion to eat and drink, and, believe me, they don't do things by halves.

The above are a few bad examples, but we have also many good examples.

D. commune in Thai Nguyen has a large population but only little land. There are many difficulties in farm production. For over a year now, US planes have repeatedly attacked various hamlets in the commune. But the people have courageously carried on their work, reorganized their life to meet wartime conditions, stepped up production to serve the anti-US resistance for national salvation and socialist construction. The 1965 autumn crop was not good, and the co-op members' income decreased. But the people encouraged each other to carry on production and achieved self-sufficiency in food. They didn't have to ask for help from the state. The villagers overcame all difficulties and for the last summer rice crop they achieved the highest-ever acreage under cultivation, average yield and total output. Vegetables and subsidiary crops increased by half or twofold. Every household has a patch of kitchen garden. The co-op management controls the crops to help needy families in pre-harvest periods. People no longer indulge in wasteful revelry on the occasion of weddings or religious ceremonies. They carefully calculate the food ration in every family and consume subsidiary cereals so as to economize rice and have enough food supplies for the whole season.

Thanks to the practice of economy and the judicious expansion of production, the D. people not only have enough food for the whole village but have also delivered more than their quota of grain to the state, while other villages have had to ask for relief from the state in the period between two crops.

So although that commune has suffered from both natural calamities and enemy destruction, its people have managed not only to be self-sufficient in food but also to discharge their duty to the state.

The 1966 autumn crop at D. was marked by repeated attacks by enemy planes in addition to serious drought and ravages by insects. Yet the D. people recorded an unprecedented success. The average rice yield rose by 400–700 kilograms per hectare in comparison with the previous years. Good rice, carefully selected and winnowed and dried, was immediately sent to the state stores. After calculating the food rations for the co-op members, five hundred kilograms more of rice were sold to the state at the incentive price. Old people in Minh Hoa and Thong

Nhat co-ops sold to the state all the rice they got from the extra land they had reclaimed. Everyone acts upon the slogan: 'To economize a grain of rice is to supply our soldiers with an extra bullet to fire at the US aggressors.'

As a result of ten air raids by enemy planes, great damage was caused to the people's property. But, thanks to good organization of civil air defence, no one was killed or wounded in the whole village. People said: 'So long as we live, we can create wealth.' They shared with each other food, clothes, pots and pans, etc., and not a dong of relief was asked from the state.

Over the past two years, D. commune has taken the lead in depositing savings in Thai Nguyen. In 1965, the average savings deposited by each villager were 13.2 dong. In 1966, by late November, the total was already 42,000 dong, not including the sums earmarked for production. The per capita average was then 31 dong. Almost all Party committee members, Party members and cadres set good examples in depositing money in their savings accounts. Many of them after selling their pigs or poultry only retained a small sum for their daily expenditures and deposited the rest in the credit fund of the village. The village schoolmasters also deposited close to 1,000 dong in the credit fund, thus contributing some more capital to farm production in the village. Many other villagers, like Mrs Le Thi Thu, have saved up to 2,000 dong each.

Thanks to those savings, the farm co-ops have had more capital for expanding production and improving the living conditions of their members. This year, the village credit co-op has granted loans totalling 2,000 dong to the farm co-ops for the purchase of production means such as husking machines and 120 piglets for breeding; it has also helped victims of air raids.

This commune is an example of good work in air defence, farm production, economy, solidarity and mutual assistance among members. Other communes should imitate it.

We should learn from good examples and avoid following bad ones.

6. We must be active in air defence and dig more trenches and shelters. Help should be given to evacuees, especially old folk and children, to victims of air raids, to families of disabled armymen, war martyrs and soldiers at the front.

Finally, I ask you to convey my greetings and those of the Central Committee and the government to our countrymen, cadres, soldiers, militiamen, young people and children. I hope you will work hard and turn your districts into 'four-good' ones.

Tet is drawing near. This is a Tet of resistance for national salvation. It must be a joyful but economical festival. Do you all promise that this will be so?

(All present answered: '*Yes, we do, Uncle.*')

47

ELEVATE REVOLUTIONARY ETHICS, MAKE A CLEAN SWEEP OF INDIVIDUALISM[1]

3 February 1969

Our people usually say: The Party members go in front, the people follow behind. This is a sincere praise for Party members and cadres.

After thirty-nine years of glorious struggle, having brought the August Revolution to triumph and the first war of resistance to victory, and at present fighting against the US aggressors to save the country while building socialism in the North, our people are confident that our party's leadership is very clearsighted and has led our nation continually from victory to victory. In the Party's history of struggle and in its daily activities, especially on the fighting and production fronts, numerous cadres and Party members have displayed great valour and exemplary conduct. They are always the first to face hardships and the last to claim rewards, and have been credited with great achievements.

Our party has brought up a revolutionary young generation of boys and girls full of zeal and courage in fulfilling every task.

Those are beautiful flowers of revolutionary heroism. Our people and our party are very proud of such meritorious sons and daughters.

However, besides those good comrades, there are still a few cadres and Party members whose morality and quality are still low.

They are burdened with *individualism* and always think of their own interests first. Their motto is not 'each for all' but 'all for me'.

Because of their individualism, they flinch from hardships and diffi- culties and sink into corruption, depravation, waste and luxury. They crave for fame and profits, position and power. They are proud and conceited, look down on the collective, hold the masses in contempt, act arbitrarily and tyrannically. They are cut off from the masses and from realities, and are affected by bureaucratism and commandism. They make no efforts to improve themselves and don't seek to improve their ability through study.

Because of their *individualism*, too, they provoke disunity, and lack a sense of organization, discipline and responsibility. They do not carry out correctly the line and policies of the Party and the state, and harm the interests of the revolution and the people.

In short, *individualism* is the source of many wrongdoings.

In order to turn all our cadres and Party members into meritorious revolutionary fighters, our party should strive to imbue them with the ideals of communism, the Party's line and policies, the tasks and morals of Party members. Criticism and self-criticism should be seriously practised in the Party. Frank criticism of cadres and Party members by the people should be welcomed and encouraged. The life of the Party cell should follow the rules. Party discipline should be just and strict. Party control should be rigorous.

Every cadre and Party member should place the interests of the revolution, the Party and the people above everything. They must resolutely make a clean sweep of *individualism*, elevate *revolutionary* morals, foster the collective spirit, and the sense of solidarity, organization and discipline. They must keep in constant touch with realities and in close contact with the masses. They must truly respect and develop the collective sovereignty of the people. They must study and train hard, and seek to improve their knowledge so as to fulfil their tasks well.

The above is a practical way to observe the anniversary of the founding of our party, the great Party of our heroic working class and people. It is also a necessary thing to do in order to help all cadres and Party members advance and make greater contributions to the complete victory of the resistance against US aggression, for national salvation, and the successful building of socialism.

48

APPEAL ON THE OCCASION
OF 20 JULY 1969

Dear fighters and compatriots throughout the country!

Fifteen years ago, after the glorious victory of Dien Bien Phu, the Geneva Agreements on Viet Nam recognized our people's fundamental rights – independence, sovereignty, unity and territorial integrity. These agreements provided for the holding of free general elections in July 1956 to reunify the whole of Viet Nam.

But the US imperialists have impudently sabotaged the Geneva Agreements, carried out aggression against our country, and unleashed the most atrocious colonial war in human history.

Throughout the past fifteen years, our armed forces and people in the whole country, united as one man, braving all sacrifices and hardships, have fought with sublime heroism against US aggression to save the country. The US imperialists' aggressive plans have gone bankrupt one after another, they have suffered heavier and heavier setbacks; our people have gone from success to success, and are sure to win total victory.

The armed forces and people in the North have defeated the US aggressors' war of destruction.

The armed forces and people in the South are defeating the US 'limited war'.

Since the spring of the year Mau Than, the situation has radically changed in our favour, to the disadvantage of the enemy. Four-fifths of South Viet Nam's territory with three-quarters of its population have been liberated. In these conditions of victory, the South Viet Nam Congress of People's Representatives met and unanimously elected the Provisional Revolutionary government of the Republic of South Viet Nam and the Advisory Council. This government has been promptly recognized by over twenty fraternal and friendly countries, and warmly hailed by the people of the world.

Betraying the American people's interests, President Nixon has continued to step up the war of aggression in the southern part of our country, intensified attacks by B52s and toxic chemicals, launched frenzied air bombings to destroy our villages and cities and massacre our compatriots, perpetrating new crimes of utmost barbarity.

Nixon is carrying out a scheme for 'de-Americanization' of the war in an attempt to use puppet troops to fight the South Vietnamese people.

At the Paris Conference, the US imperialists have stubbornly put forward extremely absurd demands, and refused to discuss seriously the reasonable and logical ten-point overall solution advocated by the National Front for Liberation and the Provisional Revolutionary government of the Republic of South Viet Nam.

Nixon plans to withdraw 25,000 US troops in an attempt to appease American and world public opinion. This is a trick.

The Vietnamese people firmly demand the withdrawal of all US and satellite troops; not the withdrawal of 25,000 or 250,000 or 500,000 men, but a total, complete, unconditional withdrawal. Only in this way will it be possible to retrieve the honour of the United States, and to avoid a useless death in South Viet Nam for hundreds of thousands of young Americans, and suffering and mourning for hundreds of thousands of American families.

After the total withdrawal of the US and satellite troops and the complete liberation of South Viet Nam from foreign invasion, the Provisional Coalition government, as provided for in the ten-point overall solution, will organize free and democratic general elections to enable the South Vietnamese people to determine themselves their own political regime, elect a Constituent Assembly, work out a constitution, and set up the official Coalition government of South Viet Nam without any foreign country being allowed to interfere. So long as US troops and the puppet administration remain in existence in South Viet Nam, really free and democratic general elections will be absolutely impossible.

The defeat of the US imperialists is already evident, yet they have not given up their evil design of clinging to the southern part of our country. Our armed forces and people throughout the country, millions as one man, upholding revolutionary heroism and fearless of sacrifices and hardships, are determined to carry on and step up the war of resistance, with the firm resolve to fight and win, till the complete withdrawal of US troops and the total collapse of the puppet army and administration, in order to liberate the South, defend the North and ultimately achieve peaceful reunification of the country.

I take this opportunity to express, on behalf of the Vietnamese armed forces and people, our sincere thanks for the great support and assistance we have received from the world. I am confident that the fraternal socialist countries, all the peace- and justice-loving governments and peoples, including progressive people in the United States, will extend increased support and assistance to the Vietnamese people's struggle against US aggression, for national salvation, till total victory is gained.

Fighters and compatriots in the whole country, march forward resolutely!

The US imperialist aggressors are doomed to defeat!

The Vietnamese people are sure to win total victory!

49

TESTAMENT

10 May 1969

Even though our people's struggle against US aggression, for national salvation, may have to go through more hardships and sacrifices, we are bound to win total victory.

This is a certainty.

I intend, when that comes, to tour both South and North to congratulate our heroic fellow countrymen, cadres and combatants, and visit old people and our beloved youth and children.

Then, on behalf of our people, I will go to the fraternal countries of the socialist camp and friendly countries in the whole world and thank them for their wholehearted support and assistance to our people's patriotic struggle against US aggression.

Tu Fu, the famous poet of the Tang period in China, wrote: 'In all times, few are those who reach the age of seventy.'

This year, being seventy-nine, I can already count myself among those 'few'; still, my mind has remained perfectly lucid, though my health has somewhat declined in comparison with the last few years. When one has seen more than seventy springs, health deteriorates with one's growing age. This is no wonder.

But who can say how much longer I shall be able to serve the revolution, the fatherland and the people?

I therefore leave these few lines in anticipation of the day when I shall go and join Karl Marx, Lenin and other revolutionary elders; this way, our people throughout the country, our comrades in the Party, and our friends in the world will not be taken by surprise.

First about the Party: Thanks to its close unity and total dedication to the working class, the people and the fatherland, our party has been able, since its founding, to unite, organize and lead our people from success to success in a resolute struggle.

Unity is an extremely precious tradition of our party and people. All comrades, from the Central Committee down to the cell, must preserve the unity and oneness of mind in the Party like the apple of their eye.

Within the Party, to establish broad democracy and to practise *self-criticism and criticism* regularly and seriously is the best way to consolidate and develop solidarity and unity. Comradely affection should prevail.

Ours is a party in power. Each Party member, each cadre, must be deeply imbued with *revolutionary morality*, and show industry, thrift, integrity, uprightness, total dedication to the public interest and complete selflessness. Our party should preserve absolute purity and prove worthy of its role as the leader and very loyal servant of the people.

The Working Youth Union members and our young people in general are good; they are always ready to come forward, fearless of difficulties, and eager for progress. The Party must foster their *revolutionary virtues* and train them to be our successors, both 'red' and 'expert', in the building of socialism.

The training and education of future revolutionary generations is of great importance and necessity.

Our labouring people, in the plains as in the mountains, have for generation after generation endured hardships, feudal and colonial oppression and exploitation; they have in addition experienced many years of war.

Yet our people have shown great heroism, courage, enthusiasm and industriousness. They have always followed the Party since it came into being, with unqualified loyalty.

The Party must work out effective plans for economic and cultural development so as constantly to *improve the life of our people*.

The war of resistance against US aggression may drag on. Our people may have to face new sacrifices of life and property. Whatever happens, we must keep firm our resolve to fight the US aggressors till total victory.

> *Our mountains will always be, our rivers will always be, our people will always be;*
>
> *The American invaders defeated, we will rebuild our land ten times more beautiful.*

No matter what difficulties and hardships lie ahead, our people are sure of total victory. The US imperialists will certainly have to quit. Our fatherland will certainly be reunified. Our fellow countrymen in the South and in the North will certainly be reunited under the same roof. We, a small nation, will have earned the signal honour of defeating, through heroic struggle, two big imperialisms – the French and the American – and of making a worthy contribution to the world national liberation movement.

About the world communist movement: Being a man who has devoted his whole life to the revolution, the more proud I am of the growth of the international communist and workers' movement, the more pained I am by the current discord among the fraternal parties.

I hope that our party will do its best to contribute effectively to the restoration of unity among the fraternal parties on the basis of Marxism-Leninism and proletarian internationalism, in a way which conforms to both reason and sentiment.

I am firmly confident that the fraternal parties and countries will have to unite again.

About personal matters: All my life, I have served the fatherland, the revolution and the people with all my heart and strength. If I should now depart from this world, I would have nothing to regret, except not being able to serve longer and more.

When I am gone, a grand funeral should be avoided in order not to waste the people's time and money.

Finally, to the whole people, the whole Party, the whole army, to my nephews and nieces, the youth and children, I leave my boundless love.

I also convey my cordial greetings to our comrades and friends, and to the youth and children throughout the world.

My ultimate wish is that our entire party and people, closely joining their efforts, will build a peaceful, reunified, independent, democratic and prosperous Viet Nam, and make a worthy contribution to the world revolution.

NOTES

INTRODUCTION

1. Pierre Brocheux, *Ho Chi Minh: A Biography*, Cambridge: Cambridge University Press, 2007, p. 144.
2. Sophie Quinn-Judge, *Ho Chi Minh: The Missing Years*, Berkeley: University of California Press, 2002, p. 256.
3. Quoted in Jean Lacouture, *Ho Chi Minh: A Political Biography*, New York: Vintage, 1968, p. 44.
4. 'Lynching: a Little Known Aspect of American Civilisation', *La Correspondence Internationale,* No. 59, 1924, in Jack Woddis (ed.), *Ho Chi Minh: Selected Articles and Speeches, 1920–67*, London: Lawrence and Wishart, 1969, pp. 20–21.
5. Pietro Masina, *Vietnam's Development Strategies*, London: Routledge, 2006, p. 18.
6. Bernard Fall (ed.), *Ho Chi Minh on Revolution: Selected Writings, 1920–66*, New York: Praeger, 1967, p. vi.
7. 'Preliminary Draft of Some Theses on the National and Colonial Question', in Helmut Gruber (ed.), *Soviet Russia Masters the Comintern*, New York: Doubleday, 1974, p. 279.
8. Ibid.
9. Ibid., p. 282.
10. Nugyen Ai Quoc, 'The Struggle against Capitalism Lies in the Colonies', in Gruber, p. 309.
11. 'During the period when the Nghe-An Soviets were being organized, Ho's attitude was somewhat ambiguous. While he most certainly did not approve of the action taken he took no steps to stop it. During a Thought Reform course in 1953, it was disclosed that Ho had voted

against the resolution calling for a peasant rising, but he was in a minority of one and submitted to the will of the majority. Whatever the truth there is no doubt that this was the first occasion on which Ho lost control of the movement under his charge.' Hoang Van Chi, cited in John McAlister, Jr, *Vietnam: the Origins of Revolution*, New York: Alfred Knopf, 1969, p. 94.

12. Ibid., p. 99.

13. Lacouture, pp. 100–01.

14. Louis Althusser, *For Marx*, London: Penguin, 1969, pp. 87–128. Analyzing the Russian Revolution as an 'overdetermined contradiction', Althusser writes: 'Russia was overdue with its bourgeois revolution on the eve of its proletarian revolution; pregnant with two revolutions, it could not with-hold the second even by delaying the first. This exceptional situation was "insoluble" (for the ruling classes) and Lenin was correct to see in it the objective conditions of a Russian revolution, and to forge its subjective conditions, the means of a decisive assault on this weak link in the imperialist chain, in a Communist Party that was a chain without weak links.'

15. Lacouture, pp. 100–01.

16. Quoted in Brocheux, p. 116.

17. Lacouture, p. 219.

18. See 'The Chinese Revolution and the Vietnamese Revolution', pp. 262–5 of this volume. Ho's connections with the Chinese Revolution included a stint as a private in Mao's Eighth Route Army.

19. Government directive cited in Brocheux, p. 153.

20. Brocheux, p. 145.

21. Ibid., pp. 158–9.

22. Bui Tin, *Following Ho Chi Minh*, London: Hurst and Company, 1995, p. 29.

23. Quoted in Robert O'Neill, *General Giap: Politician and Strategist*, New York: Praeger, 1969, pp. 166-7.

24. Bui Tin, p. 28.

25. Lacouture, p. 210.

26. Quinn-Judge, pp. 74–6.

27. Mark Moyar, *Triumph Forsaken: the Vietnam War, 1954–1965*, Cambridge: Cambridge University Press, 2006, p. 18.

28. Brocheux, p. 145; Bui Tin, pp. 28–9.

29. Quinn-Judge, p. 256.

30. 'Speech Inaugurating the First Theoretical Course of Nguyen Ai Quoc School', in Woddis (ed.), pp. 111–12.

I. SPEECH AT THE TOURS CONGRESS

1. Excerpt from the shorthand transcript of the National Congress of the French Socialist Party held in Tours (France) from 25 to 30 December 1920. The Congress saw the splitting of the French Socialist Party: the majority aligned themselves with the Third International (French Communist Party) and the remainder with the Second International (French Socialist Party). At this Congress, Nguyen Ai Quoc favoured the founding of the French Communist Party, the 'only party struggling resolutely for the liberation of the colonial peoples.' Thus, Nguyen Ai Quoc participated in the founding of the French Communist Party. He was also the first Vietnamese Communist. [Nguyen Ai Quoc, later President Ho Chi Minh]

2. INDOCHINA

1. Extract from an article by Nguyen Ai Quoc, published in the USSR review *The Communist*, No. 14–1921.

3. THE ANTI-FRENCH RESISTANCE

1. Excerpt from an article written by Nguyen Ai Quoc in the years 1921–26.

4. SOME CONSIDERATIONS ON THE COLONIAL QUESTION

1. First published in *L'Humanité*, 25 May 1922. Reprinted in *Selected Works of Ho Chi Minh*, Hanoi: Foreign Languages Publishing House, 1960–62, Vol. 1.

5. ANNAMESE WOMEN AND FRENCH DOMINATION

1. First published in *La Paria*, 1 August 1922. Reprinted in *Selected Works of Ho Chi Minh*, Vol. 1.

6. AN OPEN LETTER TO M. ALBERT SARRAUT, MINISTER OF COLONIES

1. First published in *La Paria*, 1 August 1922. Reprinted in *Selected Works of Ho Chi Minh*, Vol. 1.

7. MURDEROUS CIVILIZATION!

1. First published in *Le Paria*, 1 August 1922. Reprinted in *Selected Works of Ho Chi Minh*, Vol. 1.

8. THE MARTYRDOM OF AMDOUNI AND BEN-BELKHIR

1. First published in *La Paria*, 1 November 1922. Reprinted in *Selected Works of Ho Chi Minh*, Vol. 1.

9. ABOUT SIKI

1. First published in *La Paria*, 1 December 1922. Reprinted in *Selected Works of Ho Chi Minh*, Vol. 1.

10. MENAGERIE

1. First published in *Le Paria*, 1 February 1923. Reprinted in *Selected Works of Ho Chi Minh*, Vol. 1.

11. THE COUNTER-REVOLUTIONARY ARMY

1. First published in *La Vie Ouvrière*, 7 September 1923. Reprinted in *Selected Works of Ho Chi Minh*, Vol. 1.

12. THE WORKERS' MOVEMENT IN TURKEY

1. First published in *L'Humanité*, 1 January 1924. Reprinted in *Selected Works of Ho Chi Minh*, Vol. 1.

13. REPORT ON THE NATIONAL AND COLONIAL QUESTIONS AT THE FIFTH CONGRESS OF THE COMMUNIST INTERNATIONAL

1. Excerpt from the shorthand transcript of the Fifth Congress of the Communist International (held from 17 June to 8 July 1924). Nguyen Ai Quoc attended and spoke at the Congress as a representative of the French Communist Party and the French colonies.
2. The Third National Congress of the French Communist Party, held in Lyons in January 1924.
3. During World War One, the Tsarist government sent to France a Russian expeditionary corps to fight against the Germans. In 1917, these troops refused to fight for the interests of the bourgeoisie, set up soviets, and demanded their repatriation. Fearing the spread of revolutionary ideas among its troops, the French government withdrew the Russian troops from their positions and penned them up in a concentration camp surrounded with barbed wire and guarded by colonial troops.
4. A federation of French trade unions founded by revolutionary trade unions and active in France from 1922 to 1936. The CGTU sided with the French Communist Party in the struggle against fascism and war.

14. LENIN AND THE COLONIAL PEOPLES

1. First published in *Pravda*, 27 January 1924. Reprinted in *Selected Works of Ho Chi Minh*, Vol. 1.

16. THE PARTY'S LINE IN THE PERIOD OF THE DEMOCRATIC FRONT

1. Excerpt from a report made by Nguyen Ai Quoc to the Communist International in July 1939. In face of the danger caused by the German, Italian and Japanese fascists who were preparing for a new world war and an assault on the Soviet Union, the Communist parties changed their programme of action and set about establishing a broad popular front against fascism and war. In Viet Nam, in July 1936, the Central Committee of the Indochinese Communist Party decided temporarily to shelf the watchwords 'Overthrow French imperialism' and 'Confiscate landlords' estates for distribution to the peasants', and to set up the Indochinese Front against Imperialism (later renamed Indochinese Democratic Front). Nguyen Ai Quoc was then in

China. He closely followed the situation in the country and gave constant help to the Party's Central Committee in leading the movement.

18. INSTRUCTIONS FOR THE SETTING UP OF THE ARMED PROPAGANDA BRIGADE FOR THE LIBERATION OF VIET NAM

1. The Propaganda Brigade of the Liberation Army was founded by decision of Ho Chi Minh on 22 December 1944, from small guerrilla groups operating in Cao Bang, Bac Can and Lang Son. At the start, it comprised only 34 men equipped with rudimentary weapons. It aroused in many places a movement of armed struggle which was to culminate in the August 1945 general insurrection. It was the embryo of the Viet Nam People's Army.

19. APPEAL FOR GENERAL INSURRECTION

1. The National Congress was convened at Tan Trao (Son Duong district, Tuyen Quang province) on 16 August 1945 by the Viet Minh National Committee. It gathered 60 delegates of political parties, mass organizations and nationalities.

    The Congress adopted the Viet Minh's Ten-Point Political Programme and its Order for General Insurrection. It elected the National Liberation Committee which was to become the Provisional government of the Democratic Republic of Viet Nam, with Comrade Ho Chi Minh at its head.

20. DECLARATION OF INDEPENDENCE OF THE DEMOCRATIC REPUBLIC OF VIET NAM

1. Read on 2 September 1945 by President Ho Chi Minh at a meeting of half a million people in Ba Dinh square (Hanoi).

22. APPEAL TO COMPATRIOTS TO CARRY OUT DESTRUCTION, TO WAGE RESISTANCE WAR

1. First published 6 February 1947. Reprinted in *Selected Works of Ho Chi Minh*, Vol. 2.

24. TWELVE RECOMMENDATIONS

1. First published 5 April 1948. Reprinted in *Selected Works of Ho Chi Minh*, Vol. 3.

28. INSTRUCTIONS GIVEN AT THE CONFERENCE REVIEWING THE SECOND LE HONG PHONG MILITARY CAMPAIGN

1. First published in *Selected Works of Ho Chi Minh*, Vol. 3. The Le Hong Phong campaign was also known as the Cao Bang – Bac Can – Long Son campaign.

30. POLITICAL REPORT AT THE SECOND NATIONAL CONGRESS OF THE VIET NAM WORKERS' PARTY

1. The Third National Congress of the Viet Nam Workers' Party passed a resolution correcting the date of the founding of the Indochinese Communist Party, the predecessor of the Viet Nam Workers' Party, and fixing it as 3 February 1930.

31. THE IMPERIALIST AGGRESSORS CAN NEVER ENSLAVE THE HEROIC VIETNAMESE PEOPLE

1. First published in the review *For a Lasting Peace, For a People's Democracy* on 4 April 1952 under the penname Din. Reprinted in *Selected Works of Ho Chi Minh*, Vol. 3.
2. In 1808 Napoleon Bonaparte sent an expedition against Spain and was routed by the Spanish people. This campaign ended in 1812 in victory in favour of the Spaniards. In 1861 France (of Napoleon III), Britain and Spain waged a coalition war against Mexico. In this campaign France also suffered a pitiful defeat.

37. INSTRUCTIONS GIVEN AT THE CONFERENCE REVIEWING THE MASS EDUCATION IN THE FIRST HALF OF 1956

1. First published 16 July 1956. Reprinted in *Selected Works of Ho Chi Minh*, Vol. 4.

38. CONSOLIDATION AND DEVELOPMENT OF IDEOLOGICAL UNITY AMONG MARXIST-LENINIST PARTIES

1. First published in *Pravda*, 3 August 1956. Reprinted in *Selected Works of Ho Chi Minh*, Vol. 4.

40. REPORT ON THE DRAFT AMENDED CONSTITUTION

1. This report was presented to the 11th session of the First National Assembly (18 December 1959).

4I. THIRTY YEARS OF ACTIVITY OF THE PARTY

1. Article written for the review *Problems of Peace and Socialism* (No. 2, 1960) on the occasion of the 30th anniversary of the founding of the Indochinese Communist Party (subsequently the Viet Nam Workers' Party).

42. THE PATH WHICH LED ME TO LENINISM

1. Article written for the USSR review *Problems of the East* on the occasion of Lenin's ninetieth birthday.

43. THE CHINESE REVOLUTION AND THE VIETNAMESE REVOLUTION

1. Article written on the occasion of the fortieth anniversary of the founding of the Chinese Communist Party.

45. APPEAL TO COMPATRIOTS AND FIGHTERS THROUGHOUT THE COUNTRY

1. The four-point position of the DRVN government was as follows:
   1. Recognition of the fundamental national rights of the Vietnamese people: peace, independence, sovereignty, unity and territorial integrity. According to the Geneva Agreements, the US government must

withdraw from South Viet Nam all US troops, military personnel and weapons of all kinds, dismantle all US military bases there, cancel its 'military alliance' with Saigon. It must end its policy of intervention and aggression in South Viet Nam. According to the Geneva Agreements, the US government must end its war acts against the North, definitively end all encroachments on the territory and sovereignty of the Democratic Republic of Viet Nam.

2. Pending the peaceful reunification of Viet Nam, while Viet Nam is still temporarily divided into two zones, the military provisions of the 1954 Geneva Agreements on Viet Nam must be strictly respected: the two zones must refrain from joining any military alliance with foreign countries and there must be no foreign military bases, troops and military personnel on their respective territories.

3. The affairs of South Viet Nam are to be settled by the South Vietnamese people themselves, in accordance with the programme of the South Viet Nam National Front for Liberation, without any foreign interference.

4. The peaceful reunification of Viet Nam is to be settled by the Vietnamese people in both zones, without any foreign interference.

47. ELEVATE REVOLUTIONARY ETHICS, MAKE A CLEAN SWEEP OF INDIVIDUALISM

1. The five-point position of the South Viet Nam National Front for Liberation was as follows:
   1. The US imperialists are the saboteurs of the Geneva Agreements, the most brazen warmongers and aggressors, and the sworn enemy of the Vietnamese people.
   2. The heroic South Vietnamese people are resolved to drive out the US imperialists in order to liberate South Viet Nam, build an independent, democratic, peaceful and neutral South Viet Nam and ultimately achieve national reunification.
   3. The valiant South Vietnamese people and the South Viet Nam Liberation Army are resolved to fulfil their sacred duty, which is to drive out the US imperialists so as to liberate the South and defend the North.
   4. The South Vietnamese people express their profound gratitude to the peace- and justice-loving people all over the world for their whole-hearted support and declare their readiness to receive all assistance, including weapons and all other war materials, from their friends in the five continents.

5. Let our entire people unite, take up arms, continue to march forward heroically, and be resolved to fight and defeat the US aggressors and Vietnamese traitors.

2. Written on the 39th anniversary of the founding of the Indochinese Communist Party (Viet Nam Workers' Party) – 3 February 1969.

‍

Printed in the United States
by Baker & Taylor Publisher Services